The Moderation Dilemma

THE
MODERATION
DILEMMA

LEGISLATIVE COALITIONS
AND THE POLITICS OF
FAMILY AND MEDICAL LEAVE

Anya Bernstein

University of Pittsburgh Press

Published by the University of Pittsburgh Press, Pittsburgh, Pa., 15261
Copyright © 2001, University of Pittsburgh Press

10 9 8 7 6 5 4 3 2 1

Library of Congress Cataloging-in-Publication Data

Bernstein, Anya E., 1968–
    The moderation dilemma : legislative coalitions and the politics of
family and medical leave / Anya E. Bernstein.
        p. cm.
Includes bibliographical references and index.
    ISBN 0-8229-4157-0 (cloth : alk. paper)—ISBN 0-8229-5759-0 (paper :
alk. paper)
    1. Parental leave—Government policy—United States. 2. Sick
leave—Government policy—United States. I. Title.
    HV6065.5.U6 B47 2001
    331.25'762'0973—dc21

                                                    2001000365

For Jon

"It's Nice Work if You Can Get It"

CONTENTS

ACKNOWLEDGMENTS

I would like to begin by thanking my dissertation committee at Harvard University: Sidney Verba, Theda Skocpol, and Paul Pierson. Each member played an important role in the formation of this project. Sidney Verba was a wonderful chair, guiding the project with a deft hand even after it moved away from its original approach, keeping my "eye on the ball" methodologically, providing humor and perspective when my spirits flagged, and cheering me on when things went well. Theda Skocpol provided crucial theoretical guidance and read chapters with an eagle eye, helping me on numerous occasions to organize my thoughts and clarify my argument. She helped me to place this work within the context of scholarship on American social policy and the current political scene. Paul Pierson offered consistent support and enthusiasm, reminding me again and again why it is important to study family and medical leave. He also asked many of the toughest questions, forcing me to refine my strategy and sharpen my ideas.

Beyond my committee, a number of senior scholars at Harvard and in the Boston area consulted on the dissertation or the book manuscript; several read proposals or chapters. I especially thank Morris Fiorina, Jane Mansbridge, Cathie Jo Martin, Eileen McDonagh, Paul Peterson, and Kay Lehman Schlozman.

I received helpful comments from panels at annual meetings of the American Political Science Association, the Northeastern Political Science Association, and the New England Political Science Association. I am also grateful for suggestions offered by people who attended my talks at the Boston Area Research Workshop on Political Development, the Taubman Center for Public Policy and American Institutions at Brown University, the Harvard Women's Studies Brown Bag Lunch Series, and the Social Studies Research Colloquium at Harvard.

I am grateful to two anonymous readers whose insights prompted me to sharpen my analysis and to my editors from the University of

Pittsburgh Press. I especially thank Niels Aaboe for his confidence in the project and support for a first-time author and Deborah Styles for her enthusiasm and excellent editing.

I received financial support for this project from Harvard University and from the Mellon Foundation, which provided grants that I used to travel to conduct interviews. I thank Steve Baker, who was the coordinator of graduate studies in the Harvard Government department, and Cynthia Verba, director of fellowships at the Harvard Graduate School of Arts and Sciences, for their help in the grant-writing process and for their support throughout my graduate career.

The process of gathering preliminary data for this project would have taken much longer and would have been significantly more arduous had it not been for the efforts of librarians at Harvard and in the legislative libraries of the states I studied. Several people deserve particular mention: Mary Ellen McCarthy of the Littauer Library at Harvard, David Paul of the Government Documents Library at Harvard, Hilary Frye and Denise Jernigan from the Connecticut Statehouse Library, Martha Clark from the Massachusetts State Archives, and Cathy Martin from the North Carolina Legislative Library. Special thanks are due to Bonnie Burns of the Harvard Map Collection, who helped me to create the map of family and medical leave enactment found in chapter 1.

I also thank my interview subjects. Many of them went far beyond any call of duty to meet with me for hours on end, bending their busy schedules to accommodate mine and patiently answering my questions. Some endured follow-up phone calls, gave me access to their personal files, and vouched for me for other interview subjects. A few even fed a hungry graduate student!

Finally, I thank my friends and family. I was lucky to go through graduate school with an extraordinary group of colleagues: warm, funny, and caring people who helped me on many, many occasions to gain perspective and to overcome my doubts about the project. They came to my talks, listened to my ideas, and offered valuable suggestions and comments. I am grateful to Chris Afendulis, Page Fortna, Juliet Gainsborough, Claudine Gay, Anna Greenberg, Laura Lyndon, Andy Rudalevige, Kira Sanbonmatsu, Frank Tipton, and Chris Willemsen.

I could not have written either the dissertation or the book without the support of my family. My father, Tom Bernstein, and stepmother,

Dorie Solinger, offered invaluable encouragement from the field and provided strategic advice throughout the process. My mother, Ellen Bernstein, and my sister, Maia Bernstein, engaged me in discussions about work and family and helped to shape my ideas about the issues I study. Their belief in the importance of this project and in my ability to do it has sustained me for many years. My parents-in-law, Joseph and Nancy Bassett, also sustained me, both through their interest in my work and through much-needed breaks in the form of Sunday dinners and evenings out.

Benjamin and Sarah Bassett arrived, respectively, immediately after I finished first my dissertation and then this book. In addition to unwittingly hastening the completion of this work, they have been a source of tremendous joy and inspiration. In writing a book about work and family issues, I think it is important to acknowledge their grandparents and child care providers, who have spent countless hours nurturing them so that my husband and I could work. I am grateful to Ellen Bernstein, Joseph and Nancy Bassett, Jeanne Lothrop, and Erin Collings.

Last but by no means least, I thank my husband, Jonathan Bassett. Over the years, Jon has listened to my ideas and woes with equal interest, offering faith and perspective and an unwavering belief that I could do this. He takes a fully equal role in parenting, and cooks far more than his share of our meals. He has been my most scrupulous editor, reading every word of this manuscript over and over. This book is better for his efforts, and I am a better and much happier person for his presence in my life. I dedicate this book to him, with much love.

The Moderation Dilemma

1 ‖ THE MODERATION DILEMMA AND THE POLITICS OF FAMILY AND MEDICAL LEAVE

Enacting sweeping political reforms has always been difficult in the United States. The American system is unusually fragmented, with power distributed among three branches on the federal level and between one national and fifty state governments. Policy makers at all levels have different agendas and differing abilities to achieve what they want. As a result, the agreement required to enact the widespread changes desired by one party or group is most often achieved only in a time of crisis or war. Institutional fragmentation is widely believed to contribute to "American exceptionalism": the slow and limited development of social welfare policies in the United States.[1]

For those seeking to enact substantial policy changes, the American political system presents a significant hurdle. In addition to gaining the support of 51 percent of the House and 60 percent of the Senate (due to the filibuster rule), reformers face the necessity of either winning over the president or convincing a full two-thirds of Congress to override the presidential veto. In an era of heightened conflict deriving from weak political parties, individualistic campaign styles, and, often, divided government, these tasks may be Herculean.[2]

With few exceptions, then, the only way to pass legislation invoking a policy innovation in the United States is by compromising.[3] While this may have been the founders' intention, it presents would-be reformers with a dilemma. By accepting a compromise, or "half a loaf," advocates for policy change have an opportunity to enact at least some of what they want and often to better the lives of at least some of their

1

constituents. Further, by enacting something, advocates may be able to lay the groundwork for a future expansion of their program, especially once those who benefit from it organize to support its extension. Indeed, many social welfare programs in the United States, most notably Social Security, have been expanded after enactment. Finally, policy advocates may accept a compromise in order to establish the principle that government *should* make policy in a particular area: that a certain kind of regulation is acceptable or that money should be spent on a particular issue.[4]

Accepting half a loaf may have negative consequences for policy advocates, however. Enacting a moderate policy may decrease momentum for passing legislation based on a broader policy, either by eliminating the most visible symptoms of a problem or by satisfying some of the groups that had previously pushed for reform. This happened in the 1960s, when a movement for national health insurance was halted after the enactment of Medicare and Medicaid.[5] In addition, advocates' credibility with their constituents may be lessened if the constituents view them as having sold out and if their ability to distinguish themselves from their competitors is compromised. As John Gilmour explains, in many cases, advocates may prefer no policy to one that does not meet their needs.[6] The American political system will not necessarily produce compromise.

An excellent example of this "moderation dilemma" faced by groups determining when to compromise can be seen in the case of the movement for family and medical leave. Family and medical leave policies require that businesses of a certain size allow employees to take time off to care for newborn children, sick children, spouses, or parents, and, in some cases, for the employee's own illness. Family and medical leave was debated for eight years on both state and national levels, and policies covering private employers passed in nineteen states before the Family and Medical Leave Act was finally signed into law by President Bill Clinton in 1993. The policies were supported by a coalition of labor, church, and feminist groups as a reform needed to support working families. They were opposed by businesses and, to a lesser extent, by social conservatives as government mandates and improper intrusions into family life.

Family and medical leave policies were so controversial that on both the state and national levels legislation could be passed only through considerable compromise. As a result, the policies that did become law generally cover barely half the population. Further, they all mandate only unpaid leave, which means that many people who have access to family and medical leave cannot afford to make use of it. A congressional study conducted eighteen months after the passage of the national Family and Medical Leave Act found that while 45 percent of workers were covered by the law, nearly two-thirds of those who needed it could not afford the accompanying loss of wages.[7]

The lack of strong family and medical leave policies in the United States contrasts with policies in other countries. Nearly every other nation offers women a maternity leave that is at least partially paid,[8] and many European countries offer leave to fathers as well. Data presented by Kirsten Wever show, for example, that Austria allows new mothers to take sixty-seven weeks of leave, with sixteen of those weeks paid; Italy provides forty-six weeks of maternity leave, paid at 52 percent of the mother's former salary, and twenty-six weeks of paternity leave; and Sweden provides seventy-eight weeks of maternity leave, with seventy-two of those weeks paid at 90 percent of the former salary, and sixty weeks of paternity leave.[9]

It is important to note, as Wever does, that while leaves for new parents are far more generous in other countries than they are in the United States, few countries provide extensive leaves to care for other family members, as the American Family and Medical Leave Act does. Thus while American parents have fewer benefits than their counterparts in other industrialized countries, those who are caring for elderly or sick relatives often have better arrangements. I will argue that this is due in part to American cultural norms toward motherhood,[10] and in part to the strength of political organizing among the elderly in the United States. The power of the American Association of Retired Persons is legendary in American politics,[11] and the organizers for the national Family and Medical Leave Act helped their cause by drawing the AARP into their coalition by including elderly care as part of the policy.

The lack of a strong family and medical leave policy in the United States is also difficult to understand since it is a response to one of the most important demographic trends of the twentieth century: the entrance of women, and particularly married women, into the paid workforce. As shown by economic historian Claudia Goldin, married women's participation in the paid workforce has increased by roughly 10 percentage points during every decade since the 1940s, until now just over 60 percent of married women work.[12] Family and medical leave policies respond to the fact that women are in the workforce and thus are not constantly available to fulfill caregiving duties.

It is natural to wonder why such a dramatic demographic shift has not been accompanied by the enactment of a strong policy response, especially when it has in most other industrialized countries. Part of the explanation clearly is that the American political system is set up to make it difficult to pass broad-ranging social protections. But the existence of *some* social protections in the United States, such as laws defining minimum wage and maximum working hours and prohibitions on children's labor, which were initially enacted to protect women, children, and families, indicates that it is sometimes possible to achieve regulations in the name of "family values,"[13] even in the absence of a catalyzing crisis or war.

Why was it so hard to pass family and medical leave? First, the fragmented nature of American political institutions makes it difficult to pass any widespread change. Second is the political power of business, and third is the lack of a strong work and family movement in the United States. In many states, and for many years at the national level, institutional intransigence combined with strong opposition and weak support for family and medical leave to make it impossible to pass policies. Despite these obstacles, nineteen states and the federal government eventually did pass versions of family and medical leave. This book seeks to explain why family and medical leave policies passed in the states where they did and why the battle for the Family and Medical Leave Act was finally won.

Family and medical leave is interesting in its own right, because it is the only major policy innovation aimed at helping working families that was enacted during the 1990s. It is also interesting because it is one of only a handful of expansions achieved in an era when attempts were being made to dismantle the welfare state.[14] This study also compares policy processes at both the state and national levels, which is especially important given recent interest in devolving control of social policy to the states. Family and medical leave was the subject not only of an economic debate, but also of a cultural debate over changing gender roles and the relationship between the state and families. At a time when "culture wars"[15] are an important part of the political landscape, it is valuable to study a policy that touches both culture and economics.

The book reviews a quantitative study of state passage of family and medical leave, which shows that policies were more likely to pass in nonsouthern states under Democratic control, where the population was more supportive of women's rights.[16] These states can be thought of as providing *contextual resources* to advocates for family and medical leave policies.

Case studies chosen on the basis of these data as well as common understandings of American politics allow an examination of the effort to enact family and medical leave legislation in four states and at the national level. The study showed that family and medical leave policies were more likely to pass where the political leadership supported them and where family and medical leave bills were seen as important to achieving other goals. It also concluded that the policies were more likely to pass when the coalition supporting them had access to substantial resources: advocates who were viewed as credible and powerful were more likely to succeed.

These findings about the importance of contextual and group-specific resources reflect findings by many other scholars and are thus to be expected. While resources certainly facilitated the passage of family and medical leave policies, they were not sufficient in themselves. Advocates with access to resources had to make appropriate use of them by framing their proposals to fit with the political context and by proposing moderate bills and being willing to compromise. All of the family and medical leave bills that passed were compromised, and my study shows that these compromises took place at every step of the policy process. State and national advocates introduced weaker bills than they wanted in order to gain credibility, they worked with conservatives to frame family and medical leave as family values instead of as feminist bills, and they compromised again during the bargaining phase, agreeing to pass even weaker versions of family and medical leave. While resources were necessary, strategic adherence to resource constraints was crucial.

These strategic choices are linked to the identities of the advocates and to the type of organizations they were working for. I argue that "insider" groups, which are largely made up of and funded by elites and which enjoy strong ties to the political system, are more likely to moderate and make compromises, even if those strategies conflict with group ideology and preferences. Members of insider groups are more likely to believe that the ends justify the means and that passing incremental legislation is better than passing no legislation. They are also more likely to possess resources that will help them achieve these aims. In contrast, "outsider" groups, which are mass based and funded and only loosely connected to the political system, are less likely to be willing to accept incremental change. Family and medical leave bills passed only in places where insiders gained control of the policy process.

This study provides an explanation for policy innovation that draws together two ideas. The first is that *resources matter*: groups that operate in favorable political climates and that have power and credibility are more likely to be able to achieve their goals. The second idea is that *strategy matters*: in order to succeed, groups need to adapt their strategies to the vagaries of the political climate in which they are operating. This book asks how these two ideas are linked. Comparing groups operating with similar resources, I ask why some groups chose successful strategies while others did not, and I develop a comprehensive model showing how resources and strategy affect each other and together affect chances for policy success.

The Political Power of Business

Business opponents of family and medical leave objected to the policy as an "unfunded mandate" imposed by government. They argued that family and medical leave represented one more in a long line of attempts by government to regulate business, and they warned that the mandate could compromise profits and jobs. With regard to state-level proposals, business groups frequently invoked arguments about "competitive federalism,"[17] threatening that states that passed family and medical leave policies would find it harder to attract business investment, because businesses would search elsewhere for lower cost places to locate. Another common argument was that family and medical leave would set a precedent that would lead to more costly mandates such as paid family leave and employers' providing health care benefits for their employees (a result that was in fact desired by many advocates of the policy).

The arguments made by business groups in opposition to family and medical leave are similar to arguments made against a variety of other proposed social policies throughout the twentieth century. The strength of business is frequently mentioned as one explanation for the failure of the United States to develop a European-style welfare state. Business opposition to widespread welfare state policies is thought to be successful for two reasons. First, arguments against social welfare policies fit with the American belief that capitalism is a central good that needs to be protected or at least not interfered with[18] and with the belief that business strength is the key to maintaining prosperity. As noted by Charles Lindblom, business is granted a "privileged position" in market systems as a result of the role it plays in furthering economic development. Because political fortunes are linked to prosperity, politicians are likely to be very attentive to business concerns.[19]

Second, business arguments against social welfare policies are likely to be successful because they come from a wealthy and well-connected source. Since the 1950s, critics of pluralism have pointed out that groups with the most resources tend to be more active politically and thus better able to influence the political system. And studies of interest group lobbying have shown that business groups dominate the lobbying scene in Washington, in both their numbers and their spending.[20]

The political power of business is not absolute, however. Weighing the relationship between business and politics over the past few decades, David Vogel argues for a more interactive model, based on the fact that businesses also depend on government to safeguard property rights and improve market stability. Vogel observes that the ability of business to intimidate government varies over time and by economic cycle and that often other social objectives are able to override a concern for business.[21]

Paul Pierson argues that variance in institutional structures between different political systems will affect the power of business. He maintains that business power will be accentuated in decentralized, federal systems where capital is highly mobile, and that in fragmented institutions with many veto points it will be easier for business to block reforms but harder for it to pursue a cohesive policy agenda. Fragmented institutions will amplify the influence of particular sectors of business.[22]

A recent study by Cathie Jo Martin examining business influence on a number of recent social policy initiatives (including family and medical leave) adds a final caveat to the view of business as an 800-pound gorilla unified in its opposition to social policy. Martin distinguishes between big businesses and small businesses, arguing that big businesses sometimes want social policy innovations and are not in any case well organized to oppose them. However, small businesses are unified under several membership organizations and are highly effective at blocking or preventing the enactment of social policy initiatives.[23]

A picture of the role of business opposition in the development of family and medical leave begins to emerge from these works. Claims by business that family and medical leave would damage the economy would at the very least get a hearing, particularly where business is well organized, where capital is mobile, and where institutions are fragmented. The ability of business to block family and medical leave might vary by economic cycle, however. Opportunities to enact policies like family and medical leave present themselves when the economy is good, when the public mood is relatively pro-government, and when capital is less mobile. Advocates must take advantage of those opportunities, for example by cultivating support (or at least not opposition) from friendly big businesses and by searching for ways to respond to more vociferous opposition from small businesses.

The Weak Work and Family Movement

Who were the potential advocates for family and medical leave, and how broad was their support? How did they mobilize that support and choose their strategies? Family and medical leave appears to be the kind of policy that *should* have attracted broad support, since it provides help not only to people who are caring for newborns and young children but also to people who are sick themselves or have sick spouses or elderly relatives. It never became the focus of a broad-based social movement, however. This is in great part because the issue suffers from a double-edged collective action problem. Not only is family and medical leave a public good that is available to all who qualify

rather than only those who have worked to pass it,[24] but it also benefits people for a relatively short time when they are, by definition, extremely busy. Compared with policies like Social Security, for example,
family and medical leave offers a scattered and occasional benefit. Social Security is available to nearly everyone at a set point in their lives
(when they retire) and, from that point on, until they die. In contrast,
only a small percentage of the population will need family and medical
leave at any given time, and when they need it, they will usually only
need it for a short time.[25]

Thus it is not surprising that there was never a grassroots movement for family and medical leave, even though the public was supportive of the policy by the end of the national debate.[26] Instead, the
effort to pass legislation mandating family and medical leave was
largely elite driven, supported primarily by advocates from the feminist
and labor communities who believed that it was important.

One group that did not join the effort to pass family and medical
leave legislation was the conservative New Right. Leaders of the New
Right viewed family and medical leave with a mixture of ambiguity
and hostility. While family and medical leave ostensibly exists to help
people spend more time with their families and thus can be labeled a
family values issue, the need for it has arisen as women have entered
the workplace, a practice that members of the New Right generally do
not support. Some leaders of the New Right also derided unpaid family
and medical leave as "a windfall for yuppies," arguing that it would
give preferential treatment to two-earner families who could afford to
take time off without pay.[27] The reluctance of the New Right to support family and medical leave may reflect continuing ambiguity on the
part of the public: even as a significant percentage of the public supports working women and perceives that they have to work, many people still wish that women would stay at home, especially when their
children are young.

At the same time, national level advocates for the Family and Medical Leave Act gained crucial support for their bill from lobbyists from
the U.S. Catholic Conference, which hoped that the availability of family and medical leave would discourage women from having abortions.
Arguing that conflicts with work are one reason that women have abortions in the first place, leaders of the Catholic Conference placed family and medical leave high on their legislative agenda and helped to gain

support for the policy from pro-life members of Congress. The willingness of feminist advocates to work with pro-life advocates was extremely important in ensuring the passage of the Family and Medical
Leave Act.

Determinants of State Policy Innovation

The question of why policies pass in certain places and at certain
times has interested scholars for years. Studies of state policy development generally attempt to identify structural variables associated with
broad measures of policy innovation or with the development of specific policies. These studies can be divided into three categories: those
emphasizing socioeconomics (income, education, and urbanism),[28] those
emphasizing institutions (legislative professionalism, party competition),[29] and those emphasizing ideology and political culture.[30]

While it is important to identify the "agents of policy development" (the state characteristics associated with the likelihood that policy innovation will occur),[31] covariation studies have their limits. Most
important, while they provide measures of association, these studies do
not provide explanations. They identify features of the political, economic, or social system that provide resources for those seeking to advance a policy innovation. They do not, however, identify the *process*
by which these features facilitate policy development. In a recent essay,
Jeffrey Stonecash argues that scholars studying the development of
state policy should use case studies, which can more easily identify
venue-specific processes, to fill the void left by covariation studies.[32]
This project does exactly that by using a covariation study of family
and medical leave enactment in order to choose state case studies, and
then using those case studies as well as a study of the national effort to
pass family and medical leave to specify the role of group resources and
strategies.

Institutionally oriented scholars of interest groups, social movements, and public policy have contributed to the understanding of how
social structures can facilitate or inhibit the development of policy innovations. Over the past twenty-five years, theories of social movement emergence and evolution have been applied to movement successes
and failures to generate hypotheses about the conditions under which
groups are likely to achieve policy change. *Resource Mobilization The-*

ory, which posits that movements will emerge when potential members have access to resources such as money and elite support, suggests that groups will be most successful when they are well connected to the power structure.[33] Resource mobilization theory is complemented by *political process theory,* which specifies that while the presence of these resources may facilitate movement emergence, a convergence of broad socioeconomic processes, political opportunities, and indigenous organizational strength offers a clearer explanation not only for the development but also for the evolution and impact of social movements.[34]

The concept of a *political opportunity structure* is now used by a number of scholars (including this author) to isolate both the contextual variables and the broader institutional and political processes that facilitate or inhibit not only group formation but also the ability of groups to achieve their policy goals. As described recently by Lee Ann Banaszak, crucial features of the political opportunity structure include state structures and the formal rules governing political behavior (for example, as mentioned earlier, the fragmented federal system), the distribution of political power among various actors, and party and interest groups.[35] The political opportunity structure affects which groups form, and, crucially, *how* they form, including how they come to identify themselves and determine their goals and strategies. It also affects the capacity of states to respond to group demands.[36]

Recent studies of agenda-setting and policy innovation allow us to see more clearly how the contextual, institutional, and group resources that constitute the political opportunity structure can affect policy change. These studies suggest hypotheses about the role of the political opportunity structure in the development of family and medical leave. They also reveal the need to incorporate knowledge about group behavior and strategy into any analysis. It is not enough for groups to operate within a favorable opportunity structure and to have resources available to them. Groups must develop an agenda and adopt strategies that allow them to make the best use of these resources. This does not always happen.

The field of agenda-setting was pioneered by E. E. Schattschneider, who first argued that "whoever decides what the game is about decides who can get into the game."[37] Peter Bachrach and Morton Baratz extended this argument, maintaining that the power to keep issues off the public agenda was as important as the power to place issues on the agenda.[38] Steven Lukes built on Bachrach and Baratz's argument, positing that belief systems about the proper distribution of power and the nature of government could in themselves prevent issues from reaching the public agenda.[39]

These arguments about the role played by social structures and the distribution of power as determinants of the political agenda resonate in later studies of agenda-setting and explanations of policy innovation. Roger Cobb and Charles Elder argue that innovations are more likely to pass as legislation when they are seen as significant by members of the broad political community (on the "systemic agenda") and by "authoritative decision makers" (on the "formal" or "institutional" agenda).[40] Nelson Polsby adds that reforms must be congruent with "the intellectual convictions of experts and policymakers."[41] And Polsby and Barbara Nelson emphasize the importance of structural and political incentives for reforms in addition to the support of powerful political actors and a supportive political climate.[42]

These lessons are amplified by John Kingdon. Drawing his argument from studies of health and transportation policy, Kingdon argues that three things need to happen for an issue to succeed on the policy agenda. First, the issue must be recognized as a legitimate public problem. This can happen when systemic indicators change or when "focusing events" (such as airline crashes or an economic crisis) occur. Second, a solution that is technically feasible, ideologically acceptable, and politically possible must be available. And third, the political circumstances must be right: the national mood must be favorable, and supporters must have power. Kingdon argues that innovation is more likely to occur when the three "streams" of problems, policies, and politics come together.[43]

While Kingdon specifies aspects of the political opportunity structure that facilitate policy innovation, he tells us little about how the activities of political actors affect the agenda-setting and policy processes. Kingdon identifies as "policy entrepreneurs" those who invest resources in trying to pass a policy. He describes them as developing and floating ideas around policy communities. And he describes them as seizing opportunities that arise and facilitating the processes of "coupling" the three streams listed above. But he tells us little about *how* entrepreneurs operate, and beyond the fact that they need to be influential, little about what affects their success. Kingdon's emphasis on the external conditions required to pass policy innovations leaves us with little understanding of why entrepreneurs adopt or do not adopt needed strategies or how strategy interacts with political resources.

Later work on agenda-setting and policy development provides more detail on the role of political strategy. Deborah Stone argues that political actors often have some leverage on how the problems they identify will be defined; they can thus try to define these problems in ways that will direct the scope of solutions in a favorable direction.[44] Frank Baumgartner and Bryan Jones add that problem definition can affect not only the scope of solutions, but also the institutional venue in which a problem is considered; thus political actors may have opportunities to direct their issues to favorable venues.[45] R. Douglas Arnold describes how successful coalition leaders link their proposals to well-established ends, demonstrate its benefits, and develop procedural strategies to minimize costs and to make it easier for legislators to "claim credit" or "avoid blame" for their support of a policy.[46]

Studies of social policy and gender issues also offer analyses applicable to the passage of the Family and Medical Leave Act. Theda Skocpol suggests that policy entrepreneurs target widely, building support for programs by covering people across classes. She argues that "universal" policies tend to have more positive "moral images" and are thus more likely to succeed.[47] Writing about the women's movement, Joyce Gelb and Marian Lief Palley observe that when activists link their goals to the established American political tenet of equal treatment as opposed to role change, they are more likely to be successful. They point out that success is most likely to be achieved by groups who are perceived as "legitimate" and who are willing to work for incremental change.[48]

Many of the authors described above use concepts similar to those used in the literature on "framing" social movements developed by David Snow and his colleagues. Drawing on the concept of a frame first developed by Goffman, Snow and others define a frame as a "'schemata of interpretation' that enables individuals to 'locate, perceive, identify, and label' occurrences within their life space and the world at large." They argue that "by rendering events or occurrences meaningful, frames function to organize experience and guide action."[49] Frames are used by policy advocates, and especially by members of social movements, as ways to legitimize themselves and their goals within the cultural context in which they are operating. An example of framing used by Sidney Tarrow is of the American Civil Rights movement, which was framed by its advocates as an attempt to extend the accepted American principle of equal opportunity to black Americans.[50]

The literature on framing suggests that advocates who are able to frame their movements to associate themselves with widely acceptable beliefs and values will be more successful than those who cannot. I will show later in this book how advocates for family and medical leave in many states and on the federal level attempted to link their movement with the movement for family values, instead of using more controversial frames of women's or workers' rights. The advocates' ability or inability to frame family and medical leave as a family values issue helps to account for their success or failure.

Drawn together, the above literature suggests a number of hypotheses to explain variation in the enactment of family and medical leave policies. Family and medical leave legislation is more likely to pass in places *where the political context is favorable*. It is also more likely to pass when it is proposed by legislators and advocates who have *power and credibility*, and where there are *structural and political incentives for reform*, such as when the membership of a legislature is unified and when there are few competing issues on the agenda. Finally, advocates must make use of these resources by proposing bills that will be viewed as reasonable and moderate within the political context in which they are operating and by *framing these bills in ways that emphasize culturally acceptable values*.

However, while the literature outlined above suggests that family and medical leave legislation is likely to pass when the advocates have access to resources and also adopt strategies that allow them to make use of those resources, it tells us little about *why* certain groups adopt such strategies while others do not. If, as Theda Skocpol argues, there needs to be a "fit" between group capacities and the political opportunity structure,[51] the factors that shape group capacities and choices of strategy need to be understood.

Organizational Structure and Group Strategy

Earlier in this chapter, I noted that family and medical leave suffers from a "double-edged collective action problem": it is not only a public good but offers a scattered and occasional benefit to potential recipients. As Mancur Olson showed nearly thirty years ago, individuals have few incentives to work to achieve "collective" or "public" goods, because once these goals are achieved, they will be available to everyone. Those who worked to achieve them will receive no special benefit; they would thus be better off if public goods were achieved through the work of others.[52] The collective action problem is exacerbated as group size grows and the chance that individual action can be directly linked to the desired result diminishes.

However, and as recently shown by Sidney Tarrow, Olson's collective action problem applies much better to economic associations or interest groups than it does to social movements. As Tarrow notes, "Research has shown that people associate with movements for a wide spectrum of reasons: from the desire for personal advantage, to group solidarity, to principled commitment to a cause, to the desire to be a part of a group."[53] While this caveat is duly noted, it remains important to realize that any social movement must offer incentives to people to get them to join and stay active. Social movements by definition rely on actions by their members; when they lose their members, they die. In understanding the movement to enact family and medical leave legislation, we thus need to keep in mind both that the policy is a public good and that it is not a particularly well-defined one.

James Q. Wilson divides the incentives that can be offered by social movements or interest groups into three categories: material incentives (tangible benefits such as group discounts), solidary incentives (connections with other people developed through participation in the group activity), and purposive incentives (satisfaction from having contributed to the cause, even if one knows that one's individual effort did not in itself make the difference).[54] He also divides group behavior into two categories: bargaining, whereby the parties involved negotiate and compromise, and protest, whereby one group engages in activities designed to "raise the cost to another party of continuing a given course of action."[55] Wilson notes that many groups engage in both types of activities and that a single movement may encompass both bargaining and protest strategies. He argues that choice of strategy is associated with organizational structure and with the incentives available to participants. Wilson states that groups with relationships with their opponents and a sense of status in the community are more likely to bargain. Groups that rely on purposive incentives are more likely to protest: "Associations . . . that do rely on [purposive] inducements will attach such importance to their goals that not only will the results of bargaining seem unsatisfactory, but the very idea of bargaining, with its inevitable implications of compromise, will appear objectionable."[56]

Drawing on Wilson's argument and writing about the Equal Rights Amendment (ERA), Jane Mansbridge argues that when few tangible benefits are associated with the passage of a law, proponents may attach increased significance to the political and cultural principles associated with the policy.[57] This may lead to an unwillingness to compromise and enable a law to pass, but at the cost of sacrificing some part of the principle. In the case of the ERA, Mansbridge explains that supporters' interest in associating the ERA with widespread cultural and political change led them to agree with opponents that the ERA would lead to such policies as female conscription. She argues that supporters' insistence that they emphasize such cultural issues made it harder to pass the ERA.

The arguments offered by Wilson and Mansbridge suggest that the organization of groups advocating family and medical leave is likely to affect the development of strategies for passing the policy into law and especially for the groups' willingness to accept compromises. Because family and medical leave is a public good, its advocates are likely, as were the advocates for the ERA, to be motivated by purposive incentives. As a result, they are less likely to view an incremental reform as a victory. Only in arenas where the most pragmatic advocates are able to overcome collective action problems and seize control of the policy process will family and medical leave be likely to become law.

Advocates and the Moderation Dilemma

The literature on organizational structure and group strategy helps us to understand why advocates for family and medical leave may not pursue strategies that fit with the political opportunity structure. The incentives available to recruit and retain group members affect the formation of agendas and the development of strategy, which in turn affect how groups resolve the moderation dilemma. Policies like family and medical leave, which offer few tangible benefits, are likely to be supported by groups motivated by purposive incentives and unwilling to adopt strategies of framing, moderation, and compromise. The fact that family and medical leave legislation passed in nineteen states and on the federal level suggests that the constraints associated with organizational structure can be mitigated by other influences, however.

In an effort to explain why some advocates *were* willing to fit their strategies to the political opportunity structure by moderating and compromising, despite the fact that they were likely to be constrained by purposive incentives, I turn to a narrower literature on group strategy. The willingness of groups to engage in what Wilson labels *bargaining* and other scholars label *insider* strategies may also be associated with organizational maintenance.

Thomas Gais and Jack L. Walker Jr. define *insider* strategies as efforts to persuade those in power to act in a particular way, primarily through lobbying.[58] Successful lobbying requires developing long-term relationships with legislators and administrators, establishing credibility as providers of accurate information, and developing a sensitivity to the realities and constraints of the political process.[59] In contrast, *outsider* strategies attempt to put pressure on those in power by mobilizing public opinion through demonstrations, appeals to the media, and public speaking, with little regard for the exigencies of the political process. Writing about tactics adopted by women's organizations during the 1980s, Roberta Spalter-Roth and Ronnee Schreiber describe insider techniques as characteristic of interest groups rather than social movements.[60] Both they and Gais and Walker agree with Wilson that many groups use both types of techniques.

The above literature suggests that groups are more likely to pursue strategies of bargaining or insider activism when they share the values held by those in power, which include compromise and a willingness to accept incremental change. This is more likely to happen when groups develop lasting relationships with those in power around a number of issues. These long-term relationships are more likely to develop in groups that have long-term, professional staff than in those with an amateur, rotating staff. And they are more likely to develop in groups that are dominated by elites who share values with those holding political power than with members of the mass public. As explained by Wilson, long-term relationships generate trust and decrease the likelihood that participants will participate in disruptive action because activists "may fear that a protest today in a matter that divides them will reduce the chances of collaborative action in the future in matters that unite them."[61]

The research done by Gais and Walker also indicates that groups that are funded by "patrons" (foundations, government grants) have more incentives to pass something for which they can claim credit, just as legislators have a need to claim credit.[62] These groups must constantly justify their funding to organizations that could be giving support to any number of groups. One way to do this is to attach their names to a piece of legislation, even if that legislation is incremental. In contrast, citizen-based groups have to justify their actions to mass constituents who, as mentioned earlier, were probably motivated by purposive incentives to join their groups in the first place. Members of citizen groups are less likely to view compromise as a "win" and prefer to have their organizations stick to principle.[63]

Perceptions of the Policy Process

The literature on organizational structure and strategy indicates that the choice of insider or outsider strategy will be affected not only by the incentives available for organizing but also by advocates' perceptions of the policy process in general and of incremental change in particular. Advocates for family and medical leave who are willing to frame the policy in culturally appropriate ways and to moderate and compromise will do so both because they have incentives to pass legislation embodying a policy and because they believe that incremental change can lay the groundwork for a more substantial policy. Conversely, advocates who are unwilling to moderate may lack incentives to do so and may also fear that incremental change will decrease momentum for a widespread policy. Evidence to support both of these approaches can be found in the recent history of American social policy.

Much of what happens to an incremental bill depends on how it feeds back into the political system. The idea of a policy feedback is that once a policy is enacted to respond to an issue, it can shape the politics of that issue and in turn affect the evolution of later policies.[64] As shown by Theda Skocpol and Paul Pierson, policies can affect politics in two ways. First, they can transform state capacities, creating new administrative arrangements or expanding existing ones so that state intervention in new areas is deemed legitimate. Second, they can affect the development and capabilities of advocates devoted to continuing and expanding the policy.[65]

The classic example of policy expansion through feedback is Social

Security, which began as a modest policy covering relatively few people but over time expanded to become a nearly universal policy offering broad benefits. Scholars of Social Security attribute its success in part to the strong support it enjoyed from administrators who were dedicated to expanding it incrementally and from advocates within the congressional committees that oversaw it. Overcoming initial resistance, these administrators carefully engineered the expansion of Social Security to the point where it gained widespread approval from a public now accustomed to receiving old-age support from the government.[66]

The advocates for family and medical leave in the late 1980s and early 1990s faced considerable uncertainty about whether any incremental policies that they passed would, as many hoped, be a "first step," or whether that would be all they could get. While scholars and advocates can now look back from the vantage point of history at the successful incremental expansion of Social Security, it is very difficult to predict at the time a policy is enacted into law how it will feed back. Advocates for national health insurance during the 1960s accepted Medicare and Medicaid with the expectation that these programs would quickly be expanded. Advocates must, therefore, "muddle through,"[67] as they attempt to determine how valuable incremental change will be.

In the absence of clear guidelines, the literature suggests that group characteristics will be associated with ideas about incremental change in the policy process just as they are with the choice of insider or outsider strategies generally. Groups whose members share the values of the American political system are more likely to believe in the incremental change that is the hallmark of that system. These groups are more likely to be professional and elite than mass-based.

In the case of family and medical leave, the fact that many of the lead advocates identified themselves as feminists shaped their perceptions of the policy process. Attracted to family and medical leave as a response to the rapid increase of women, and particularly mothers of young children, in the workforce, these activists feared that if the legislation were not designed properly, the resulting policies would stigmatize women as needing "special" protection and might make it more difficult for women to achieve equality in the workplace. Furthermore, many of the advocates were committed not only to a society free of sexism but also to a society free of classism. If family and medical leave remained unpaid, these advocates realized, they would not be accessible to all and might exacerbate the division between rich and poor. These concerns meant that in places where proposals were for unpaid leave or involved special treatment for women, any commitment to sweeping change was sorely tested and the moderation dilemma was exacerbated.

Measuring the Passage of Family and Medical Leave

As explained above, part of this book is devoted to explaining why some states passed laws mandating family and medical leave policies while others did not, and why the battle to pass the Family and Medical Leave Act was finally won. Before a full discussion is possible, however, it is necessary to explain what I mean by "passing a family and medical leave policy," as the types of policies that were passed in states before 1993 can be differentiated in two major ways. First, some laws cover private employers, while others cover only state employees. Some laws cover pregnant women only for the period before and after childbirth, when they are technically "disabled," while others cover parents caring for newborn and newly adopted children and people caring for ill family members or tending to their own illness. Not surprisingly, advocates generally had an easier time passing less far-reaching pregnancy-only laws and laws covering state employees than laws covering private employers and laws requiring family leave provisions.

TYPES OF FAMILY AND MEDICAL LEAVE POLICIES

Type of policy	Covers state workers only	Covers private employees
Pregnancy leave only	easiest to pass	harder to pass
Family and medical leave	harder to pass	hardest to pass

A third way that family and medical leave policies can vary is by providing some amount of wage replacement, or "paid family leave." I do not include this aspect on the above chart because before the 1993 passage of the Family and Medical Leave Act, paid family leave was deemed so controversial that it had been introduced in only one state, Massachusetts, where it failed (see chapter 3). By 2000, no state had passed paid family leave legislation either, but bills had been proposed in eighteen states (see chapter 6).

This book focuses on efforts to pass family and medical leave policies covering private employers; the category of policy that is labeled
"hardest to pass" in the table above. The analysis excludes those states
that passed family and medical leave policies that only covered state
employees [see figure 1].[68] Thirteen states had passed such laws by
1993, the year the national Family and Medical Leave Act was passed.
While these bills frequently represent the only step that those states
have taken toward recognizing and responding to work-family dilemmas, they are substantively different from and less interesting than
laws that require private employers to provide leaves for their employees. Providing state workers with family and medical leaves is essentially a benefits decision made by states, which affects their own
personnel practices and budgets. While there is clearly a symbolic benefit in having states allow their workers to take time off to attend to
family and medical matters, these laws do not regulate business, which
was the central issue in the debates over family and medical leaves.

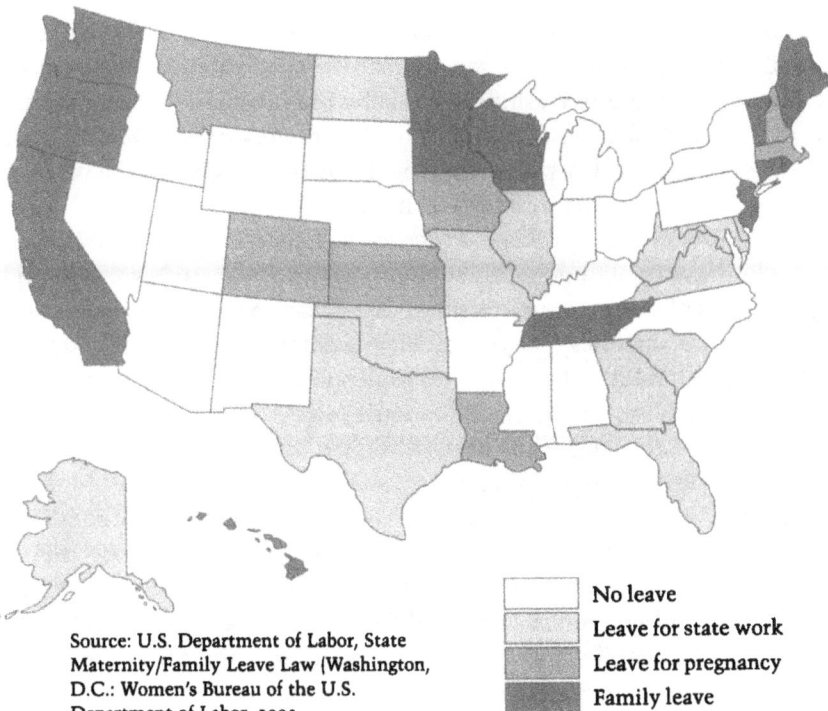

Source: U.S. Department of Labor, State
Maternity/Family Leave Law (Washington,
D.C.: Women's Bureau of the U.S.
Department of Labor, 1993.

No leave
Leave for state work
Leave for pregnancy
Family leave

The book does not focus on pregnancy disability leaves covering private employers, which were passed by seven states. An example of a pregnancy disability leave is Colorado's law, which requires businesses with one or more employees to provide female employees with a "reasonable period" of leave, or Iowa's law, which requires all businesses to provide employees with eight weeks of leave for disabilities caused or contributed to by pregnancy and childbirth. While these policies represent a step beyond those that only cover state workers, they do not provide substantial benefits beyond those required of employers who already offer disability leaves to other workers as required by the Pregnancy Discrimination Act of 1978.[69]

The focus of this study is family and medical leave laws, which had been passed in twelve states and the District of Columbia by 1993. Family and medical leave laws mandate that private businesses of a certain size give their employees time off to attend to family and medical needs. An example of a family and medical leave law is Maine's statute, which requires that employers of twenty-five or more people give those employees ten weeks of unpaid leave within any two-year period for the birth or adoption of a child, to care for the illness of a child, spouse, or parent, or to care for that employee's serious illness. Another example is Washington's law, which requires that employers of one hundred or more people give those workers twelve weeks of leave during any two-year period for the birth or adoption of a child or to care for the terminal illness of that child.

James Garand and Pamela Monroe develop a model of family and medical leave policy adoption in the states using logistic regression and three sets of independent variables. They examine the effect of *institutional-elite* variables ("characteristics of state policy-makers likely to be related to state adoption of family leave policy"), *constituency-demand* variables ("attitudes and identifications held by the state population that are thought to increase support for family leave policies") and *contextual-demand* variables ("demographic characteristics of the state population that are expected to increase or decrease the likelihood that family leave policy will be perceived by a substantial proportion of the population as being in its self-interest").[70] Garand and Monroe find that nonsouthern states controlled by Republicans were less likely to have enacted family and medical leave policies, while urban states that had ratified the ERA and had higher percentages of women in their legislatures were more likely to have enacted family and medical leave policies.

Garand and Monroe's study provides important information about the kind of states and the Ddistrict of Columbia that are likely to have passed family and medical leave, and their findings resonate with other models of state policy innovation. Essentially, they argue that family and medical leave policies are more likely to pass in liberal states (as shown by the importance of Democratic party control and by urbanism, which is usually correlated with liberalism), which are more sympathetic to feminism (as shown by their ratification of the ERA and their election of more women to state legislative office). While these findings are not surprising, given the nature of family and medical leave as a policy that is usually supported by liberals and feminists but not conservatives, it is nonetheless valuable to see that Garand and Monroe's findings are congruent with intuition about the nature of support for family and medical leave.

Selecting the Case Studies

The four state case studies described in chapters 3 and 4 move beyond the contextual data, providing insight into the debates over family and medical leave that cannot be obtained through quantitative studies alone. I chose the case studies based on the data from Garand and Monroe's quantitative study in order to understand why advocates in some states with contextual resources (being liberal, supportive of feminism) still did not manage to pass a policy, while others did, and why advocates in some states with few resources managed to pass a policy, while advocates in others did not. In addition to selecting case studies based on political liberalism and support for feminism, I divided the cases by region, choosing two southern and two nonsouthern states. I wanted to find out whether the well-known maxim in American politics, that "the South is different"[71] applied to policy making for family and medical leave.

My four case studies are thus divided into two pairs of states. Each pair is in the same region and is similar both ideologically and in support for feminism. Within each pair, one state passed a family and medical leave while the other did not. Using this methodology allowed me to control as much as possible for the contextual factors and to allow a narrower focus on the political opportunity structure, on the resources available to coalitions of supporters, and on the strategies they chose.

The first pair of case studies are Connecticut and Massachusetts, New England states that are similar ideologically and that were dominated by Democrats in the late 1980s.[72] Both states have a strong record on women's rights; both ratified the ERA within a year of its passage. Finally, Connecticut and Massachusetts were among the first states in the nation to enact maternity disability laws in the early 1970s. While a family and medical leave law passed in Connecticut in 1989, however, in Massachusetts proponents tried and failed to pass a family leave law that included wage replacement throughout the 1980s.

The second pair of case studies is Tennessee and North Carolina, two southern and relatively conservative states. Both states had bitter debates during the struggle to ratify the ERA: North Carolina never ratified it,[73] while Tennessee ratified it and then rescinded ratification. Neither state had a maternity disability law in place in 1987, when family and medical leave bills were introduced for the first time in both states. Tennessee passed a wide-ranging maternity leave law in that year, but bills introduced each legislative session in North Carolina between 1987 and 1993 failed to pass.

This book compares the debate over family and medical leave in the four states with the debate over the federal Family and Medical Leave Act, which passed in 1993. The study was conducted largely through the use of 128 interviews conducted between April 1995, and June 1996, plus an additional ten follow-up interviews conducted in the summer and fall of 1999 (see appendix 1 for a description of the selection process and appendix 2 for a list of interview subjects). Interview data were supplemented with an examination of bill drafts, hearing and committee transcripts (where available), briefing papers, memos, personal files, and news accounts.

Plan of the Project

Chapter 2 provides a historical context for studying family and medical leave policy and for understanding the moderation dilemma faced by advocates. A history of political responses to working women in the twentieth century serves as background for a discussion of the first efforts to pass work-family policies during the 1960s and 1970s.

The chapter focuses on the historic tension between achieving special protection for women and families and providing opportunities for them to achieve equality. This tension emerged again during the debate over family and medical leave.

Chapters 3 and 4 present the findings from the state case studies. Chapter three describes the findings from case studies of Connecticut and Massachusetts, where in the mid-1980s, conditions were excellent for passing legislation on family and medical leave. Success in Connecticut is attributed both to the resources possessed by the major proponent of the bill there and to the willingness of the proponents to compromise until the bill covered only employers of seventy-five or more people. The proponents in Massachusetts did not possess the requisite political clout and also hurt their chances by introducing a bill with a wage replacement provision attached. The initial proposal for "paid family leave" stigmatized the proponents and made it impossible for them to bargain and compromise successfully.

Chapter 4 presents findings from case studies of Tennessee and North Carolina. The quantitative data suggest that it should have been difficult for both of these states to pass family and medical leave legislation, yet in 1987 Tennessee became one of the first states to do so. The key to success in Tennessee lies in a combination of resources and strategy. The bill was introduced by two moderate, well-respected legislators and by a well-established interest group. A maternity leave covering women only was proposed, and the bill was compromised to cover only employers of 100 or more people. In contrast, an effort to pass legislation mandating a parental leave policy in North Carolina failed, but more as a result of a dearth of resources available to proponents and to political chaos at the time than to strategic decisions.

Chapter 5 presents findings from the case study of federal family and medical leave. The advocates for national family and medical leave comprised a bipartisan group of legislators and a coalition of labor, church, and professional women's groups adept at using insider tactics. Like their counterparts in Connecticut, these groups were willing to compromise, in this case from originally covering employers of five or more people for twenty-six weeks to covering employers of fifty or more people for twelve weeks. They were also willing to eschew paid leave. Unlike their counterparts in Tennessee, however, these organizations were unwilling to propose a maternity leave bill covering women only, even though they knew that it would be easier to pass. While this strategy is thought to have lengthened the time to pass the law, it left the proponents with their desired gender-neutral bill when it finally did pass.

A number of scholars have suggested that states may serve as laboratories for one another and for the federal government. This suggests that once a number of states passed family and medical leave policies and the benefits of these policies could be shown, other states and the federal government would be more likely to adopt policies themselves. The laboratories hypothesis is considered in the second half of chapter 5. While respondents thought that states that enacted family and medical leave policies early did serve as models for other states and for the federal effort, they argued that this effect was tempered by the unwillingness of policymakers in a number of states (especially in the South) to emulate policies enacted elsewhere. Further, while advocates for the federal Family and Medical Leave Act stated that they used state examples to show that the policy would benefit people without significant costs to business, they argued that this had a limited impact and that it was offset by the ability of opponents to frame family and medical leave as a states rights issue and to argue that there was no need for a federal bill.

Chapter 6 examines the impact of the federal Family and Medical Leave Act since its passage. The leaders of the coalition that passed the FMLA hoped that the bill they had passed would be a first step, and that they would soon be able to pass legislation covering more workers and providing some wage replacement. More than seven years after the passage of the FMLA, these goals have not been accomplished, but organizing for a paid family leave has begun in a dozen states. In 1999 advocates for paid family and medical leave gained a boost from President Clinton, who issued a directive to the Department of Labor permitting states to use surplus unemployment compensation funds to provide leaves for the parents of newborn or newly adopted babies. However, as of the fall of 2000, no state had passed a paid family leave bill.

Chapter 6 evaluates the effort to pass a paid family leave within the context of the moderation dilemma. As explained earlier, advocates who agree to a compromise have no way of knowing whether they are, in fact, achieving the best policy possible, or whether they should hold out for a better policy down the road. Using the hindsight that the advocates could not have had, I analyze the compromises made in the process of passing the Family and Medical Leave Act. I argue that while the policy cannot be considered an unqualified success because it has not yet been expanded, it has helped to legitimize government involvement in work-family issues and it has laid important groundwork for the enactment of paid family leave.

Chapter 7 discusses implications of the moderation dilemma and concludes the project. The moderation dilemma affects activists on many issues. It is exacerbated on issues around which there are severe collective action problems or divided public sentiment. In the case of the women's movement, the dilemma has increased as the movement matures and makes the transition to interest groups. While radical and reformist approaches may in fact complement each other, this does not diminish the tension felt among activists over what can and cannot be accomplished. This tension is unlikely to be resolved soon.

2 EQUALITY AND DIFFERENCE
The Historical Context for Family
and Medical Leave

Family and medical leave bills have roots as far back as the Progressive Era, when modern labor regulations were first being developed. Because of constitutional constraints, the dominance of laissez-faire ideology, and the strength of business interests, the ability of progressive reformers to enact comprehensive regulations was limited. Unable to improve everyone's working conditions, many reformers narrowed their scope and, basing their arguments on Victorian ideas about the importance of women's roles as mothers, lobbied successfully to enact regulations covering women only. But these benefits came at a cost, which was recognized by some even then: focusing on women's status as mothers and attempting to gain special treatment to accommodate that status made it harder for women to achieve equality. This dilemma about how to respond to motherhood has divided feminists ever since.

Throughout the twentieth century, the percentage of women in the workforce steadily increased until in 1960 the participation rate for married women was 30.5 percent, and the participation rate for married women with children under six was 18.6 percent. Between 1930 and 1960, these increases in women's participation in the workforce, punctuated by the participation of "Rosie the Riveters" during World War II, were generally not accompanied by cultural change: the idea that women belong in the home persisted. But between 1960 and 1988, as the participation rate in the labor force for married women increased 86 percent, from 30.5 to 56.5 percent, the participation rate for married women with children under six increased 207 *percent*, from 18.6 percent to 57.1 percent. This latter change, prompted both by declining wages and by the ideas of the reemerging women's movement, led to an intensification of the debate over governmental responses to the problems of working women and a renewal of the equality versus difference dilemma.

This chapter traces the history of political and regulatory responses to working women in the twentieth century. Efforts to develop labor policies for women are examined, and the debate among feminists over strategy and tactics is analyzed. Particular attention is paid to the activities of feminists during the two decades preceding the introduction of family and medical leave. It was during this time that the modern equality versus difference debate emerged and family and medical leave came to be seen as the type of policy that both sides could agree on.

The Progressive Era: Success through "Maternalism"

The industrial revolution brought about many changes for American workers. The locus of work moved out of the home and into the factory. With this move came a number of well-publicized abuses in working conditions and the impetus for progressive reform. But efforts to enact such reforms as the minimum wage or maximum working hours were challenged in the courts, and many early regulations were struck down as violations of freedom of contract.[1] The most notable case was *Lochner v. New York*, a 1905 Supreme Court decision prohibiting New York State from limiting the working hours of bakers to ten hours a day, six days a week. The Court declared that the interest of the state in the bakers' health was outweighed by the right of the bakers to choose to work as many hours as they wanted.[2] As Theda Skocpol notes, *Lochner* had a chilling effect on progressive reformers, who after 1905 no longer focused on "broad hours laws for male workers."[3]

Unable to achieve the broad reforms they desired, advocates began to propose narrower reforms. One group they turned to was women workers. While women had entered the paid workforce during the Industrial Revolution, their participation had led to considerable social discomfort, associated with the emergence during the nineteenth century of a "cult of true womanhood," which considered women physically frail but morally pure and determined that "a woman's place is in the home."[4] As a result, only poor women entered the workforce during the early industrial period, and even they did so only once their families were assured that their working conditions would be clean and that they would remain "pure."[5]

As the industrial revolution progressed, however, the desire for profit, combined with the fact that so many women workers were poor, black, or immigrants,[6] led to the dropping of standards. Employers found that women could be paid less than men, both because of their "frailty" and because they were assumed to be supported by men.[7] This latter assumption that women were working for "pin money" instead of for desperately needed wages prevailed for much of the twentieth century and in part accounts for the widespread failure of labor unions to organize women workers. Alice Kessler-Harris observes that at the beginning of the Progressive Era, conditions for women at many work sites were as bad as those for men. "A restraining ideology rooted in revered familial relationships forbade effective solutions to the dilemma facing female wage workers. Having been placed out of bounds through no fault of their own, they had been denied women's traditional protections and left to fend for themselves."[8]

While organized women workers were unable to achieve substantial reforms, middle-class Progressives were more successful. Basing their claims directly on the Victorian notions of motherhood and drawing on both cultural and legal precedents,[9] these reformers argued that women deserved special protection not just because of their status as women but because of their status as mothers.

Many scholars emphasize that in Victorian society, influenced by the "cult of true womanhood," mothering took on the characteristics of a political avocation. Paula Baker states: "Mothering was crucial: by raising civic-minded, virtuous sons, [women] insured the survival of the republic."[10] During the late nineteenth century, a movement for "educated motherhood" grew among middle-class women. The leaders of this movement, who founded the National Congress of Mothers in 1897, argued that an important task such as mothering required training and that social institutions should be structured to emphasize the importance of children and, in particular, the importance of contact between mothers and children.[11]

The activities of maternalist reformers were widely approved, and their arguments became powerful political tools. Where labor activists could not get a hearing, reformers emphasizing women's special role as mothers could. A good example of this phenomenon is the 1908 Supreme Court case *Mueller v. Oregon*, a case involving the working hours of female laundresses. *Mueller* is especially interesting because of the degree to which it contrasts with *Lochner v. New York*, decided only three years earlier. In *Mueller*, the Court found that the state had a compelling interest in a woman's working conditions because of her maternal role. "Woman's physical structure and the performance of maternal functions place her at a disadvantage in the struggle for subsistence. . . . This is especially true when the burdens of motherhood are upon her. . . . As healthy mothers are essential to vigorous offspring, the physical well-being of woman becomes an object of public interest and care in order to preserve the strength and vigor of the race."[12]

Basing its decision on a brief filed by the soon-to-be justice Louis Brandeis, the Court found that the state's interest in women's health justified restrictions on women's working hours, even when similar restrictions on men's working hours had been rejected. In Justice Brewer's words, a working woman is "properly placed in a class by herself."[13]

Most progressive reformers rejoiced at the *Mueller* decision, delighted by the fact that they had been able to gain protections for at least some of the population and hoping that the decision would set a precedent for further reforms.[14] And indeed, by 1917, nineteen states had passed laws limiting women's working hours.[15] One reason for this enthusiasm was that many reformers disapproved of women's working and hoped to limit it as much as possible; they were seeking to protect those women who had to work instead of opening the door for more women to do so. One reformer stated: "Under justly ordered social and industrial conditions, women would not have become wage-earners at all. . . . But since, under the present industrial system, they have become a permanent factor in industry, their condition, wages, hours, and physical fitness . . . is one of the most vitally important questions of the time."[16] Other reformers were less enthusiastic, arguing that while protections benefited many, they also further differentiated women from men in the workplace, thus threatening women's equality.

Many critics of the *Mueller* decision were members of the National Woman's party. The NWP, which introduced the Equal Rights Amend-

ment (ERA) in Congress in 1923, was among the first women's organization to actively seek equal rights for women.[17] The NWP's emphasis
on equality led the group to consider the idea that protective legislation
constituted sex discrimination. At first, members of the group were reluctant to accept this idea, for a time embracing *both* the principle of
equal rights and the principle that women's physical characteristics
and status as mothers warranted special treatment. But over time many
members came to believe that "enacting labor laws along sex lines is
erecting another handicap for women in the economic struggle."[18]

The approach taken by the National Woman's party was opposed
by reformers from groups like the League of Women Voters and the
Women's Trade Union League, which had a long history of distrust and
animosity toward the NWP.[19] Fearing that an equal rights amendment
would undo the achievements of protective legislation, members of
these groups waged an all-out war against the ERA. They were joined
by the National Consumer's League, led by former NWP member Flo-
rence Kelley, by organized labor, and by the director of the newly created Women's Bureau of the Department of Labor, Mary Anderson.
Arguing that the National Woman's party activists were "theoretical"
feminists "talking about things and conditions entirely outside their
own experience or knowledge,"[20] Anderson guided a controversial 1928
study that found that women suffered few discriminatory effects as the
result of protective labor legislation.[21]

And so was born the debate over equality and difference within the
feminist movement. This debate continued throughout the twentieth
century and remains salient today. Policy advocates have struggled to
reconcile the desire for women to achieve equality with the fact that
motherhood, due to some combination of biology and culture, bestows
on women a distinctly different experience.

The Depression-Era Experience

Women's participation in the workforce increased steadily during
the Depression and World War II, though it was not accompanied by
significant changes in public conceptions about women's roles. Rather,
with few exceptions, the ideal of domesticity and motherhood that had
been established during the Victorian Era and that had served as a basis
for Progressive Era protective reforms was maintained. In great part be-

cause of the persistence of these cultural norms, the policy effects of the New Deal and World War II were limited for women. The legitimacy of women's participation in the labor force was challenged anew during the Depression, and while New Deal reforms set important regulatory precedents, women received fewer immediate benefits from these reforms than did men. Further, during World War II, the United States government made its first concerted effort to encourage women to work, but this campaign was designed to maintain the ideal of domesticity and to limit women's work to wartime only. However, the New Deal legitimized the role of the state in protecting all workers rather than just women, and the experience of World War II demonstrated that even pregnant women and mothers were capable of engaging in paid work.

During the Depression, a major defense for discrimination against women was the fact that they were competing with men for scarce jobs. Relying on the Progressive Era idea that most women were working for superfluous "pin money" and that they should not ideally be working for pay, employers and policy makers alike agreed that in times of economic scarcity, women and particularly married women with employed husbands should be the last to be hired and the first to be fired. One historian quotes a magazine editor's proposal to fire women as a way to end the Depression: "Simply fire the women, who shouldn't be working anyway, and hire the men. Presto! No unemployment. No relief roles. No depression."[22] And despite the fact that the view that they did not need to work was almost certainly erroneous (Kessler-Harris estimates that "nearly one-third of married women who worked were entirely responsible for their families, while 55.6 percent shared the responsibility with others"[23]), married women were seen as selfish for keeping jobs that men were thought to need more.

As a consequence, many married women lost their jobs during the Great Depression. The greatest losers were women in jobs that were not strictly defined as women's work. These jobs, which included teaching and social work as well as government service and manufacturing, were the most desirable to unemployed men. Many of the losses were facilitated by municipal decision making: 77 percent of school districts surveyed in 1931 said that they would not hire married women, while 84 percent of insurance companies, 65 percent of banks, and 63 percent of public utility companies limited the employment of

married women in some way. And on the federal level, a provision of
the National Economy Act of 1932 prohibited both spouses from being
employed by the federal government.[24] The public largely supported
these actions: a 1936 Gallup poll found that 82 percent of Americans
approved of employer discrimination against married women.[25]

Female elites were divided in their responses to this treatment.
Many thought that well-off women did, in fact, have a duty not to take
jobs from those who needed them more. In a commencement speech in
1931, the dean of Barnard College told the graduating class that if it is
not "necessary for you to be gainfully employed, . . . [then] perhaps the
greatest service you can render to the community is to . . . refuse to
work for gain."[26] But other feminists protested what they considered to
be arbitrary dismissals of women. Officials from the National Women's
Trade Union League, for example, argued that economic situation
rather than marital status should be the important criterion.[27]

Major labor unions also did little to help women seeking to keep
their jobs or to participate in the expansion of the welfare state that
came with the New Deal. As a result, many occupations traditionally
held by women were exempted from the National Recovery Act's minimum wage and hour codes.[28] Despite these impediments, women's
employment actually rose during the 1930s, and their economic situation improved relative to that of men. There are several reasons for
this. First, employment in traditionally women's occupations did not
drop as quickly as employment in traditionally men's occupations,
and even unemployed men were sometimes loath to take "women's
work."[29] Second, in a time of economic difficulty, some employers
were eager to hire women, who could be paid lower wages.[30] And third,
although NRA codes did exempt many traditional women's occupations from minimum wage and hour laws, the fact that women held a
larger proportion of the remaining low-paid jobs meant that their status became disproportionately better.[31]

The fact that the New Deal greatly expanded the capacity of the
U.S. government to respond to social problems affected the situation of
working women in both the short and the long term. In addition to creating historically unprecedented social programs, the New Deal expanded the concept of government function to include both social
provision and business regulation; in short, it redefined the state.[32] The
experience of the Depression had expelled the idea that social problems

are always individual in origin, and should rarely if ever be solved by the government. Overturning the precedent set in *Lochner v. New York*, Congress and the Court established the right of the government to set standards for wages, hours, and working conditions for all workers, rather than just for women.[33] This meant that even though some occupations in which they were clustered were not covered, women could, for the first time, lay claim to protections on an equal basis with men.

Women in the Workforce during World War II

Following the bombing of Pearl Harbor and the declaration of war, millions of American men and women were mobilized to fight. The result was a massive labor shortage on the home front, exacerbated by the need to manufacture the machinery of war. While jobs could be filled by unemployed people and by migrants from the South (particularly blacks), within a year these people were not sufficient.[34] The only group left consisted of previously unemployed women.

The mobilization of women into the workforce during World War II delineates the era as a watershed for working women.[35] As Claudia Goldin points out, however, more than half of the women who entered the workforce after Pearl Harbor left it between 1944 and 1950.[36] While women were urged to work for the duration of the war, their continuation in the workforce after the war was not encouraged.

Mobilizing women into wartime production, which ran counter to the norms of the period, required a tremendous recruiting effort. Many employers and many of the women themselves were prejudiced against women's participation in the workforce, and most of the open jobs were in what had traditionally been considered male occupations. In response, government and industry leaders orchestrated a sophisticated public relations campaign to encourage women to work, but only for the duration of the war. This campaign suggested that women should have patriotic rather than financial motivations for entering the workforce. Ignoring the fact that at least half of the women who worked during World War II were already working before it started, wartime propaganda showed women working in order to "do their part" and to support boyfriends and husbands fighting abroad. The classic image in both music and art was of "Rosie the Riveter" protecting her boyfriend

Charlie ("Charlie, he's a marine") by "working overtime on the rivet-ing machine."[37] Popular imagery portrayed Rosie as remaining true to her womanhood even while she is engaged in the dirty and distinctly unfeminine work of fighting fascism. Gluck describes the famous Nor-man Rockwell drawing of Rosie the Riveter that appeared on the cover of the Saturday *Evening Post*: "The double message was clear: her loafer-clad foot was firmly planted on *Mein Kampf*, symbolizing her role in stamping out fascism, but she could still remain feminine, as the powder puff and mirror peeking out of her coverall pocket re-minded."[38]

However, most women were drawn to war work primarily because it offered steady employment and better wages. And while much of the propaganda depicted young women and mothers eager to return to their family responsibilities, in actuality most entrants to the workplace were either single or beyond childbearing age.[39] While certainly the most significant growth among women in the workplace during World War II was among married women, resistance among women and the public at large prevented many women with young children from par-ticipating.[40]

The campaign to recruit women into wartime production also em-phasized that women entering the workforce were doing so only tem-porarily. This subject drew considerable attention from government, literary, and commercial sources. Many advertisements included ap-peals to motherhood and family as they promised equal efficiency and quality from items that would be produced for home use after the war. One such advertisement for the ADEL Precision Products Company, published in *The Saturday Evening Post* in May 1944, showed a little girl asking her riveter mother, "Mother, when will you stay home again?" The small print states that "in her post-war home she'll want the same high degree of precision and she will get them when ADEL converts . . . to products of equal dependability for home and industry."[41]

Employers and unions accepted these assumptions about women workers in developing policy toward them. Viewing women as tempo-rary workers, employers were often loath to invest in them by giving them more than cursory training.[42] And many unions, which could have viewed the new women workers as potential constituents, pre-ferred to remind them that they were holding jobs for men and that they would be expected to give those jobs up after the war was over. Women needed to keep up standards for men, but that was all.[43]

Despite these efforts, however, a "considerable number" of women who were surveyed toward the end of the war said that they would like to keep their jobs.[44] This posed a problem for business and government leaders, who had to explain why, if women were doing these nontraditional jobs well, they should not be allowed to compete for them in the future. Until the war, women had been considered incapable of doing much of the work that they were suddenly found to be eminently capable of doing. Their obvious ability made it hard to explain why they should suddenly stop.

Many scholars agree that the campaign to persuade women to leave their jobs was as powerful as the one to persuade them to take them in the first place. Several methods were used. The first, which is described above, consisted of putting pressure on women to persuade them that going back home after the war was the right thing to do. The second involved the application of the new field of psychiatry. Studying child and family development, psychologists and pediatricians (notably, Dr. Benjamin Spock) offered expert confirmation of what reformers had worried about since mothers began to enter the workforce: that children raised in group settings were disadvantaged compared with those whose mothers stayed home.[45] Mothers who had joined the workforce during World War II were thus subject to social pressures that defined them as selfish and uncaring if they continued to work outside the home.

The process was facilitated by the wartime experience of segregating women into certain kinds of jobs (such as riveting) that were categorized as "suitable" for women workers.[46] When the war ended, employers making the transition from war production to domestic production could argue that most women's jobs were, "unfortunately," the ones that were not needed in the postwar economy. This practice made it easy to lay off thousands of women workers while simultaneously hiring returning male veterans with less experience and seniority.[47] However, a study of employment patterns at a Ford plant in Michigan found that many of the jobs commonly held by women during the war did not disappear at the end of it. Furthermore, women employed during the war were concentrated in a number of jobs (such as assembly) that were, for the purposes of wartime employment, relatively unimportant; with the shift to postwar automobile production at Ford, they actually became more important. Acknowledging that riveting, the most stereotypical women's job during the war, *did* become obsolete afterward, Kossoudji and Dresser argue: "Anna the Assembler and Millie the Machinist performed work that was as functional to automobile production as it was to the production of bombers. Yet when Rosie [the Riveter]'s job disappeared, Anna and Millie too found themselves unemployed. Occupational shifts cannot be presented as the entire story of the disappearance of women industrial workers."[48]

Thus Kossoudji and Dresser join a group of scholars who argue that despite the fact that the 1940s was a break point in women's employment (and particularly married women's employment), the experience of the war did not in itself do much for women.

The World War II era remains significant, however, because it represents the first national experience of accommodating work and family. While certainly most women with young children still did not work even during wartime, many did. The result of this, as Karen Anderson notes, was "the largest commitment to public child care in the nation's history," with the federal government spending more than $50 million dollars to fund approximately 3,000 child care centers serving more than 600,000 children.[49] Many of these centers were badly managed and subject to public disapproval, and most of them closed down for lack of funds after the war. But the mere fact of their existence provided an important precedent for the future.

The issue of family leave was also raised by the Women's and Children's Bureau of the Department of Labor. Early in the war, the Women's Bureau issued guidelines for employers, which were remarkably similar to those offered by the proponents of family and medical leave forty years later. The recommendations were that pregnant women be given a total of three-and-a-half months leave, six weeks before birth and eight weeks afterward, and that they be guaranteed reinstatement and seniority rights.[50] Following a study of employer practices toward pregnant women in 1942–43, the Children's Bureau argued that "aesthetic and moral misgivings" rather than concern for genuine health risks were the basis for discrimination against pregnant women.[51]

While these recommendations were obviously not adopted and fell by the wayside after the war, their existence set an important precedent for the future. Despite the fact that the World War II experience did not definitively establish that women *should* be in the workforce or that government could effectively play a role in developing work-family policies, some groundwork for both of those goals was laid. In later decades, advocates of work-family policies would invoke the positive aspects of the World War II experience (that women performed well, that they needed day care and family leave, and that some success in providing these benefits was achieved) to support their arguments that government could and should get involved in work-family issues.

The Postwar Period

As a result of national and international rebuilding, the postwar years witnessed unusually high economic growth, with median family income increasing a dramatic 42.5 percent between 1949 and 1959.[52] For the first time in almost two decades, people had money to spend and something to spend it on. As Stephanie Coontz points out, "For most Americans, the most salient symbol and immediate beneficiary of their newfound prosperity was the nuclear family: overwhelmingly, people spent their new wealth on homes in the suburbs, furniture, clothing, and appliances."[53] One consequence of this trend toward displaying prosperity in the home meant that living up to cultural norms required women and particularly mothers to remain out of the workforce more than ever before. The ideal family, as portrayed in television shows such as "Leave It to Beaver" and "Ozzie and Harriet," comprised a father earning a family wage, a stay-at-home mother, and between two and four children. Following the expert advice, the mother in this ideal family was a nurturer and care giver and as such was the "moral guardian of civilization itself."[54]

Thus, culturally speaking, the decade of the 1950s was a period of retrenchment for American working women. The similarities between the family ideal of the 1950s and the Victorian "cult of domesticity" are unmistakable, with some scholars suggesting that the family ideal was a response to insecurity prompted by the cold war, just as the cult of domesticity was prompted by the insecurity of the early industrial period.[55] Women, and particularly mothers who worked, were disregarding the important role that society had given them. Like the domestic ideals of the nineteenth century, this modern ideal was unrealistic. Contrary to myth, married women's employment actually increased during the 1950s, in part because the standard of living had been increased and even during that decade could not be maintained by all single earner families.[56] Furthermore, as it became painfully clear in Betty Friedan's work *The Feminine Mystique,* many women who stayed home were miserably unhappy in their confined roles as housewives and mothers.[57]

Friedan's identification of "the problem that has no name" was one catalyst for the women's movement that emerged during the 1960s and 1970s. For the first time in this century, and particularly for middle-class, college educated women, the idea of pursuing a career even at the expense of family became a popularly accepted alternative and indeed a worthy political goal.[58] The ideal of woman as the family nurturer was challenged, and the acceptability of such things as group child care was, for the first time, supported by a substantial segment of the population. Partly as a result of these new norms, workforce participation for married women, and particularly for mothers of young children, increased 64.2 percent and 142 percent respectively between 1960 and 1980, compared with only 39.5 percent for single women.[59]

Although feminism facilitated women's participation in the workforce by prompting changes in women's thinking and, to some extent, changes in public and elite acceptance of working women, it should not be seen as the only reason why women entered the paid workforce. Many women who entered the workforce during the 1960s and 1970s, and many women who work outside the home today, do not identify themselves as feminists and do not support the goals of the women's movement. In fact, many of these women are not even in the paid workforce by choice.[60]

The other reason that women and particularly mothers of young children entered the workforce in such high numbers was that after 1973, American real wages began to decline.[61] This made it much more difficult for one earner (the man), working a standard forty-hour work week, to earn a "family wage." As a result, as Juliet Schor demonstrates, two things happened. First, men increased their work hours, putting in more overtime or working more than one job, to make up for the decrease in their real wages. And second, women went to work to supplement family incomes.[62]

Modern Movements to Accommodate Work and Family

Between 1970 and 1980, the percentage of married women with children under age six in the paid workforce increased from 30.3 percent to 45.1 percent.[63] This rapid increase in conjunction with activism by feminists and social policy experts led to a modern movement for policy responses to the problems encountered by working parents.

The modern movement to accommodate work and family began at about the same time as the feminist movement during the early 1960s, with the release of a 1963 report by the President's Commission on the Status of Women. Appointed by a reluctant President John F. Kennedy, the commission called for policy changes including better child care services for "those who decide to work" and an end to discrimination in the workforce.[64] The next year, Title VII of the Civil Rights Act of 1964 was passed, banning among other things employment discrimination based on sex. While members of the Commission on the Status of Women supported Title VII,[65] the bill cannot be said to have come out of the commission's work, as it passed largely in an attempt to block support for the larger civil rights bill.

The Civil Rights Act of 1964 created the Equal Employment Opportunity Commission (EEOC), which was charged with implementing the new laws. Although the EEOC was initially reluctant to get involved in pregnancy discrimination,[66] it became more active as the women's movement grew and congressional passage of the Equal Rights Amendment (ERA) became certain. In 1972 the EEOC issued guidelines interpreting Title VII as prohibiting pregnancy discrimination. Lower courts responded by ruling for plaintiffs in dismissal and denial-of-benefit cases.[67]

But starting in 1974, the Supreme Court dealt a blow to those seeking to equate pregnancy discrimination with sex discrimination. In two cases, *Geduldig v. Aiello* (1974) and *General Electric v. Gilbert* (1976), the Court ruled that despite the fact that only women get pregnant, insurance and disability programs that exclude pregnancy do not discriminate on the basis of sex. The decisions emphasized the fact that pregnancy is a "physical condition" that does not affect all women categorically. In *Geduldig*, the Court majority determined that disability plans not covering pregnancy do not "exclude anyone from benefit eligibility because of gender but merely remove one physical condition from the list of compensable disabilities."[68] And in *Gilbert*, Justice Rehnquist argued, "While it is true that only women can become pregnant, it does not follow that every legislative classification concerning pregnancy is a sex-based classification."[69] The decisions in both cases were accompanied by vigorous dissents, emphasizing that, despite the fact that not all women become pregnant, only women experience pregnancy-related discrimination.

Given the political climate of the 1970s, in which the ERA had just been passed in Congress and was still expected to be ratified by the states, it was not surprising that Congress acted quickly to amend Title VII and prohibit pregnancy discrimination.[70] As Joyce Gelb and Marian Lief Palley describe, within days of the *Gilbert* decision in December 1976, a coalition of more than three hundred groups, including women's groups, labor unions, and even right-to-life organizations, had developed to petition for an amendment to Title VII.[71] And as befit the political climate of the time, hearings on the bill emphasized the idea that it would provide pregnant women only with equal opportunity, rather than special treatment.[72] The resulting Pregnancy Discrimination Act of 1978 amended the Civil Rights Act to prohibit discrimination in employment on the basis of pregnancy, and required that any health or disability plan cover pregnancy as it covered other medical conditions.[73]

Because the Pregnancy Discrimination Act (PDA) mandated that pregnancy be treated on an equal basis with other disabilities, it was ideologically acceptable to the "equality feminist" descendants of the National Women's party who in the 1970s had emerged as a significant force within the women's movement and who feared that classifying pregnancy as a special condition could make it more difficult for women to achieve equality in the workplace.[74] But the PDA did not require employers to provide disability or other benefits to pregnant women. As a result, millions of women whose employers did not provide disability benefits were left without job protections should they become pregnant. Arguing that this *effectively* meant that pregnant women were being discriminated against, a group of advocates began a movement to pass legislation to require employers to give women maternity leaves. Members of this movement were the ideological descendants of the "difference feminists" of the Progressive Era, who had argued that because only women become pregnant they should be entitled to special treatment in the workplace.

Within several years of the passage of the Pregnancy Discrimination Act, a number of states had enacted laws requiring that employers of a certain size provide maternity benefits to all women. The laws in two of these states, California and Montana, were challenged as violations of the equal treatment provisions of Title VII of the 1964 Civil Rights Act and of the Pregnancy Discrimination Act.

As the two lawsuits wound their way through the courts, they were subject to conflicting decisions. In *Miller Wohl Company v. Commissioner of Labor and Industry*, the Montana Supreme Court found that the Montana Maternity Leave Act enhanced rather than contradicted the Pregnancy Discrimination Act, and that "by removing pregnancy-related disabilities as a legal ground for discharge from employment, the MMLA places men and women on more equal terms."[75] But in *California Federal Savings and Loan v. Guerra*, the California Supreme Court found that that state's maternity disability leave law violated the Civil Rights Act of 1964. However, this decision was promptly overturned by the Ninth Circuit Court of Appeals and was subsequently appealed to the Supreme Court.

Both the *Miller Wohl* and the *Cal Fed* cases split the feminist legal community, just as the special protection statutes had divided the feminist community sixty years earlier. The debate intensified as the advocates waited for the Supreme Court to review *Cal Fed*. Many advocates, including the sponsor of the California law and local feminist and civil liberties groups, supported the California maternity leave law and proposed passing a national maternity leave law to override the lower court decision. They argued that maternity leave laws do not "'protect' women from the workplace, but instead *enable* women to be in the workplace."[76] But another group of advocates, led by national women's organizations and by the national ACLU, was more equivocal. While not directly opposing the California maternity leave law, they emphasized the costs of protective legislation and suggested that the best solution would be to enact disability legislation covering all workers.[77]

This new approach, championed by feminist legal scholars Wendy Williams and Susan Deller Ross, reflected new thinking among advocates for working women and served as the foundation for the family and medical leave proposal. These feminists saw clear risks involved in passing protective, maternity-only legislation: for them this legislation was associated not only with the lack of economic opportunities for women, but also with stereotypes of women as primarily mothers. This view was in turn linked to an emerging belief that women's childbearing role was a major source of women's global oppression.[78] Thus for these advocates, a policy that responded to pregnancy and child rearing in the workplace needed also to respond to the historical linkage between women and the domestic sphere and to provide a new model through which both men and women would be regarded as legitimate members of both the public and private spheres. Williams quotes Ann Scales: "True equality requires not just women in men's jobs and operating men's institutions, but also that those institutions be replaced by others broad enough to accommodate the full range of human activities."[79]

Family and Medical Leave and the Equality/Difference Dilemma

For both equality and difference feminists, family and medical leave offered a solution to the century-long debate over equal protection and special protection for women workers. By situating pregnancy within a variety of personal needs, gender-neutral family and medical leave emphasizes what women of childbearing age have in common with men and with women beyond childbearing age, rather than "singling out women or mothers as a separate class."[80] Furthermore, by providing leave benefits for either parent for the purpose of tending to a newborn or sick child, family and medical leave sends the message that while only women can become pregnant, men are just as able as women to perform child rearing duties. Family and medical leave thus provides a needed benefit for pregnant women without singling them out as needing protection and thus compromising their drive for equality.

The advocates who introduced the first family and medical leave bill in Congress in 1985 insisted on introducing a gender-neutral bill instead of a national maternity leave bill that would cover women only. These advocates persisted with their gender-neutral bill even after the Supreme Court overturned *California Federal Savings and Loan Association v. Guerra*, ruling in 1987 that mandated maternity leaves did not violate the Pregnancy Discrimination Act of 1978.[81] But the decision to introduce family rather than maternity leave was a difficult one, in which the advocates were pitted against those who worried that, while appeals to maternalism might work as they had in the past, a broader bill would be considerably more difficult to pass.

While the advocates on the national level were pursuing their effort to pass a gender-neutral family and medical leave bill, some state level advocates proposed bills covering women only. Most of these bills mandated that employers provide some disability leave for pregnant mothers, usually for a six- or eight-week period (doctors typically define a woman as "disabled" for six weeks after a normal childbirth). The bill enacted in Tennessee, which will be discussed in chapter 4, is an exception to this general rule: it provides four months of leave both for recovery from childbirth and for the purpose of encouraging "bonding" between a mother and child.

The national level family and medical leave bill was from the beginning unpaid, requiring that employers allow their employees to take leave, but not requiring that they pay them. The fact that the family and medical leave proposal was unpaid caused considerable debate both at the time it was introduced and during the nine years it was being debated. This controversy reflects a dispute among the middle-class feminists who have dominated the movement throughout the twentieth century over whether they were truly representing working women. On one side of the paid family leave debate were activists who argued that paid family leave would face even more opposition than unpaid leave, probably dooming proposals to failure. On the other side of the debate were activists who argued that without wage replacement, family and medical leave would be a meaningless benefit for millions of lower-wage workers who cannot afford to take time off without pay.

Advocates in only one state, Massachusetts, decided to introduce a paid family and medical leave during the 1980s. Their decision and the subsequent political process will be analyzed in chapter 3.

Conclusion

Family and medical leave has roots extending back nearly a century, to the origins of work-family policies in the United States. It represents one solution to the debate among feminists about how best to help women achieve equality in the workforce and to have their "different" experiences as mothers accommodated. While some feminists attempted to provide women with special protections, others expressed concern that any special protection stigmatizes women and makes it difficult for them to achieve equal status in the workforce.

Family and medical leave represents a way to reconcile the two perspectives. As noted above, by placing the experience of childbearing within the larger context of caring for family members, family and medical leave emphasizes that giving birth is only one of many family-related tasks that may need to be accommodated at the workplace. Since men can care for children or sick relatives just as easily as women can, a gender-neutral family and medical leave policy minimizes the chance that women will be stereotyped and discriminated against as a result of their making use of the law.

But as the next three chapters will show, passing a gender-neutral family and medical leave bill proved to be difficult in many states and on the national level. Except where the advocates for family and medical leave had access to an exceptional array of resources, advocates had to weigh carefully the importance of having a gender-neutral bill against the fact that maternity-only bills enjoyed more legislative support. One reason for this is that maternity-only bills adhere to traditional norms whereby women are the primary care givers for their children. In contrast, gender-neutral bills emphasize the fact that many care-giving duties can be performed by men. As Gelb and Palley point out, it is generally harder to pass legislation promoting role change.[82] A second reason is that maternity leave bills cover fewer people for only one condition. Because fewer people are eligible to take maternity leaves, they are generally the subject of less opposition.

Advocates for family and medical leave on both the state and national levels thus had to make a difficult choice. Ideologically, most of them preferred to try to pass gender-neutral bills. But practically, they were faced again and again with the fact that it would be easier to pass maternity-only bills. The choices made by advocates reflect their identities, the resources that were available to them, and their beliefs about incremental change and the political process.

3 POLICY MAKING IN A LIBERAL CONTEXT
Connecticut and Massachusetts

If one were going to predict in the early 1980s which states would pass family and medical leave policies, Connecticut and Massachusetts would certainly be at the top of anyone's list. Both states are historically liberal and supportive of women's rights; both were among the first to ratify the Equal Rights Amendment (ERA). Both states had maternity disability laws in place, dating back to the 1970s. Finally, both states were dominated by Democrats during the mid-1980s, and Democrats have historically been more supportive of policies like family and medical leave. However, while family and medical leave policies were introduced in both states in the mid-1980s, a policy passed in Connecticut but not in Massachusetts. This chapter seeks to explain why.

As noted in chapter 1, I studied family and medical leave in Connecticut and Massachusetts primarily by conducting interviews with participants in the political processes there. In keeping with the goals of this project and with the hypotheses described in that chapter, I attempted to identify the resources that were available to advocates for family and medical leave and the constraints they were working under, and I examined the strategies they used to place and advance family and medical leave on the public agenda. I was particularly interested in the choices the advocates made about what to propose, how to frame family and medical leave, how to build coalitions, and when and how to compromise. In both Connecticut and Massachusetts, I found that these strategic decisions, in combination with resources, affected the proponents' ability to attract support and credibility for their bills. This in turn was crucial to their ability to bargain and compromise successfully.

The Proponents in Connecticut: Inside the Political Establishment

Family and medical leave got on the political agenda in Connecticut because it attracted the attention of John Larson, the president pro-tem of the Connecticut Senate. Larson, a senator from Hartford, was physically attractive (many observers noted his resemblance to John F. Kennedy), charismatic, and ambitious; in the mid-1980s he was widely regarded by those around him as an upcoming political star. Larson was clearly looking toward a run for an even higher office, and in the mid-1980s, both his supporters and detractors thought he was searching for political positions from which he could support this move.[1]

As recalled by Cecilia Woods, the director of research for senate Democrats, Larson became interested in work-family issues during hearings on child abuse, in which testimony emphasized the stress felt by working parents.[2] Soon after his election as president pro-tem of the senate, Larson and his staff crafted a holistic "work and family agenda," which comprised some thirty-five bills providing funding for child care, prenatal health programs, before-and-after school programs, and welfare-to-work programs. The cornerstone of the work and family agenda was family and medical leave.

The coalition for family and medical leave that emerged in Connecticut was centered on John Larson. It consisted largely of his staff, the staff of the Democratic caucus, and members of organizations sponsored by the state government: the Permanent Commission on the Status of Women, the Commission on Children, and the Social Services Commission. Women's organizations and labor groups from outside government, who played a crucial role in the effort to pass family and medical leave in Massachusetts, were invited to participate in the political process in Connecticut, but they were emphatically not the leaders and were not relied on to provide crucial support to the movement.

The fact that the leaders of the movement to pass family and medical leave in Connecticut came from inside the political system meant that they had strong incentives to craft legislation that would pass, even if that legislation did not accomplish all that they wanted. Larson, his staff, and his allies wanted to pass a family and medical leave policy for which he could claim credit to support his run for higher office.[3] And the members of the commissions that worked on the bill were professionals, paid to develop policy, rather than volunteers with many other issues and concerns occupying their time. Many of them viewed themselves as working for Larson, and thus had every incentive to cooperate with his objectives.

In contrast, members of women's and labor groups (such as the National Organization for Women [NOW] and the Connecticut AFL-CIO) outside of government had less of a stake in the Connecticut family and medical leave bill. Because their energy and resources would not make the difference between passage and nonpassage, these advocates never had to decide whether the bill was sufficiently "ideological" for them to commit resources. Thus when Larson and his colleagues decided to introduce an unpaid rather than a paid family and medical leave policy in order to boost the chances that the bill would pass, the groups outside of government did not dissent strongly. As one respondent who would have preferred to see a broader bill get introduced explained to me, "Since we were not the lead group, it would have been a little odd if we had said no."

Resources and Strategies

With the position of president pro-tem comes the power to create committees. In the winter of 1987, Larson used this power to create a committee on family and the workplace. While both supporters and detractors of family and medical leave were on the committee (and hearing transcripts reveal considerable dissent), the committee nevertheless provided an institutional mechanism to give special consideration to the policy. As shown by Frank Baumgartner and Bryan Jones, the venue where a bill is considered can be crucial to its success or failure.[4] Having a committee that was not only sympathetic to the idea of family and medical leave but was specifically created to support bills like it by the most powerful person in the senate was an important resource.

In addition to providing a supportive venue for introducing family and medical leave, the Committee on Family and the Workplace also helped to frame the policy as a family issue by situating it within a group of other family-oriented bills. As noted in chapter 1, there are essentially three ways to frame family and medical leave: as a women's issue, as an economic issue, and as a family issue. The public policy literature described in chapter 1 suggests that there are costs associated with framing issues as women's issues.[5] The advocates in Connecticut were aware of this, and they consciously made an effort to frame their proposal for family and medical leave as assistance to the beleaguered family. Grouping family and medical leave with other family-oriented bills was one way to do this, and sending all the bills together through one committee helped make this grouping stick.

Using the resources of committed advocates and the Committee on the Family and the Workplace, Larson and his staff set about devising a three-pronged strategy to get family and medical leave passed. The first part of the strategy involved passing a leave covering state employees only during the 1987 legislative session; this less controversial leave eventually served as a laboratory for the bill covering private employers. The second part of the strategy involved creating a task force to study family and medical leave in the private sector, which included both child development experts and a number of moderately sympathetic representatives from the business community. These representatives provided a hole in the wall of business opposition, making it more difficult for businesses to unite and making it easier for swing legislators to discredit business opposition. The third part of the strategy was to propose a moderate bill exempting many employers and then to bring business to the table and negotiate, on the one hand making it clear that something was going to pass and on the other hand showing a willingness to respond to the most stinging critiques and to compromise on many key provisions.

Debating Family and Medical Leave in Connecticut

In March of 1987, the Committee on Family and the Workplace held its first hearings on the family and medical leave proposal for state employees, considering a bill that would grant state employees unpaid leaves of absence of up to twenty-four weeks over a two-year period to care for a newborn child or a sick family member. Participants in the political process remembered that there was little opposition to the state employees' leave bill, although one staff member mentioned that it was hard to get advocacy groups to testify about the importance of the bill, since it did not affect the public. The bill, and an accompanying bill authorizing a task force to study work and family roles and private sector parental leave, passed the committee and then the entire legislature easily.

According to respondents on both sides of the issue, the law authorizing family and medical leaves for state employees served a number of purposes for proponents of a private-sector bill. First, it legitimized family and medical leave as a public policy issue, changing it from a private issue to be negotiated between employers and employees to something in which the state should involve itself. This set a precedent for further state intervention. Second, passing family and medical leave for its own workers allowed the state to create a "laboratory" with which it could show that the consequences of the policy would not be as disastrous as opponents claimed. Using the experience of 50,000 state workers, proponents of family and medical leave were able to show that an unpaid policy would not be abused and that productivity would not decline substantially as a result of having the policy in place. Third, having enacted a policy to cover its own employees made it easier for the state to legitimize its mandate that other employers do the same.

The Task Force to Study Work and Family Roles started meeting and holding public hearings in early 1988. The task force was chaired by John Larson, and while it included a number of opponents of the legislation, it was clear that the purpose of the task force was to support the passage of a private-sector family and medical leave law. According to most respondents, however, the crucial contribution of the task force was not that it was bipartisan, but that it included a number of representatives of businesses that already had their own family and medical leave policies.[6] While none of the business representatives on the task force supported the policy mandate publicly, their willingness to sit on the task force and to testify that family and medical leave had not hurt their companies helped lend credibility to arguments made by proponents of family and medical leave that the bill would not cause significant harm and might actually be beneficial to both employers and employees.

Of the three supportive business representatives on the task force, the most active was Jeanne Kardos, the director of employee benefits at the Southern New England Telephone Company (SNET). Kardos, who also testified about SNET's experience with family and medical leave on the national level, agreed to serve as co-vice chair of the task force and provided considerable time, support, and information about SNET's experience. As Cecilia Woods explained, "She really made our job much easier, because here's a corporate executive who came in and said, 'We've had this for years, and . . . this has worked.' She said, 'we have happy employees, and they are better employees, and you are very unwise not to consider this possibility.'"[7]

While the presence of other business representatives on the task force also lent credibility to the task force as a whole, Kardos's presence was crucial because she was willing not only to sit on the task force but also to testify in hearings while the other business representatives were not. However, the presence of the latter group was also helpful, my respondents agreed, if not in supporting the bill that came out of the task force, then in not opposing it. The three companies that sent representatives, and other companies that did not send representatives to the task force but were in communication with proponents of family and medical leave, were commonly known to be important members of the business community in Connecticut. While these businesses did not actively support the policy, neither did they oppose it. This weakened the opposition.

The ability of the Connecticut proponents to bring some businesses to the table on family and medical leave was crucial to the success of the bill and stands in contrast to the experience of the proponents in Massachusetts. While part of the explanation for the proponents' ability to get businesses to come to the table must be attributed to Larson's personal clout, part of it seems to be associated with the moderation of the advocates and their willingness to compromise. Included in this moderation was the proponents' decision not to propose a paid family and medical leave bill.

In my discussions with respondents in Connecticut about paid family and medical leave, I was struck by their unanimity. While many of the supporters of the policy expressed a desire for paid family and medical leave in the ideal, all except one described paid family and medical leave as not attainable, and some described it as not even desirable. Business representatives, including those who sat on the task force, drew a line between paid and unpaid family and medical leave policies, arguing that a provision for pay would not only make the leave far more costly for businesses, but might also increase the possibility of abuse. By and large, the lead advocates in Connecticut did not challenge these perceptions.

Respondents on both sides of the issue agreed that while paid family and medical leave was mentioned occasionally during the political process leading up to the enactment of family and medical leave, it was not seriously considered by anyone. In explaining why this happened, they used terms like "realism," citing their understanding that while the business community was somewhat divided over unpaid leave, it would have united and fought fiercely against a paid family and medical leave. As a result, the lead advocates for the Connecticut bill described a movement for paid family and medical leave as "suicide" and asserted, "It never would have happened."

I pushed the proponents a bit on this point, reiterating for them a list of the resources they had, and asking why, given these resources, they did not try harder for something they clearly wanted. Essentially, I was told that while the proponents realized that they had considerable resources, they did not think they had enough to pass a paid family and medical leave. Further, they were committed to passing *something*, and they feared that if they had proposed a paid family and medical leave, they would have incited their opponents and alienated moderates to the point where nothing would go through. Larson explained, "I think that part of leadership or part of politics is understanding, pick your fights, and pick the fights that hopefully you can win."[8] Finally, the proponents stated that they hoped to pass an unpaid leave and expand on it later to provide wage replacement.

The proponents' assertion that they would not have been able to pass a paid family and medical leave bill is validated by the fact that even their proposal for unpaid family and medical leave was opposed by conservative members of the legislature and by some business groups. The original family and medical leave bill introduced by John Larson provided up to twenty-four weeks of family and medical leave every two years to employees in businesses employing twenty-five or more workers. Despite the fact that it exempted small businesses (and 20 percent of the workforce), and despite the fact that the Connecticut economy was doing very well, opponents emphasized their fear that placing a new mandate on business might drive them, and the jobs they provide, away. To underscore the connection between mandates and unemployment, the Connecticut Business and Industry Association ran an advertising campaign against family and medical leave entitled, "Don't Kill the Golden Goose."

Larson and his colleagues reacted to the opposition first with surprise and then with outstretched hands. Through the spring of 1989, they met with leaders from the business and business advocacy communities, so that by the final debate in early June, they were prepared to compromise. The final bill looked very different from the original, but it passed: it provided for sixteen weeks of family and medical leave over two years, phased in over four years from covering employers of 250 or more workers to covering employers of 75 or more workers. This excluded all small and medium-sized businesses in Connecticut and more than 50 percent of employees.

Massachusetts Proponents: Outsider Activists

The movement for family and medical leave in Massachusetts began in 1985 on the initiative of Phyllis Segal, a former legal director of the NOW Legal Defense Fund, and Mary Jane Gibson, the assistant majority whip in the Massachusetts House of Representatives. Both women had been active in a referendum fight in Massachusetts over abortion, which was won by the pro-choice side. In a conversation soon after the referendum, Gibson and Segal discussed the future of the women's movement and agreed that more attention needed to be paid to issues of economic equality. Their attention turned the Massachusetts maternity leave law, which at that time required that businesses with more than six employees allow workers to take eight weeks off around childbirth. Arguing that the policy was both insufficient and sexist in that it excluded fathers, the women decided to try to extend leaves to fathers and to expand the amount of time covered. They were eventually joined by a group of Massachusetts legislators and by a coalition of thirty-seven interest groups.

Gibson's position as assistant majority whip in the Massachusetts House of Representatives suggested that, like John Larson, she would possess substantial political resources, would build the same kind of coalition as he did, and would use strategies similar to the ones used in

Connecticut. But in interviews, respondents describing Gibson explained that while she certainly had some authority and access to political resources, her tenure came at a time when the Massachusetts House of Representatives was unusually decentralized and dominated by committee chairs rather than the legislative leadership. Several respondents stated off the record that Gibson's appointment was largely symbolic, and that she was not a strong whip. And further, Gibson's effort to pass family and medical leave was supported not by insiders, as Larson's was, but by outsider groups including the National Organization for Women, the Coalition of Labor Union Women, and the Massachusetts American Civil Liberties Union (ACLU). These groups made up the core of the coalition supporting family and medical leave in Massachusetts.

Respondents describing early mobilization for family and medical leave in Massachusetts emphasized the fact that in contrast to the organizers in Connecticut, who wanted to pass a bill to help a leader develop an image as a supporter of family values, the organizers in Massachusetts were primarily motivated by the goal of feminist policy change. They developed and framed their proposal for family and medical leave accordingly.

Resources and Strategies

As noted above, the advocates for family and medical leave in Massachusetts had some but not all of the resources available to the advocates in Connecticut. Gibson's position as assistant majority whip in the house of representatives afforded them enough credibility and political clout to obtain early funding for a Commission on Parenting Leave to study the feasibility of family and medical leave. In addition, the advocates in Massachusetts during the mid-1980s, like the advocates in Connecticut during that same period, were operating in a strong economy, which makes it theoretically easier to pass a business mandate like family and medical leave. And finally, the state government was unified under a Democratic legislature and the governorship of Michael Dukakis. While certainly none of these resources ensured that a bill like family and medical leave would pass, they helped the advocates in 1985 to feel optimistic about their chances.

This optimism influenced the advocates for family and medical leave in Massachusetts to make an important strategic decision. Early in the agenda-setting process, the advocates determined that they would propose a paid family and medical leave bill, instead of an unpaid leave as was proposed in Connecticut and indeed in every other state. This decision reflected the advocates' identities as feminist organizers who believed that they needed to represent the concerns of all women, not just the high-income women who can afford to take time off from their jobs without pay. One advocate stated: "I think there were a number of us who had direct experience with . . . very low-income families [and] working class women . . . And just felt very strongly that [if the] leave remained unpaid, . . . it was really going to be something that was an entitlement for a very small group of families, a very small group of working women."

Another activist put it more succinctly: "Without it [wage replacement] it [paid leave] is elitist." As a result of these beliefs, the first family and medical leave bill filed by Representative Gibson (introduced in 1986, before the Commission on Parenting Leave even started meeting) included a "wage replacement fund," which would finance leaves up to twelve weeks at 66 percent of the state average weekly wage. It was to be funded by a .025 percent tax on employee wages between $10,000 and $40,000.

Interviews with the lead advocates revealed considerable (although not uniform) consensus about the importance of introducing a paid family and medical leave in Massachusetts, just as there was considerable consensus about the importance of introducing an unpaid leave in Connecticut. But in contrast to Connecticut, the Massachusetts advocates differed widely in their perceptions of the political process: some believed at the outset that they could achieve paid family and medical leave while others did not. Those who stated that they thought paid family and medical leave was achievable cited demographic changes such as the increase in the number of women in the workforce and the development of a "sandwich" generation caring for both children and elderly parents. In an interview, Gibson commented: "We just felt that it was so apparent . . . that that's what needed to happen, and everybody cared about families and everybody just wanted to do what's best for families."[9] Others were doubtful that paid family and medical leave would pass right away, but believed that putting the issue on the table was important and thought it might result in a compromise unpaid leave that could then be expanded to provide some wage replacement. A third group of advocates was unsupportive of paid family and medical leave, stating that they realized from the beginning that there was a risk involved in lobbying for the policy.

Debating Family and Medical Leave in Massachusetts

From a political standpoint, in the end this last group was proven right. H.B. 5200, the first parental leave bill with a wage replacement provision, quickly died in the Commerce and Labor Committee, to which all parental leave and wage replacement bills were sent.[10] Proponents of paid family and medical leave soon realized that attaching a wage replacement provision to the parental leave proposal was not going to succeed, so they tried another tactic: forming a commission to study the feasibility of developing a temporary disability insurance (TDI) program in Massachusetts that would cover both disability and dependent care. As explained by Gibson, TDI, which currently exists in five states as an insurance program for disability but *not* for dependent care, seemed to be a way both to ensure wage replacement and to build a coalition large enough to get something passed.

The TDI commission started meeting in early 1988. Representatives were chosen from business, labor, women's groups, and government. After a number of meetings (and considerable dissent by the business representatives on the commission, most notably representatives from the Associated Industries of Massachusetts and the National Federation of Independent Businesses), the commission proposed a law that would tax employers and employees at approximately $75 a year each and would provide a sliding scale of benefits for both temporary disability and dependent care, capped at 60 percent of the state average weekly wage. The resulting bill, introduced in early 1989, was "An Act Establishing Employment Leave Insurance," which was introduced simultaneously with but separate from a bill proposing unpaid parental leave beyond the scope of the current maternity leave law. By separating their proposal into two bills, the advocates hoped to be able to pass at least unpaid leave alone, while at the same time affirming their commitment to paid family and medical leave.

But even the approach of proposing temporary disability insurance separately from unpaid leave did not work. With the exception of the parental leave law in 1988 (at the end of the TDI commission's work and before the introduction of the employment leave insurance bill), and again in 1991 (after the employment leave insurance bill had died), none of the above-mentioned bills even passed out of the Commerce and Labor Committee. The two bills that did pass died in the next committee to take them up, Ways and Means. By the early 1990s, it was clear that no family and medical leave bill was going to pass in Massachusetts.

In explaining why *both* proposals for paid and unpaid leave failed in Massachusetts, many respondents cited the early attachment of wage replacement to the bill. Respondents on both sides of the debate argued that the wage replacement provision made it easier for business opponents and moderate and conservative legislators to dismiss the bill and its proponents as not serious. Even in the mid-1980s, when the Massachusetts economy was booming, a significant number of legislators worried that paid family and medical leave might actually put an undue burden on business. For its part, the business community quickly united against the bill, and proponents were unable to find "friendly" business partners who already had family leave policies to testify in support of the policy or at least describe the value of the policy to their companies, as the advocates in Connecticut had.[11] In interviews, proponents conceded that a few "friendly opponents" would have helped their cause significantly. Gibson stated:

> In the 1980s, . . . the high technology companies around Route 128 [near Boston] that used highly skilled women . . . had very generous leave policies, and some of them had parental leave, . . . but they didn't write them down, and they didn't talk about it, and it wasn't in their brochures, and you couldn't get them on the phone to tell you what it was . . . out of solidarity with their colleagues or whatever [they] would never join us.

Many respondents argued that as a result of their advocacy for paid family and medical leave, the proponents were stigmatized so that even the unpaid leave bills they introduced later in the political process were not considered feasible. One supporter of paid family and medical leave commented: "In order to make them [business] approachable, you have to seem very large and powerful and about to win something. I don't think we ever reached that sort of plateau." As a result, with the exception of Gibson, the leadership of the Massachusetts legislature distanced itself from the legislation and stayed distanced even when proponents offered to compromise. One respondent stated, "The leadership didn't go to the wall on this one."

In addition, the proponents of family and medical leave in Massachusetts faced challenges from within their own ranks. One challenge came in the form of dissension on the issue of how to achieve paid family and medical leave. Both Gibson's early proposal and the proposal that came out of the TDI committee split the cost of wage replacement insurance between employers and employees; this had the effect of angering not only business groups but also unions, which argued that wage replacement should be funded entirely by employers. This disagreement among the proponents (which is ironic, since this was probably the only place where the coalition leadership was willing to compromise) meant that mainstream unions, which were already not making family and medical leave a priority in Massachusetts,[12] became even weaker supporters of the bill.

Finally, many of the women's groups that constituted the strongest part of the family and medical leave coalition had other priorities to attend to besides this bill. A number of proponents mentioned that the continuing struggle over abortion on both the state and the national levels and the goal of achieving civil rights for gay men and lesbians as other issues that distracted from attention to family and medical leave.

When one considers the identities of the groups attempting to pass family and medical leave in Massachusetts and the nature of the issue they were organizing around, the strategic decisions made by the advocates become easier to understand. The major proponents were political outsiders who were largely motivated by ideology rather than by practical considerations; they thus had few incentives to compromise. But their decision not to introduce an unpaid family and medical leave made it harder to find allies from the business community and cost them the support of moderates in the legislature and, ultimately, the legislative leadership. To compound these problems, the proponents themselves were divided with regard to how paid family and medical leave should be administered, and were committed to lobbying for other policies as well. In some ways, the political process around family and medical leave in Massachusetts can be summarized by this saying, which was quoted to me by one supporter of the legislation: "The Republicans never defeat the Democrats, because the Democrats, if you give them a bunch of rifles and ask them to form a firing squad, they'll form a circle."

It is also important to realize that while many of the proponents' problems can be attributed to their strategic miscalculations, others were not of their making. A number of respondents observed that while they were not confident that a paid family and medical leave would pass, they thought that over time, they would be able to pass something, and it is indeed possible that, had political and economic conditions remained the same as they were in the mid-1980s, these respondents might have been right. But while conditions for passing family and medical leave seemed ideal in 1985, they changed rapidly over the next five years. To use John Kingdon's term, the "policy window" (a period of time when circumstances are ripe for passing a particular piece of legislation)[13] for family and medical leave closed. In interviews, respondents cited three factors that caused the window for family and medical leave to close more quickly than advocates expected. These were the distraction of a universal health insurance proposal in 1988, Governor Michael Dukakis's failed presidential bid in that year, and the political and economic fallout from the collapse of the "Massachusetts Miracle" in the late 1980s.

In April 1988, the Massachusetts legislature passed the country's most comprehensive health insurance plan, mandating that employers provide coverage for their workers and levying a tax to cover unemployed workers. Several legislators stated that the bill, which passed by a narrow margin, was supported in large part to help Governor Michael Dukakis win his presidential bid. While the health care bill (which was never implemented) was considered an important victory by both health care and public interest organizations and by the women's and labor groups supporting family and medical leave, it also proved to be a distraction from family and medical leave. One legislator explained that "Health care sort of overtook [family and medical leave]. . . . There are only so many bills you can get through."

Then in November of 1988, just as the TDI task force was preparing its recommendations and the employment leave insurance bills were starting to take shape, Governor Michael Dukakis lost his bid for the presidency. Within a few months, the "Massachusetts miracle" had collapsed: the budget was in deficit, the economy was headed for a recession, and Dukakis, by then unpopular, had announced that he would not seek reelection. Although the proponents for family and medical leave kept introducing bills, an opportunity had been lost.

Commenting in retrospect, almost all the respondents (including the chair of the Commerce and Labor Committee in 1985) agreed that if an unpaid family and medical leave had been introduced in 1985 or 1986, it probably would have passed. And from this perspective, it makes sense to view as a mistake the decision made by the advocates to introduce a paid family and medical leave at that time and not immediately make it clear that they were willing to compromise. But it is also important to remember that the respondents had no way of knowing in 1985 how long their window would be open and whether it would be wide enough to accommodate paid family and medical leave. Given their ideological positions (and the possibility that they may not have fully understood that in politics, opportunities are often fleeting), it is easy to understand why the Massachusetts advocates proposed paid family and medical leave.

When asked why paid family and medical leave was introduced so early and why the proponents did not make it clear that they were willing to compromise, respondents offered three explanations. One was that there was not sufficient support in the coalition to lobby for unpaid leave alone. One supportive legislator, a self-described "compromiser," explained:

> I can't tell you how many hours I spent just trying to gain consensus. . . . The advocates were so committed to the world that it was exceedingly hard to get anyone to agree to anything. . . . They didn't want to be practical. No matter what you did for them, if it wasn't 100 percent they didn't want it. They were so sure they could do better, and we haven't been able to do anything.

From the other side of the coalition, members admitted that they had been "ambitious" but explained that in the early years, there had seemed to be little reason to compromise. For many advocates, the decision not to moderate was based on both their agenda and their belief that they did not need to do so.

A second explanation came from advocates who noted that during the time that the coalition was working for a state family and medical leave policy, members were also lobbying for a national family and medical leave policy. Because the national level policy was always going to be unpaid, and because in the early years there was considerable optimism that the national bill would pass quickly (in fact, it did not pass until 1993), some of the advocates did not see a need to be so timid on the Massachusetts proposal.

A third explanation is especially interesting. This argument was that it is not fair to label the movement for family and medical leave in Massachusetts as a failure simply because the advocates were not able to *pass a policy*. Several people explained that when groups introduce and lobby legislation like family and medical leave, they may have two goals in mind. First, they want to get a policy passed, but second, and sometimes in contradiction with the first goal, they want to effect cultural change. By introducing family and medical leave, the advocates who were feminists were attempting to publicize distinctions between men's and women's roles and to illustrate how in a time when women increasingly work outside of the home, these roles come into conflict. With this goal in mind, introducing paid family and medical leave, even in light of how difficult it would be to pass, made sense because it allowed the advocates to highlight conditions experienced by working-class women and, as one proponent explained, "to create debate [and] discussion." Another proponent stated that just introducing paid family and medical leave "might change people's consciousness."

Some advocates also argued that circulating an idea like paid family and medical leave might pay dividends in the long run, even if it did not lead to the passage of a policy immediately. This notion is supported by Kingdon, whose research indicates that ideas may need to be around for a long time before policy communities can be "softened up" sufficiently to seriously consider them.[14] Thus the true value of introducing even a paid family and medical leave that could not pass might be in getting people to debate it, setting the stage for its passage later.

Analysis

The contrast between the movements for family and medical leave in Connecticut and Massachusetts is stark, despite a preponderance of ideological, cultural, and economic similarities between the two states. The different outcomes in the two states can be attributed both to the different resources available to the proponents for the policy and to the different strategies adopted by these coalitions. The proponents of family and medical leave in Connecticut had the advantage of the leadership of senate president John Larson, who believed that the bill would provide him with an issue with which to launch a run for higher office. Larson united the legislature in support of the proposal and created a committee solely to consider work and family bills. The advocates had an advantage in their coalition's leadership by insiders who accepted the principle of incremental change and who were willing to fit their strategies to the political opportunity structure by proposing unpaid family and medical leave and by framing the bill as a family rather than a feminist issue. [15]

In contrast, the advocates for family and medical leave in Massachusetts lacked a strong, united leadership and further harmed their chances by introducing a paid family and medical leave bill. While they were initially operating in a strong political and economic climate, their insistence on introducing a more ambitious bill stalled the political process, diminishing their credibility and making it difficult to pass anything until after political and economic circumstances had changed and their policy window had closed.

But it is important to remember that in comparison with other early state enactors, the Connecticut family and medical leave law was quite limited in scope.[16] Considering the substantial political resources available to Larson and his colleagues, the possibility arises that the advocates in Connecticut may have compromised too much, just as the advocates in Massachusetts, who possessed fewer resources, appear to have compromised too little. While it is clear that paid family and medical leave was not feasible in Connecticut, it is not clear that advocates there had to compromise to the degree that they did, exempting all but the largest businesses. The fact that, to date, the business-size threshold has not been lowered shows the degree to which compromise has its risks as well.[17]

The coalition leaders in Connecticut justified their actions by arguing that by establishing the principle of government support for working families, they laid the groundwork for a later expansion of family and medical leave. This approach assumes that an incremental policy will generate group and administrative support and that, as a result of its passage, the capacity of the state to become involved in a particular policy area will be expanded. But more than ten years after the passage of the Connecticut family and medical leave act, it is unclear whether these goals have been accomplished.

And it is also important to analyze more fully the argument made by advocates in Massachusetts that by introducing a more widespread bill, they changed the terms of the debate and set the stage for the enactment of a more widespread policy. Respondents in both states argued that the policy process itself increased awareness of the need for family and medical leave even among the businesses not affected by the law. If they are right, and the introduction of family and medical leave had the effect of "teaching" both legislators and members of the business community about the issue, then perhaps adding wage replacement to the proposal might have added an additional element to that lesson.

Even if introducing paid family and medical leave did not educate influential people in the legislature and business community, it might have educated the general public. As mentioned earlier, one tenet of the women's movement is "consciousness raising," whereby women (and men) learn to associate formerly private concerns with public problems and solutions.[18] Introducing legislation is one way of raising consciousness, as the legislative process itself involves identifying and publicizing an issue as a public problem demanding a public solution.[19] Thus one can argue that introducing and publicizing family and medical leave might have led members of the public to consider their own situation and perhaps to see the work-family problems they were experiencing as worthy of public response. It follows that introducing a paid family and medical leave might encourage people, for the first time, to imagine that they could have access to wage replacement when they needed to take family and medical leaves. Over time, an expanded public imagination might catalyze further policy development, just as enacted policies sometimes feed back and lead to other policies.[20]

The possibility for a movement that fails to pass a policy still to meet educational goals is described by Jane Mansbridge. Explaining that the ERA became a "symbol of demands for change in women's position in the workplace and the family," Mansbridge states:

When the ERA was in the newspaper, when co-workers went to an ERA demonstration, or when advocates debated the ERA in the school gym, women who normally thought little about these issues seem to have begun to ask themselves about the amount of housework they were doing, about their pay, and about the kind of person they wanted to be. The result was both creeping feminism and creeping anti-feminism. But most of those who pondered these issues have moved in a feminist rather than an anti-feminist direction.[21]

Making an argument about a feedback in the public imagination and comparing the actions of proponents of family and medical leave in Massachusetts with those of advocates for the ERA has, however, one major drawback. In order to influence the public imagination, a movement must attract considerable attention and debate. While this clearly happened with the ERA, there is little evidence to suggest that it happened with family and medical leave in Massachusetts, where the movement was never grassroots and quickly became marginalized. There was little media coverage of the movement for family and medical leave in Massachusetts, and it is doubtful that most of the public was aware of what was being proposed, let alone actively considering its application to their own lives. This suggests that even to achieve cultural change, a certain feasibility threshold must be reached. The fact that it was not reached in Massachusetts makes this justification for the introduction of paid family and medical leave less understandable. But it is well worth considering as a theoretical justification for introducing a desired bill instead of a compromise.

Finally, the advocates in Massachusetts argued that since an unpaid leave bill was being proposed at the federal level at the same time, they had nothing to lose by introducing a paid family and medical leave, and they were making a valuable contribution to the national debate. As will be described in chapter 5, several national advocates for family and medical leave validated that claim, arguing that it was helpful to have a proposal in one state for paid family and medical leave. But they also stated that part of their argument for a federal policy rested on their being able to show that the economies in states that had passed family and medical leave policies had not suffered unduly; this in turn depended on a number of states' actually passing something. Thus if it was helpful for advocates on the national level to have a paid family and medical leave proposal in Massachusetts, failure to enact legislation there meant that the national advocates had one less state to use as an example to build the case for a national policy.

Conclusion

In both Massachusetts and Connecticut during the mid-1980s, political and economic conditions appeared to be strong for passing family and medical leave policies; these conditions served as resources for advocates for the policy. But the similarities end there; this chapter clearly shows that while political and economic resources are helpful in passing legislation like family and medical leave, they are not sufficient. Other resources, such as the power and clout of an insider advocate such as Connecticut's John Larson, were essential both because power matters and because insiders are more likely to use moderation and compromise, which were deemed essential to passing family and medical leave. Larson used his clout to secure a supportive venue for debating family and medical leave; he lobbied his fellow legislators; *and* he organized a coalition of insiders who crafted a pragmatic bill and compromised from there. In contrast, the advocates in Massachusetts were led by the majority whip of the house of representatives, Mary Jane Gibson, who did not enjoy substantial power *and* who was working with a coalition of outsiders who were not predisposed to compromise. Motivated by goals of feminist policy change, the advocates in Massachusetts introduced an ambitious, inclusive bill. But following their hearts cost them credibility, and they were ultimately unable to pass anything.

Advice for Advocates

The above comparison of the policy processes for family and medical leave in Connecticut and Massachusetts suggests several things for advocates seeking to enact contested policy innovations. Advocates need to take advantage of opportunities like those described above before they disappear, which they are apt to do quickly and suddenly. They need to be careful about who they choose to lead a movement for policy change, keeping in mind both the importance of power and clout and the importance of being an insider, with a strong command of what it will take to pass legislation. Finally, advocates need to develop and frame their proposals to maximize their credibility and their ability to build a broad coalition. This will, very likely, involve moderating the proposal and being willing to compromise over time.

However, this process may conflict with the advocates' goals, and there may be good reasons for refusing to compromise. In particular, it may be important to introduce idealistic bills in the hopes of educating elites and the public and setting the stage for passing more expansive public policy. But as suggested above, this educating process will work only if advocates have enough resources to get attention.

In retrospect, it appears clear that paid family and medical leave could not have passed in either Connecticut or Massachusetts in the mid-1980s, barring an exceptional change of circumstances. The question becomes, then, whether it is better to compromise by passing an incremental bill, as the advocates in Connecticut did, or whether it is better to pass no bill at all, as happened in Massachusetts. This question will be explored in later chapters and will be one focus of chapter 6, which examines the movement since 1993 to pass a paid family leave.

4 ||| POLICY MAKING IN A CONSERVATIVE CONTEXT
Tennessee and North Carolina

The first dictum in American politics is that "the South is different." And indeed, comparative state politics studies have found considerable differences between politics and policy in the eleven states of the former Confederate South and the rest of the country.[1] These differences are also confirmed by a quick glance at the map showing passage of state family and medical leave legislation that appears in chapter 1. Only two of the eleven southern states, Louisiana and Tennessee, passed policies covering nonstate employees. And only Tennessee passed a policy that required employers to provide more than a maternity disability leave. In contrast, all of the New England states passed at least a maternity disability leave, and four of the six passed a family and medical leave policy.

It appears, then, that the South somehow provided a less hospitable climate for supporters of family and medical leave than did the New England states or the states in the upper Midwest and the far West. The quantitative study conducted by Garand and Monroe and described in chapter 1 suggests that this is because southern states are more conservative and less supportive of feminism than are other states. But a quantitative study cannot explain exactly *how* these contextual factors affected the ability of advocates to pass family and medical leave. And it does not explain how the advocates in Tennessee managed to pass a widespread maternity leave policy, despite an apparent lack of contextual resources.

In an attempt to answer these questions, I turn to case studies of two southern states: Tennessee, which passed its maternity leave law in 1987,[2] and North Carolina, where efforts to pass family and medical leave between 1987 and 1993 failed. Tennessee and North Carolina are ideal for a comparative study of state policy enactment because, like Connecticut and Massachusetts, they are similar to one another. They are geographically close and were, in fact, both once part of the single colony known as Carolina. They are ideologically conservative, but their progressive (for the South) traditions were hailed by many respondents. They have historically been dominated by Democrats but are becoming more Republican. And they have similar and conflicted histories with regard to the Equal Rights Amendment (ERA): Tennessee ratified the ERA but then later rescinded ratification, while North Carolina was the target of a long and bitter battle, which supporters of the ERA ultimately lost.

As in Connecticut and Massachusetts, I studied family and medical leave in Tennessee and North Carolina primarily by conducting interviews with participants in the political processes there. But the studies had very different findings. While supporters of family and medical leave in the two New England states both enjoyed substantial political resources, the advocates in Tennessee and North Carolina faced stronger cultural and political opposition to their proposals. In Tennessee, the advocates were able to win by piecing together a coalition of influential moderates who were willing to make substantial compromises. However, the advocates in North Carolina did not have access to virtually any political resources, and in addition were operating in an unusually difficult political environment. They did not offer substantial compromises, but most respondents did not consider this to be the key to explaining their inability to pass family and medical leave. Instead, the North Carolina case suggests that compromise is valuable only when advocates have enough resources to ensure being taken seriously.

Proponents in Tennessee: Insider Moderates

In contrast to the successful effort in Connecticut to pass a family and medical leave policy, which was led by a powerful legislator, the effort to pass a maternity leave policy in Tennessee was led by an advocacy group. However, this advocacy group, the Tennessee Women's Political Caucus, was an "insider" group, just as Senator John Larson of Connecticut was an insider legislator. As noted in the first chapter, groups that are most likely to adopt insider tactics are those that have an elite membership and a professional staff, and they often are funded by foundation or government grants rather than membership dues. The staff members of these elite groups develop long-term relationships with legislators and members of the bureaucracy and are more likely to view working within the system as legitimate and to view incremental change as progress. In addition to having more political clout, insider groups are more likely to propose moderate bills and to be willing to compromise.

The Tennessee Women's Political Caucus, which was founded in 1982, was by 1987 well known as a moderate feminist organization consisting of professionals and people connected with government: judges, legislators, and members of the administration. The caucus thus enjoyed credibility by virtue of its membership. In addition, it had a reputation for sponsoring moderate, family-oriented bills such as child abuse legislation and legislation to protect homemakers who get divorced. While the caucus was certainly adept at sponsoring legislation that would help women, it made considerable efforts to frame that legislation as "pro-family" rather than "feminist." One caucus leader stated: "I don't think we've ever had any legislation that negatively impacted men."

According to the interviews I conducted, the caucus's paid lobbyist, Mary Frances Lyle, was herself a substantial asset to the caucus's efforts to pass legislation. Lyle, who is also a partner in a Nashville law firm, was described in respectful terms by every single person I interviewed (proponents and opponents): common adjectives for her included "effective" and "influential." Together with the credibility associated with the membership of the Tennessee Women's Political Caucus and the caucus' history of sponsoring moderate, "family values" legislation, Lyle's leadership meant that the caucus was in an excellent position in 1987 to sponsor a family and medical leave bill.

The Tennessee Women's Political Caucus further aided its cause by persuading moderate and influential legislators to sponsor their family leave proposal. In interviews, caucus members noted that choosing credible legislators was a crucial part of their strategy. In this case, the caucus persuaded a pro-business Republican, Karen Williams, in the house of representatives, and a male Democrat, Joe Haynes, in the senate, to sponsor their family leave bill. The bill was cosponsored in the house by a particularly influential male Democrat, Bill Purcell.

Resources and Strategies

The major resource available to the proponents of family leave in Tennessee was, as described above, the proponents themselves. As the literature on policy innovation suggests and the case studies of Connecticut and Massachusetts show, having credible, powerful sponsors who are seen as moderate and reasonable was crucial to attempts to pass family and medical leave. These resources were all the more important in Tennessee, where, as previously mentioned, the political context was hostile to the development of policies like family and medical leave. Even before the recession of the early 1990s, when states began paying more attention to being friendly to business, Tennessee was comparatively reluctant to enact regulations on business. For example, it has no minimum wage and is a right-to-work state that does not permit closed shops. Respondents (including opponents of the legislation) agreed that compared with other states, Tennessee imposes relatively few tax and regulatory burdens on businesses.

Many respondents did refer to a progressive tradition in Tennessee.[3] One respondent mentioned the fact that Tennessee was the deciding state in the ratification of the nineteenth amendment, guaranteeing women the right to vote, and several noted that despite a general trend against enacting regulations, Tennessee had in recent years passed several important pieces of regulatory legislation, including a plant closing law and a hazardous material right-to-know law.

However, both proponents and opponents agreed that due to both the strength of business and the predisposition of the legislature, it was (and is) generally difficult to pass regulatory legislation in Tennessee. And the sponsors of family leave in Tennessee noted that in addition to these constraints, Tennessee is a culturally conservative state where they knew it would be difficult to pass legislation that challenges traditional gender and family role norms. One supporter of the legislation stated: "They can understand a woman taking care of babies, but they don't yet understand men taking care of babies. Even though, of the younger men, . . . in the legislature, the ones that are in my age group, are great daddies. . . . But as a whole, I don't think Tennessee is ready yet to see the daddy as a co-equal with momma."

Given these constraints, the proponents of family leave in Tennessee decided to propose a maternity leave law covering women only instead of a parental or family leave law that would cover both men and women. They reasoned that a proposal for maternity leave would attract support from cultural conservatives and that business would less strongly oppose a bill that covered fewer people (that is, only women). Their effort was prompted by the 1987 Supreme Court decision in *California Federal Savings and Loan v. Guerra* (described in chapter 2) upholding the constitutionality of a California maternity leave law that had been challenged as a violation of the equal protection statute of the 1978 Pregnancy Discrimination Act. In a decision written by Justice Thurgood Marshall, the Court found that the California maternity leave law did not violate the intent of Congress in passing the Pregnancy Discrimination Act.[4]

The Tennessee Women's Political Caucus had been considering proposing maternity leave for a number of years before 1987 but had not done so pending the outcome of the *Guerra* case. Advocates for family and medical leave on the national level viewed the *Guerra* decision with mixed feelings, fearing that maternity-only laws would lead to more rather than less discrimination against women, but the advocates in Tennessee were delighted with the outcome. In interviews, Lyle and most of her colleagues stated that they would have liked to introduce a gender-neutral bill, but they did not believe that such a bill could pass in Tennessee. Clearly viewing *any* leave bill, even one that just provided benefits for women, as a step forward, they filed maternity leave legislation "within days" of the Supreme Court decision.

Political Process

While proposing maternity leave and securing strong sponsors ensured that the advocates in Tennessee would be taken seriously, it was not enough to ensure that their bill would move through the legislature easily. Maternity leave was opposed by conservative legislators and by business organizations including the Tennessee Business Roundtable, the Tennessee Association of Business, and the National Federation of

Independent Businesses. The arguments made by opponents were similar to the arguments made by opponents of family leave in Connecticut and Massachusetts: as a mandate on business, the bill represented an unreasonable intrusion of government into employer-employee relations and would make it difficult to attract business to Tennessee. Somewhat ironically, the opponents of the Tennessee bill argued that a maternity leave policy might result in discrimination against women of childbearing age.[5]

Like the advocates for family and medical leave in Connecticut, the Tennessee Women's Political Caucus responded to the opposition by compromising. In addition to attempting to preempt the opposition by proposing a maternity leave only, they accepted an amendment to change the bill's language to leave "for the purposes of bonding," which they feared would expose it to lawsuits and possible repeal because, as Lyle explained, "either parent can bond."[6] As in Connecticut, the advocates in Tennessee accepted a compromise that reduced the number of covered employers from those employing fifteen or more people to those employing one hundred or more, a tiny percentage of Tennessee's population.

Despite these compromises and the fact that the Tennessee legislature was unified under Democratic leadership, the opposition to the Tennessee maternity leave bill was strong enough to stall the bill until nearly the end of the legislative session. At this point, Lyle and other members of the Tennessee Women's Political Caucus decided to try to obtain the support of the popular and pro-business governor, Ned McWherter. Although he was only in his first term, McWherter enjoyed considerable political clout as a result of having served for the previous fourteen years as speaker of the Tennessee House of Representatives. He was known for his political skills and for his support for economic growth. Moreover, as a governor with a working-class background, McWherter was known as a populist and an occasional supporter of labor.

Two members of McWherter's staff were also members of the Tennessee Women's Political Caucus. In interviews, they remembered that Lyle had kept them apprised of the progress of the maternity leave bill during the early months of the legislative session. One of the staff members, Betty Anderson, remembered that she had told Lyle that if the bill ran into trouble, McWherter might be a source of help.[7] And so, in mid-April of 1987, with approximately one month left to go in the legislative session, Lyle approached Anderson and her colleague Betty Haynes. The two women, who enjoyed strong relationships with McWherter, asked him to publicly support and lobby for the bill.

Members of the Tennessee Women's Political Caucus, observers, and McWherter himself remembered that three factors were important in attracting McWherter's support, which was universally viewed as crucial. The first factor was, as noted above, the credibility of the caucus and particularly of the two staffers for McWherter who were members. The second factor was that by the time the caucus members approached McWherter for help, they had already compromised the bill significantly, limiting their proposal to maternity leave only and agreeing to exempt all but the largest businesses from coverage. This helped to convince McWherter that he was not supporting a lost cause, and it made the bill more attractive to the governor, who saw himself as a moderate and a supporter of traditional values. In an interview, McWherter stated that he had been attracted to the fact that the bill would help mothers and would not significantly harm business. He saw the bill as an innovation that would affirm important values even as it responded to the modern phenomenon of women working outside the home. And he stated that he would not have been as supportive if the bill had covered men as well as women: "Although I want to be on the cutting edge when we go into the 21st century, I guess I have to say I'm a little old fashioned. So my priority was on the mother. . . . I'm not opposed to the men, but I wouldn't go to the wall on men like I would with the mother."[8]

Finally, the advocates for the Tennessee maternity leave bill were aided by serendipity of sorts. At the same time the bill was stalled in the legislature, Governor McWherter's mother was terminally ill. McWherter, whose mother had worked outside the home when he was young, was convinced by his staff that the bill would be a fitting tribute to her. This led him not only to support the bill but also to do so enthusiastically.

While nearly all respondents cited the credibility of the Tennessee Women's Political Caucus and their willingness to compromise as essential to the passage of the maternity leave bill, most cited McWherter's support as crucial. Lyle and sponsors Williams, Haynes, and Purcell all stated that the bill would not have passed, despite their efforts, had it not been for McWherter's support. While they recognized that their re-sources and strategies had been necessary to attract that support, they argued that the support itself was a necessary factor. As a powerful and pro-business governor, McWherter led people who ordinarily would have been hesitant to support maternity leave. Another legislator said: "The impact was that people trusted him, and they thought, well, if the governor is for this, then I don't have any problem with it. He's a con-servative businessman, just as the sponsor of the bill [is], and this is something we ought to do."

McWherter's support, and his stated reason for his support, solidi-fied the efforts of the Tennessee Women's Political Caucus to frame their maternity leave bill as a motherhood issue rather than a feminist or labor issue. Opponents remembered that once McWherter stepped in, the issue became a gut-level emotional issue rather than a bill that one could argue had both pros and cons. Within a month of McWherter's an-nouncement of support, the bill had passed by wide margins in both the house and senate. At the signing ceremony, McWherter paid tribute to his mother and ate pickles and ice cream, the foods traditionally craved by pregnant women.

The situation in Tennessee had an interesting parallel to that in Connecticut: nearly all respondents agreed that despite overwhelming support at the end, there had not been enough resources to pass a gender-neutral parental or family and medical leave. Many cited Mc-Wherter's motives as one piece of evidence. Most respondents, how-ever, focused on the agenda-setting period and the initial effort to persuade legislators to support the bill. They noted that the bill had to achieve a certain level of support before its supporters could appeal to McWherter. Like the supporters of paid family leave in Connecticut, they worried that parental leave would have sent the wrong signals about the seriousness of the proposal and would have invited stronger opposition from businesses and from culturally conservative members of the legislature. One moderate legislator argued: "The old curmud-geons are sympathetic to motherhood, but being fathers themselves, they were thinking, God, I wouldn't have wanted to stay home for six months! Their own personal experience said, This is not something I would have done."

Respondents emphasized that proposing maternity leave helped to head off opposition from traditionalists *within* the legislature rather

than helping to head off opposition from culturally conservative interest groups. Despite the best efforts of the proponents, conservative
Christian groups like the Eagle Forum and the Christian Coalition did
oppose the maternity leave bill, but, in part because they were just getting organized in the late 1980s, it was not a major priority for them.
This finding underscores the fact that the need to adapt the family and
medical leave proposal to traditional norms in Tennessee resulted from
an analysis of the general political situation rather than the strength of
opposition groups.

As in Connecticut, several groups would have preferred proposing
a more widespread bill, but did not attempt to do so because they did
not want to oppose the efforts of the Tennessee Women's Political Caucus. But while these groups, which included the Tennessee chapters of
the National Association for Women (NOW) and the American Civil
Liberties Union (ACLU), supported the efforts of the caucus on maternity leave, they also did not make the issue a priority. In an interview,
however, a member of one of these groups expressed concern that the
Tennessee Women's Political Caucus is too closely aligned with "the
establishment" to achieve substantial policy innovations.

Two legislative efforts were made to propose bills beyond the scope
of maternity leave. According to most respondents, neither of these efforts was taken seriously. The first was a bill filed in 1987 by a legislator who also signed on to the Tennessee Women's Political Caucus bill.
This bill provided *all* employees (both men and women, with no exemptions for small businesses) with twenty-six weeks of medical leave
in any twelve-month period and eighteen weeks of family leave in any
twenty-four-month period.[9] While I was unable to reach the sponsor of
this bill, other respondents indicated that they thought it had been filed
for educational purposes, to remind people that the maternity leave
proposal could have been more widespread. In an interview, Lyle remembered that the sponsor of the second bill did not "push" it, and
that she thought that having the second bill out there was helpful
because it made the Tennessee Women's Political Caucus bill look
moderate by comparison.[10] This perception is reflected in one of the
legislative debates over maternity leave, in which the sponsor of the
maternity leave bill that eventually passed distinguished her "pro-family" bill from the bill described immediately above, and the house ma-

jority leader stated that if the sponsor of the second bill will "agree to drop that terrible bill she's got, . . . this [the maternity leave bill] is a good alternative to it."[11]

The story of the passage of maternity leave in Tennessee is, over-whelmingly, the story of how insider advocates and legislators were able to overcome a challenging political and cultural environment through their credibility, their political clout, and their willingness to moderate and compromise. While the resulting bill was restricted to women and covered only businesses employing one hundred or more people (a tiny percentage of Tennessee's population), it provides the most widespread maternity benefit in the country: four months of job-guaranteed leave. As noted earlier, the amount of leave guaranteed in Tennessee distinguishes that state from seven other states (including Massachusetts, in the early 1970s) that guarantee the jobs of pregnant women, but only for six to eight weeks.

The Tennessee advocates succeeded where advocates in numerous other states (including every other southern state) failed because they adapted their proposal to fit with the political culture in which they were working and because they framed their bill as a "motherhood" bill; this allowed them to tap into Tennessee's progressive tradition rather than becoming mired in an equally powerful tradition of eco-nomic and cultural conservatism.[12] Their story is similar in many ways to the story of the development of family and medical leave in Con-necticut. It is strikingly different from the story of the effort to pass parental leave in North Carolina.

Advocates in North Carolina: Outside Activists

As noted earlier, North Carolina is culturally and economically similar to Tennessee: it is a "New South" state with a rapidly growing economy and a reputation for being a "progressive plutocracy," which has often taken the lead on social issues like civil rights.[13] While North Carolina's regulatory burdens are generally considered low and, like Tennessee, it is a "right to work" state, which prohibits closed shops, it has one of the highest corporate tax rates in the nation. In the area of women's rights, North Carolina was the focus of a bitter battle over the ERA in 1981–82, which the pro-ERA side ultimately lost.[14] But it has, historically, been one of the only states in the South to have a fund to provide for Medicaid abortions, although that fund has been cut drastically in recent years. When asked to compare North Carolina with Tennessee, many respondents rated them as similar both culturally and economically.

The political context in North Carolina, as in Tennessee, was probably somewhat more hospitable to policies like family and medical leave than it was in other states in the South. As in Tennessee, however, resources for this type of policy innovation were tenuous at best. While in Tennessee these resources were exploited by influential advocates and legislators, in North Carolina the movement for family and medical leave was started by a representative who was clearly an "outsider" in the legislature. The legislator, Annie Brown Kennedy, introduced parental leave bills, allowing both men and women to take up to twelve weeks of unpaid leave for the birth or adoption of a child, in the legislative sessions of 1987, 1989, and 1991. In 1993 she introduced a state family and medical leave act identical to the bill that had just passed at the federal level.

Just as the leadership of Senator John Larson in Connecticut and the leadership of the Tennessee Women's Political Caucus and representatives Karen Williams and Joe Haynes in Tennessee provided instant credibility for their proposals, the association between Kennedy and the North Carolina family and medical leave bills instantly cost the proposals credibility. Kennedy was described by liberals and conservatives alike as "not taken seriously"; some respondents ventured to call her "angry" and "a radical." In stark contrast to descriptions of Mary Frances Lyle, the lobbyist for the Tennessee Women's Political Caucus, Kennedy's lack of influence was mentioned in nearly every interview. Respondents emphasized that proposals offered by Kennedy would be viewed by many legislators as suspect and would have little chance of passing. As a result, few people felt that it was worth expending energy on a bill she was sponsoring.

Further, while Kennedy did obtain support from a number of other legislators, no legislators or groups made family and medical leave a priority until 1991, when a group called "North Carolina Center for Laws Affecting Women" (NCC-LAW) won a grant from the Z. Smith Reynolds Foundation to conduct research on the need for family and medical leave in North Carolina and to draft a new bill. This group, however, was *also* described by a number of respondents as not very influential; it was primarily a research group and, again in contrast to the Tennessee Women's Political Caucus, had little experience lobbying. One advocate described the president of the NCC-LAW as "brilliant and well respected . . . but advocating something at the grassroots is not something she does."

There were, however, groups and legislators that could have become more involved but did not. One group was North Carolina Equity, which appears to be similar to if somewhat less influential than the Tennessee Women's Political Caucus. Like the Tennessee Women's Political Caucus, NC Equity has a small, elite membership and a paid staff, and it is funded largely by foundations (including, like the NCC-LAW, the Z. Smith Reynolds Foundation). NC Equity conducts research and "educates" legislators (meaning that they are a tax exempt group that cannot lobby officially) about a variety of women's issues, including work and family issues. Several respondents indicated that if Equity had made family and medical leave a priority, it would have had a better chance of passing. Others argued that Equity is too closely tied to the business community to be a major force behind controversial legislation. One advocate stated:

> I think NC Equity is respected on some levels, but there's respect and then there's effectiveness, there's respect and then there's victory. I mean Citizens for Business and Industry [a leading business group] would certainly think Equity is a worthy group, and they are glad they are there, they bring them in on things and they have them on their panels, but as far as putting another mandate on their members, I don't think these groups have done a good enough job.

Regardless of how effective they could have been if they had made family and medical leave a priority, in the late 1980s and early 1990s, NC Equity and other women's organizations had other priorities besides family and medical leave. High on their list was fighting an attempt to limit North Carolina's abortion fund, which until the early 1990s provided one million dollars in Medicaid assistance every year to poor women seeking abortions. In addition, respondents remembered a domestic violence project and an effort to require health insurers to cover mammograms.

Another group that respondents mentioned as a possible source of support for family and medical leave was the Caucus of Women Legislators, a newly formed bipartisan organization. But in the late 1980s and early 1990s, when the North Carolina family and medical leave proposals were being debated, this group was just establishing itself. In order to maintain cohesiveness, a caucus leader said, "We only brought up things that were not divisive." Given the dearth of momentum and the pro-business climate in North Carolina, the Caucus could not risk making family and medical leave a priority.

Unions formed another natural constituency for family and medical leave, but as many respondents pointed out, unions are weak in North Carolina.[15] During the late 1980s, the state AFL-CIO was working on a right-to-know bill requiring employers to provide information about hazardous materials in the workplace. The president of the North Carolina AFL-CIO, Chris Scott, said, "We put all our eggs into that basket."[16]

In part because of the lack of grassroots support, the advocates for family and medical leave in North Carolina were unable to find anyone to even introduce the bill in the more conservative senate until 1993. When they did, they were unable to find a legislator who had substantially more credibility than Kennedy in the house. Minutes from a December 1992 meeting of the coalition formed by the NCC-LAW show that the coalition had hoped to get one of the three leaders in the senate to introduce the bill.[17] But none of these leaders would do so, and the bill was eventually introduced by a senator who, like Kennedy, did not enjoy a reputation for effectiveness.

Thus, while there was certainly interest in family leave in North Carolina, the proposal lacked both the sponsorship of influential legislators and the support of credible advocacy groups. In the words of one supporter, "This . . . bill . . . was not at the top of anyone's agenda." In part, this was because the issue early became identified with a weak legislator and an uninfluential advocacy group. It was thus seen as a losing cause. The lack of support for family and medical leave in North Carolina can also be attributed, however, to an unusually weak political opportunity structure in the state at the time.

Resources and Strategies

In contrast to the advocates for maternity leave in Tennessee, the advocates for parental leave and, later, for family and medical leave in North Carolina possessed few individual resources. In addition, they faced a number of political constraints, including a leadership crisis in the 1989 legislative session. North Carolina had long been a one-party, Democratic, state. In 1989, however, the speaker of the house of representatives was overthrown in what was described as a coup by a coalition of Republicans and conservative Democrats. The overthrow resulted in such a bitter atmosphere that virtually nothing could be accomplished for the rest of the term. As one representative said, "There was chaos for the [whole] two year period."

In 1991 a new speaker of the house, Dan Blue, was elected. Advocates for parental leave rejoiced because Blue was a well-known liberal. But while Blue supported parental leave, it never became a priority for him. This was, in part, because he had been elected by a slim margin and was inundated with requests for support on a number of issues from environmental legislation to health care. His former press secretary stated: "When you remove the power [of the speaker], what you basically had was a very conservative House of Representatives. . . . So he couldn't twist an arm on every vote. And in fact he had very few chips to pull in, he had less than you think."[18]

In addition, Blue and the 1991 North Carolina legislature were almost immediately faced with a crisis of a different sort: the state budget that year ran a $1.2 billion deficit. Because the North Carolina constitution requires a balanced budget, the legislature was forced to cut services by $600 million and to raise taxes, including corporate taxes, by the same amount. Not surprisingly, this caused considerable consternation in the fiscally conservative legislature and made legislators extremely reluctant to do anything else that could be perceived as harming business during that term. One legislator stated, "I think folks who had bit the bullet to raise taxes, rightfully so, were very hesitant to bite the bullet on other things that could have been ammunition to be used against them."

According to most respondents, these constraints (in addition to the conservative climate in North Carolina) would have made it difficult to pass any type of family and medical leave legislation before the

1993 session, and especially legislation with little political clout behind it. Many respondents saw the 1993 session as the best hope for
family and medical leave in North Carolina: political upheaval had
been resolved, the budget crisis was over, and the NCC-LAW had obtained a grant to conduct research on family leave and to draft a new
bill. But in 1993, family and medical leave in North Carolina ran into
a final challenge: when Bill Clinton was elected president in the fall of
1992 and promised to sign the federal Family and Medical Leave Act,
the state bill was deemed unnecessary.

Political Process

As noted above, Annie Brown Kennedy first introduced parental
leave in the North Carolina House of Representatives in 1987, but no
companion bill was introduced in the senate that year, or in any year
until 1993. In a process typical of North Carolina, the legislature that
year created a "Parental Leave Study Commission," which was sup-
posed to report back with recommendations to the house within a year.
The commission never filed a report.

In an interview, Kennedy said her interest in parental leave came
from her experience practicing family law and her belief that "North
Carolina should be aggressive in the workplace."[19] She also said she
knew that she did not have the votes but that because the issue was important to her, she "rushed to . . . make sure that [she] was the one who
introduced it."[20] Kennedy said she did not think that a more moderate
bill (such as a maternity leave bill) would have had a chance of passing,
given the strength of the opposition to any mandate. Finally, she said
she had been firmly committed to the idea of a gender-neutral bill and
had been unwilling to seriously consider covering women only.

Many advocates concurred that given Kennedy's sponsorship and
the political circumstances in North Carolina at that time, it was unlikely that moderating the proposal would have made a significant difference. Several also stated that they knew that Kennedy and women's
organizations like the NCC-LAW and NC Equity were philosophically
unlikely to support maternity leave only. But other respondents argued
that had there been different sponsors, and, had the political circumstances of the time been different, maternity leave would at least have
had a somewhat better chance of passing, because in a culturally as well

as an economically conservative state, it would have been easier to sell.

When asked what they would do differently if they were going to try to pass a family and medical leave bill in North Carolina, respondents emphasized the importance of finding strong sponsors, and they described other controversial bills on which this had happened. Several explicitly stated that someone would have had to wrestle control of the bill from Kennedy if family and medical leave were to pass in North Carolina. Second, respondents emphasized that strategy, and particularly a family values strategy, would have made a difference for family and medical leave in North Carolina, *if there had been some resources in place first.* If the sponsor had been different, if political circumstances had been different, *and* if sponsors and advocates had been willing to use a strategy similar to the one used in Tennessee, many respondents believed that they would have had a very good chance at succeeding.

Respondents cited two cases from the preceding five years in which they had felt that this baseline of resources had been present and in which they thought that strategy had made a significant difference. Like family and medical leave, both of these bills were mandates on business, and both were proposed and lobbied mainly by women legislators and women's interest groups. One was a bill to require health insurers to cover mammograms. This bill was sponsored by a powerful and credible woman legislator, and was lobbied extensively by a "Life-Savers" coalition headed by NC Equity. The bill was framed as legislation that would benefit families from the start, so that, in the words of one advocate, "right from the outset it would be an unpleasant task to oppose a bill like that."

Another bill that passed the Republican-dominated legislature in 1995 required health insurers to allow women to stay in the hospital for forty-eight hours after giving birth. This bill was proposed by a Republican woman legislator whose daughter had been discharged from the hospital early. According to respondents, the legislator made excellent use of her own experience and made such a strong case that the bill passed overwhelmingly. The legislator managed to frame the bill as a "motherhood and apple pie" issue, and most business groups did not bother to oppose it. One business leader stated with regard to this bill: "We were torn because our overall philosophy of government is not mandating it, but I'd say that the insurance companies brought that one on themselves. Now a few of our members got upset with me [for not opposing the bill], but number one, I didn't agree with them, and number two, it was hopeless. . . . It was going to pass so why get into something like that."

One can, of course, argue that the mammogram and "drive-through deliveries" legislation passed while family and medical leave did not because they were substantively different bills: their costs were targeted at only one industry (health insurers), and they tangibly benefit a wide group of easily identifiable people (women and mothers).[21] In comparison, as described in chapter 1, family and medical leave provides a less tangible benefit, and its costs will be felt by many industries. In their explanations of why these bills passed, however, respondents repeatedly emphasized that they were sponsored by credible legislators who emphasized family values and that grassroots organizing made a difference. They argued that even motherhood and apple pie bills like these could have failed if sponsors had not had enough resources and if the wrong strategies had been used. And finally, one has only to look to the experience of Tennessee to see similarities between the bills that did pass in North Carolina and family and medical leave. In Tennessee, the proponents succeeded by fitting their proposal to the local culture, emphasizing benefits, and minimizing costs.[22]

The absence of political resources for family and medical leave in North Carolina meant that business groups had to expend virtually no energy to fight the proposals. According to most respondents, the final blow to family and medical leave in North Carolina was Clinton's election, which came at a time when, because of the external and internal resources available to the advocates, the bill would have had the best chance to pass. While the advocates argued that passing family and medical leave on the state level would make it easier to litigate claims, the imminent passage of family and medical leave on the federal level made it harder to persuade legislators or interest groups to make the issue a priority and to expend political capital to pass it.

Analysis

The case study of the development of maternity leave in Tennessee suggests lessons that are similar to the lessons learned from the passage of family and medical leave in Connecticut and the failure of paid family and medical leave in Massachusetts. In each of those cases, proponents had political resources available to them. In the successful states, however, they had more political resources than in the unsuccessful states, and, crucially, they capitalized on these resources by proposing a moderate bill, adopting insider tactics, framing the bill to fit with the political culture, and compromising. Using these tactics, the advocates in Tennessee and Connecticut managed to transform what could have been a marginalized, special interest issue into a majoritarian bill ostensibly providing broad gains in exchange for widely distributed (and minimal) costs.[23] Comparing the passage of family and medical leave policies in Tennessee and Connecticut highlights the importance of political context in mediating this process: in conservative Tennessee, the proponents and their strategy needed explicitly to be considered not feminist, and moderation meant proposing a maternity leave covering women only.

The North Carolina case study, however, is different. In North Carolina, there was such an absence of resources that strategy became virtually insignificant. While respondents in North Carolina cited examples of policy innovation in which strategy *did* matter, they suggested that strategy is only important once some political resources are present. In the North Carolina case, the association of family and medical leave with an uninfluential legislator, the fact that the bill never became a priority for any major interest group, and the political chaos of the time meant that family and medical leave became unalterably viewed as a bill with significant costs and few tangible benefits. While a strategy of moderation might have made a difference if resources had been more substantial, the dearth of resources in this case was so extreme that no strategy would have been sufficient.

The North Carolina case study thus provides an important addendum to the model developed in this project in which policy innovation is viewed as the product of both political resources and a moderate, insider strategy. This characterization arises not only in considering the fate of the bill, but also after examining the arguments offered by respondents, who offered examples of similar policy issues sponsored by proponents who had more political resources and who successfully used insider, moderate strategies. Similarly, the respondents in Tennessee and Connecticut emphasized that resources were crucial, but that a combination of moderation and resources was necessary to achieve policy success.

As in the Connecticut and Massachusetts case studies, it is important to consider the normative implications of the outcomes in Tennessee and North Carolina. Here again, if the variable measured is the ability to pass the policy proposed, then the model suggested by the experience in Tennessee of an insider strategy combined with moderation is certainly the successful model. But it should also be noted that dissenters in both states, like dissenters in Connecticut and Massachusetts, argued that proposing a more widespread bill may be important even if the bill does not pass, and that passing a moderate bill has costs as well as benefits.

The first argument, which was made by advocates in Massachusetts, was also made by Representative Annie Brown Kennedy in North Carolina. Kennedy argued that regardless of the outcome, it was important to introduce parental leave: "I still feel that [the proposal for parental leave] contributed in some way to helping to move some of the legislators and business people's thoughts further into the necessity to do at least something to help families, their employees, better perform their work."[24]

The efficacy of this argument—that simply introducing a bill will produce educational benefits—depends on the ability of advocates to make their proposal known to the public and to have it debated by elites. This did not happen in either North Carolina or Massachusetts. In Massachusetts, respondents attributed this to the proposal's being perceived as not serious; in North Carolina the fact that family and medical leave was never seriously debated was attributed to the sponsor's not being taken seriously and to the state's chaotic politics. Thus, while the sponsors in both Massachusetts and North Carolina may be correct that there are educational benefits to proposing more wide-ranging policy innovations, it is unlikely that these benefits were felt in their particular cases, because they were not considered credible. Moderation at the beginning of the political process and the presence of some substantial political resources are necessary if proposals are to serve even an educative purpose.

Some dissenting respondents also argued that regardless of the benefits associated with proposing a more widespread bill, there are costs associated with proposing an incremental one. As noted earlier, the Tennessee bill only covered women working for employers of one hundred or more people. Given this and the fact that no serious attempt has yet been made to expand the bill, dissenters argued that the passage of maternity leave in Tennessee is a symbolic victory rather than substantial change. Further, while maternity leave is certainly an important benefit for those with access to it, the fact that the bill provides a benefit only to women perpetuates the stereotype that only women need leaves. One activist expressed this point of view: "I think the goal, at least from my perspective of what feminism should be about, is to try to change the system and change perceptions about what is acceptable or not. So to just assume that it's women who need the leave, not men, is in the long run, I think, the wrong way to go."

As in Connecticut, however, proponents of the moderate Tennessee bill made strong arguments that the existence of the costs described above (if, they argued, they do exist) should not mean that an incremental bill should be considered a failure. First, all of the respondents in Tennessee agreed that maternity leave was the strongest bill that could have passed. This argument is supported by the fact that only one other southern state passed a bill covering private employers, and that state (Louisiana) mandated only a maternity disability leave. It appears that regardless of group resources and strategy, the political context in the South simply would not permit the passage of a gender-neutral bill.

Second, advocates emphasized that more time will have to pass before assessing whether the Tennessee bill has, in fact, led to discrimination against women of childbearing age and whether it will lead eventually to the passage of more extensive policies. The second part of the argument is more credible than the first, because it is certainly true that many social policies take years to evolve from the limited form in which they are passed. But as dissenters in all four states and on the national level noted, the symbolism of passing a bill covering women only has great potential to cause more harm than good.

Conclusion

The case studies of the movements for family and medical leave in Tennessee and North Carolina help to clarify the theory of the moderation dilemma. The contrast between the two states illustrates the degree to which having a base of political resources is essential before strategic choices will make the difference between policy success and failure. While the advocates in both states were working in political climates where there were fewer resources for family and medical leave than in Connecticut and Massachusetts, the advocates in North Carolina faced the additional hurdles of having an uninfluential sponsor and working during a time of political chaos. These hurdles proved to be insurmountable: respondents on both sides of the issue agreed that no amount of compromising would have led to the passage of a family and medical leave bill in North Carolina. In contrast, members of the Tennessee Women's Political Caucus, who were the main advocates for family and medical leave in Tennessee, were able to overcome the handicap of operating in a conservative state through their own reputations, through their ability to attract the support of moderate legislators and the pro-business governor, *and* through their willingness to frame their bill as a motherhood bill and make substantial compromises in its content.

The fact that resources are necessary before a strategy of moderation will make a difference in the passage of contested policy innovation does not, however, diminish the value of the moderation dilemma as an explanation for advocates' success or failure in passing policies like family and medical leave. Nearly every respondent in North Carolina argued that if the advocates there had access to better resources, moderation would have made a difference. They discussed two instances in the past five years in which, they felt, advocates with those resources had used moderation to pass their policy. While the respondents in Tennessee argued that the resources possessed by advocates there—their insider status, their clout, and their connections to Governor Ned McWherter—had been crucial to their success, they also argued that if the advocates had not moderated early, they would not have been able to make use of these resources.

Advice for Advocates

The movements for family and medical leave in Tennessee and North Carolina suggest factors that may be important to advocates of similar policy innovations, particularly in states where the advocates have access to few contextual resources. First and foremost, the experiences in Tennessee and North Carolina indicate that advocates must find credible and powerful sponsors, and, if possible, interest group advocates who are political insiders and can work with those sponsors to frame their proposals to fit the political climate and to moderate and compromise. Second, as with Connecticut and Massachusetts, the experiences of family and medical leave in Tennessee and North Carolina indicate the degree to which timing and luck are important. In the late 1980s and early 1990s, the advocates in North Carolina faced an extraordinarily difficult political climate, in which it was going to be difficult to pass *any* business regulation and especially one that challenged traditional gender norms and that was sponsored by an uninfluential legislator. One might advise advocates to consider carefully whether they have an open policy window[25] before they introduce legislation, waiting, as the advocates in Connecticut did, until they have not only the right sponsorship but also the right political climate.

The problem with this recommendation is that it may be difficult for advocates to know exactly when a policy window will open. The factors that contribute to a policy window, as described by John Kingdon, may shift suddenly: a problem may be redefined through a focusing event, or economic or political circumstances may suddenly change for the better, just as they changed for the worse in Massachusetts. To paraphrase Kingdon, an idea's time may "suddenly come."[26] And advocates must be ready to make use of new opportunities, as the advocates in Tennessee were when Governor Ned McWherter was searching for a way to pay tribute to his dying mother.

In addition, as dissenters in both North Carolina and Massachusetts argued, there may be a value in introducing legislation that will not pass. Even if the legislation is not publicized enough to educate the public, it may educate legislators, and an unsuccessful bill may lay the groundwork for a successful one down the road. Given the dismal political circumstances in North Carolina in the early 1990s, when no other legislator or major interest group expressed a strong interest in family and medical leave, it is doubtful that Kennedy's introducing the bill actually *harmed* prospects for policy innovation in North Carolina.

The Tennessee case study also serves as an example of how difficult the moderation dilemma can be for advocates of policy innovation. While the advocates for family and medical leave in Connecticut had to limit the number of employees and the number of weeks covered, the advocates in Tennessee had to fundamentally change the nature of the policy, defining it as something that only women take. This meant enacting a law that recognized and legitimized stereotypes of women as the primary care givers for children, something that was of great concern to advocates for women's equality. While this certainly has to be balanced against the value of the policy for those women who could take advantage of it, it is an important caveat.

5 | THE PASSAGE OF THE NATIONAL FAMILY AND MEDICAL LEAVE ACT

Interesting parallels can be identified between the successful movements to enact family and medical leave legislation in Connecticut and Tennessee and the long and ultimately successful movement for the national Family and Medical Leave Act. As in the successful states, family and medical leave was supported early by legislators with considerable political clout. As time passed, the bill attracted legislators with moderate records and bipartisan experience. As in Connecticut and Tennessee, the Family and Medical Leave Act was supported by a coalition that was willing to limit its proposal in order to gain credibility and to alter its proposal over time to widen its coalition base and to attract the support of moderate legislators. The proponents of the Family and Medical Leave Act did not introduce a paid family and medical leave bill, and they agreed to limit the number of weeks of leave and the number of employers who were covered by the law, to exclude key employees from coverage and to exclude coverage for abortion. They would not, however, do the one thing that both they and their opponents agreed would have helped the bill to pass more quickly. They refused to compromise the bill to a maternity leave covering women only.

This chapter examines the development of family and medical leave on the national level between 1985, when the first bill was introduced, and 1993, when the Family and Medical Leave Act became law under President Bill Clinton. The success of federal family and medical leave can be attributed to many of the same factors that led to the success of proposals in Connecticut and Tennessee, but the unwillingness of the national proponents to compromise *everything* allowed them to find a balance between staying true to their principles and offering enough compromises to remain credible in a challenging political atmosphere.

States that passed family and medical leave policies early served as resources for advocates in other states and on the national level. Studies of early state innovators showed that the policies passed were virtually costless to business; these studies were used to refute business arguments about the harms caused by family and medical leave. Legislators from states that passed family and medical leave were more likely to support the federal bill, regardless of their own ideological leanings. But these factors were of only moderate importance, because many legislators (particularly in the South) did not believe that the experience of states that passed family and medical leave was applicable to their own states, and some federal opponents of the policy made states rights arguments, asserting that the passage of state bills made federal passage unnecessary. Finally, as the federal family and medical leave bill moved toward passage, momentum decreased and states were likely to develop bills that conformed to the federal bill rather than developing more far-reaching bills.

The Formation of the National Family and Medical Leave Coalition

The coalition that emerged in support of family and medical leave in the early 1980s had a history going back to a series of legal battles over pregnancy and the workplace during the 1960s and 1970s. As described in chapter 2, an end to discrimination in the workforce and provisions for working parents were goals adopted by members of the women's movement of the 1960s and by the 1963 President's Commission on the Status of Women. In 1972, the Equal Employment Opportunity Commission issued guidelines interpreting Title VII of the 1964 Civil Rights Act as prohibiting discrimination based on pregnancy. But the Supreme Court quickly overturned these guidelines, ruling in 1974 and 1976 that insurance and disability statutes excluding pregnancy but including "comparable" conditions did not constitute discrimination.[1] A large and diverse coalition emerged to pass the Pregnancy Discrimination Act (PDA) of 1978, an amendment to Title VII stipulating that any health or disability benefit plan that covers comparable conditions must also cover pregnancy. Coalition members emphasized the importance of the PDA in providing "equal access" in the workforce for women, as opposed to special treatment.

Soon after the Pregnancy Discrimination Act was passed, questions began to emerge in the women's policy community about whether equality could be achieved without some active provision for pregnancy. While some feminists were concerned that such provisions would be similar to the paternalistic policies that had held women back during the early part of the twentieth century, others felt that equality could be achieved only through some acknowledgment of women's special status as mothers. The debate intensified when several states passed laws mandating maternity leaves. Court cases challenging laws in California and Montana as violations of the equal treatment provisions of Title VII of the 1964 Civil Rights Act and the Pregnancy Discrimination Act split the feminist policy community, with some arguing that maternity disability constituted paternalism and others arguing that it was a necessary prerequisite to gender equality.

As described in chapter 2, family and medical leave came to be seen as the type of policy that could solve the dilemma of how to treat women and men equally, while at the same time responding to the fact that only women bear children. By proposing laws that would allow people to take leave for a variety of family and medical reasons, advocates could accomplish their goal of accommodating the needs of pregnant women, while at the same time emphasizing that these needs are equivalent to many other workforce needs.[2]

Two themes emerge from interviews with members of the coalition that developed to lobby for family and medical leave in the early 1980s and from the literature on the bill. First, the experience of lobbying for workplace equality in the 1970s cemented relationships so that there was a particularly high level of trust among activists and between activists and supportive members of Congress.[3] In interviews, coalition leaders argued that this level of trust facilitated agreement on the specifics of the proposal and made the compromise process easier. Second, many of the organizations, and particularly the women's organizations, that formed the family and medical leave coalition were reeling from a series of defeats and setbacks in the early 1980s. These setbacks included the loss of the Equal Rights Amendment (ERA) in

1982 and a lack of support from the Reagan White House. A number of advocates remembered that members of the women's policy community were chastened, and thus were more attuned than usual to the importance of crafting a bill that would have a good chance of passing. In the words of one lobbyist: "In 1981 only one bill passed Congress that helped women, and that was women's history week. And then in '83 not much more, so . . . we needed something we could feel upbeat and positive about."

The Agenda-Setting Process

In 1984, the California Supreme Court ruled that a state law requiring employers to provide maternity disability leave violated the equal protection statutes of the 1964 Civil Rights Act and the 1978 Pregnancy Discrimination Act. Soon after, two members of the California congressional delegation, Representatives Howard Berman (who as a state representative had crafted the California maternity leave law) and Barbara Boxer, met with members of women's groups to draft a national maternity leave law that would overturn the court's decision. But in early meetings, the activists made it clear that they wanted a law that would apply to both male and female parents, and possibly to other groups as well.[4] They were concerned that a maternity-leave-only law would constitute special treatment of women, which would perpetuate stereotypes and might encourage employers to discriminate against women of childbearing age. Berman and Boxer, whose primary interest was in overturning the California Supreme Court's decision, responded with the concern that it would be much more difficult to pass a gender-neutral or family leave act, but the advocates, as one respondent put it, "were stubborn" on the issue of gender neutrality.

As a result of Berman and Boxer's hesitancy, control over drafting family and medical leave shifted to Representative Patricia Schroeder and to the staff of the Congressional Caucus for Women's Issues, which she headed. The first bill, entitled the Parental and Disability Leave Act of 1985, required that all employers provide eighteen weeks of unpaid leave within a two-year period to employees of either sex who stay home with a newborn, newly adopted, or seriously ill child. It also provided twenty-six weeks of unpaid disability leave, and it called for a commission to study paid leave. The bill was introduced on April 4, 1985.

Hearings were held on the Parental and Disability Leave Act of 1985, but no action was taken, in part because Schroeder voted that year against a plant-closing bill sponsored by Representatives William Clay and Augustus Hawkins, the chairs of the Education and Labor Committee.[5] The next year, however, when a reformulated family and medical leave act was introduced, Clay, who had supported the concept all along, became a cosponsor of the bill. The new proposal applied only to employers of fifteen or more people. For the first time, it was accompanied by a companion bill in the Senate, sponsored by Senator Christopher Dodd of Connecticut.

Legislative leaders Clay and Dodd provided additional credibility for the bill and prompted the first concerted opposition from business groups. In the political process that followed, it was crucial that members of Congress were joined by skilled and experienced members of insider advocacy organizations. The lead organization working to pass family and medical leave was, from the beginning, the Women's Legal Defense Fund. It was joined in the early years by the National Women's Law Center, the Women's Equity Action League, the National Federation of Business and Professional Women, and the National Association of Junior Leagues. Faced with opposition from business, the advocates for national family and medical leave began to compromise almost immediately. Overwhelmingly, both proponents and opponents of the Family and Medical Leave Act attributed its ultimate success to the willingness of the advocates to accept compromise.

The Politics of Compromise

Some of the compromises made by the advocates of the national Family and Medical Leave Act were made during the drafting stage. While these compromises may not have been necessary to attract the first liberal sponsors of the bill, they were necessary to appeal to moderate members of Congress. Indeed, even some of the sponsors thought that the initial proposal should be compromised, as they did not want to be associated with a bill that would have absolutely no chance of passing.

The first and perhaps most important compromise was not to propose a paid leave. Many respondents remembered that the decision was
prompted by Schroeder, who was deeply concerned that the bill be perceived as credible. They also remembered that the leadership and most
members of the coalition had agreed with the decision, believing that
it would be better first to establish the principle of guaranteed job protection and then try to enact a paid leave later. One advocate stated
that there was "a recognition from those in the coalition that [paid
leave] would be dead on arrival, but the way they argued it within the
groups was, we'll introduce this prototype that voices principles, and
then we'll go to paid."

In choosing this approach, the advocates for the Family and Medical Leave Act committed themselves to the principle of using incremental change. As noted earlier, this approach is usually adopted by
groups using insider techniques and working within the system. This
finding applies to the federal case as well. As in the states, the decision
to pursue an insider strategy on family and medical leave was opposed
by groups who argued that the compromising process happened too
early and that the resulting legislation undermined momentum for a
broader policy.

The most significant dissent was expressed by members of the National Organization for Women, which was joined by the Children's
Defense Fund[6] and, later, by the Fund for a Feminist Majority. At one
of the earliest hearings on family and medical leave, NOW president
Eleanor Smeal (who later became president of the Fund for a Feminist
Majority), testifying on behalf of a number of women's groups, diverged
from her prepared testimony to note that NOW would have liked to see
the proposed bill establish paid leave. Several years later, after the proposed family and medical leave act had been compromised and still
continued to call for unpaid leave, NOW became an inactive member
of the coalition.

In interviews, dissenters from the coalition expressed frustration at
decisions like the one to compromise family and medical leave during
the agenda-setting process. While acknowledging the need to compromise in order to pass legislation, they argued that many liberal groups,
and women's groups in particular, often compromise too early in an effort to respond to anticipated opposition. While acknowledging that
most proposals are compromised eventually, one respondent said, "I
don't understand why we would ever want to start out asking for less

than what we want." Another respondent compared the approach taken by insider women's organizations with the approach taken by advocates for military spending who, she argued, always ask for more than what they want because they know it will be cut. In addition to charging that insider advocates for policies like family and medical leave are too quick to try to preempt their opposition, dissenters argued that because insiders are connected with the system, they may lose touch with the needs of their constituents. Part of this, the dissenters indicated, involves taking a narrow view of what is possible and being unable to imagine widespread change. It also involves cozying up to legislators and focusing on relationships with them more than on doing the job. One lobbyist who has worked for both insider and outsider groups described insiders using this anecdote:

> Kent Conrad [a senator from North Dakota] says, "I can't vote for the Family and Medical Leave Act because there is a drought in North Dakota," and you start worrying about Kent Conrad getting reelected rather than worrying that he won't get reelected if he doesn't stand for the Family and Medical Leave Act. So you start defending Kent Conrad to the women of North Dakota. When instead, you should be talking to the women of North Dakota and then marching up to Kent Conrad and saying "&%@$ the drought! You have to take a stand up here, buddy."

Members of the dissenting groups argued that the source of the difference between themselves and the leaders of the family and medical leave coalition can be found in the structure and funding mechanisms of their respective groups. Their arguments conform to the literature on group structure and strategy outlined in the introductory chapter. The dissenters noted that in contrast to many of the groups that led the family and medical leave coalition, their own organizations are grassroots. In the case of NOW, the national staff comes from regional offices to Washington on a rotating basis, which makes them less likely to develop long-standing relationships with the power structure. NOW leaders are also primarily responsible to a mass membership, which in turn is likely to be motivated primarily by ideology and thus is less likely to view a compromise as a win.[7]

Further, while NOW and the Fund for a Feminist Majority obtain most of their funding from their dues-paying members, many of the groups in the family and medical leave coalition had only a token membership and were dependent on foundation, government, and sometimes corporate support. The dissenters pointed out that funders expect tangible results in a way that members do not, and that since the funders themselves work within the power structure, they are likely to view an incremental bill as a success. As suggested by the literature on insider and outsider strategies described in the introductory chapter, receiving outside funding can exacerbate the need to claim credit and can thus prompt compromise.

In response to the dissent, the leadership of the family and medical leave coalition echoed Representative Patricia Schroeder's argument that if a bill is to have a chance of passing, it must be perceived as credible. When asked about the value of introducing paid family and medical leave just to get an idea considered in the public discourse, one insider advocate said, "I think we thought [that] that isn't the way you get an issue considered in Congress. In fact if we had put [paid leave] out there, it would have sunk like a stone." Several activists emphasized that the eight years that it took to pass an unpaid family and medical leave policy is not an unusual length of time for a contested innovation to pass. They argued that while there might be a value in introducing the idea of paid leave, there is greater value in encoding the principle that people should be entitled to a leave. Coalition leaders emphasized that they viewed their efforts as a first step that would eventually (but perhaps not in their lifetimes) lead to a paid leave.

The Process of Compromise

The decision to pursue a gender-neutral bill was virtually the only issue on which the leaders of the national family and medical leave coalition refused to compromise. The bill was designed to attract the kind of support that would make it not only feasible but also competitive. The decision not to pursue paid family and medical leave was part of this approach, but the coalition also expanded and defined its bill specifically to attract the support of powerful groups who would provide financial and lobbying assistance and who would help frame their bill as a family rather than a feminist bill.

One decision, made about a year after the Family and Medical Leave Act was introduced, was to widen the bill beyond parents to cover people tending to their own medical needs or to the medical needs of spouses or elderly parents. Despite concerns that widening the bill would make it more difficult to explain and would prompt stronger opposition from business because more people would be eligible to take advantage of the policy, proponents made this change in order to attract stronger support from unions. While maternity leave was part of many union contracts, few included family and medical leaves. They included care for elderly parents in the bill in part to attract the support of the powerful American Association of Retired People (AARP), which along with the unions provided most of the financial support for the coalition.

A second decision was to make it clear that the Family and Medical Leave Act would not be used by women seeking or recovering from abortions. This allowed the United States Catholic Conference to embrace the bill as pro-family and pro-life, just as the decision years earlier not to include abortion in coverage under the Pregnancy Discrimination Act of 1978 had also led to Catholic support. The Catholic Conference was attracted to family and medical leave as part of its general interest in supporting working families, but would not have supported the bill if it had allowed leave for abortion. Many respondents labeled the involvement of the Catholic Conference crucial, because in addition to bringing substantial resources to the movement, the Catholics provided credibility. The conference's participation helped to frame family and medical leave not only as a feminist and labor issue, but also as a family values issue that could be made attractive to pro-life social conservatives.

In an interview, the policy advisor on economic issues for the Catholic Conference, Thomas Shellabarger, discussed the resources that the Catholic Conference offered. Quoting from a Bishop's policy letter, Shellabarger stated:

We took [family and medical leave] and wrapped it in a different mantle, building on what the women's groups had done and building on what labor had done and said yeah, it's both of those. Bishop Malone writes, ". . . the family and medical leave bill will be helpful for two fundamental reasons. It would send a message that our nation is prepared to act on our often stated commitment to family life. Second, the bill would protect people who take time off from work for important family responsibilities. Parents should not have to choose between the job they need and the[ir] children.'"[8]

The ability of the Catholic Conference to emphasize the family values aspect of the Family and Medical Leave Act was enormously helpful to the leaders of the family and medical leave coalition. In interviews, respondents mentioned that the Catholic Conference provided public relations support. They also mentioned the fact that lobbyists for the Catholic Conference could reach conservative legislators whom the feminists and labor activists could not. They noted, however, that working so closely with the Catholic Conference was a source of tension for some of the feminist activists, who were accustomed to opposing the Catholics in debates over abortion. Donna Lenhoff of the Women's Legal Defense Fund observed that the tension was eased somewhat by the fact that the lobbyist for the Catholic Conference on family and medical leave was not the same person who lobbied on abortion.[9]

The most important legislator who decided to support family and medical leave as a result of Catholic Conference lobbying was pro-life congressman Henry Hyde of Illinois. As described by Elving and remembered by several coalition members, the Catholic Conference was in discussion with Henry Hyde for some time before he was finally persuaded to support the bill. Hyde announced his support in a dramatic moment during the House debate in 1990: "We get down to the fact that society should have a policy of encouraging motherhood, not encouraging abortion. It seems to me that if a working woman becomes pregnant she needs to have job security and have an incentive to have that child, not to exterminate that child so she does not lose her job."[10]

Donna Lenhoff remembered that while the family and medical leave coalition knew that the Catholic Conference had been lobbying Hyde, she did not know exactly what Hyde would say when he came to the House floor. She said, "It was your basic great moment. . . . It had gone from [being] a kind of liberal pipe dream."[11]

A third decision was to be flexible with regard to the number of employees covered, the type of employees covered, and the number of weeks provided. As mentioned above, coalition leaders emphasized that their agreed-on central goal was to establish the principle of guaranteed job protection. While they wanted to cover the maximum number of people for the maximum amount of time, they were willing to compromise in both areas. Thus, while the original bill required all employers to provide eighteen weeks of parental leave and twenty-six weeks of disability leave in each two-year period, the final bill was considerably watered down. It provided for twelve weeks of leave for full-time workers employed by companies having fifty or more people. And it exempted, as key employees, the top 10 percent of earners in each firm. The willingness of the leaders of the family and medical leave coalition to both broaden the bill and soften its impact made it harder for those opposing the bill to make credible arguments. Over time, moderate Republicans and conservative Democrats began to support the Family and Medical Leave Act. One convert was Marge Roukema, a New Jersey Republican who became one of the bill's strongest supporters in 1987 after the proponents agreed to exempt businesses employing fewer than fifty people. Roukema's cosponsorship of the bill was cited by many respondents as crucial, because it made the bill bipartisan for the first time, and because Roukema was well known as a supporter of business. Among other things, Roukema's sponsorship of the bill helped dispel business arguments that the bill would be the first step toward a paid family and medical leave, since Roukema argued firmly that she would not support that.

The Opposition

Despite the willingness of its advocates to compromise, the Family and Medical Leave Act had attracted substantial opposition from the business community by 1987. Although a substantial number of businesses (and a majority of big businesses) were already providing family and medical leaves voluntarily by the 1980s, business organizations felt that the bill represented a dangerous precedent. If government could mandate family and medical leave, it might also be able to mandate paid leave, health benefits, or paid vacation. As in the states, business opponents of family and medical leave frequently invoked the argument that the bill would be "the first domino" or "the camel's nose under the tent."

Two opponents of family and medical leave were John Motley of the National Federation of Independent Businesses and Mary Tavenner of the National Association of Wholesalers. In 1987, Tavenner founded the Concerned Alliance of Responsible Employers (CARE), which became the central organization devoted to fighting family and medical leave. CARE focused primarily on the mandate argument, stating that while family and medical leave might be a fine policy, it should not be mandated, and if this mandate was allowed to pass, other more costly mandates might follow.

Members of the CARE coalition essentially adopted two strategies. The first was to focus on the same group that the proponents were targeting: moderate Republicans and conservative and southern Democrats. The second strategy was to count on first a Reagan and then a Bush veto, thus ensuring that the proponents would need the support of not just a majority but two-thirds of Congress. A number of opponents noted that later in the Bush presidency, after the bill had passed Congress and when it was being used by the Democrats to show that Bush was "out of touch," they were constantly fearful that Bush would change his mind. But Bush never wavered, and he vetoed the bill twice.[12]

The opponents agreed that as compromises were made, it became harder to fight the Family and Medical Leave Act. In interviews, they stated that family and medical leave *did* come to be seen as a family issue rather than a feminist or liberal issue. One congressional staff member explained, "This benefit sounds so positive, I think it is much more difficult when you are the one who has to explain an issue and explain the pitfalls." Another said: "It's very hard to oppose motherhood up here, literally. This was portrayed as a kind of motherhood, apple pie kind of benefit, and so they all had the emotions on their side. And of course they could portray the coalition opposed to it as a group of greedy businesspeople."

However, in part due to the substantial resources that were spent opposing family and medical leave by the CARE coalition and by individual groups like the National Federation of Independent Businesses (NFIB), the mandate issue continued to resonate. Even as states began to pass family and medical leave policies of their own and as a major study by a nonpartisan organization showed that unpaid family and medical leave policies did not harm business, business opposition continued.[13] In part, this was because many businesses, and especially many small businesses, saw family and medical leave as a precursor to other fights such as health care. As John Motley of the NFIB put it, "The whole idea of fighting to the bitter end . . . was to show them that the employer mandate battle was going to be bitter, it was going to be bloody."[14]

One compromise that was offered by moderate legislators was to shrink the bill to cover only maternity leave. As noted earlier, most respondents thought that if a maternity leave bill had been accepted by the proponents, it would have passed with relative ease. A number of proponents remembered that they had been afraid that the opponents of family and medical leave would at some point compromise with the moderates, and a maternity leave bill would pass despite the concerns. These concerns can be seen in the congressional debate over family and medical leave: in 1989, Representative Patricia Schroeder was quoted in the *Congressional Quarterly Almanac*: "The worst rumor we hear up here is that the administration will ask us to schedule the bill [for floor action] around Mother's Day and then take men out of the bill."[15]

As in the southern states, while business groups were not the only opponents of family and medical leave, they were the major ones. Cultural and religious conservatives also opposed the bill, but both they and other respondents agreed that the issue was not a major priority for them. In part, this was because they were working on other issues. Phyllis Schlafly's Eagle Forum, for example, was focused on trying to defeat the ABC child care bill, which was also being debated in the late 1980s. Several respondents argued that the lack of strong opposition by the New Right resulted from ambivalence. On the one hand, family and medical leave was a government mandate and reflected societal acceptance of the fact that many women work outside the home. On the other hand, it was also a bill that encouraged families to spend more time with each other and was supported by a number of prominent socially conservative legislators.

By 1989 the Family and Medical Leave Act had 20 cosponsors in the Senate and 136 in the House. In 1990 the bill passed the House for the first time but failed to reach the Senate floor. In 1991 both the House and the Senate passed the bill, but the House failed to override a veto by President George Bush. By this point, however, the bill had achieved credibility: it had support from both Republicans and Democrats, and it had the support of the Democratic leadership, which began to see the issue as one that could be used effectively against George Bush and Republicans. As one legislative staff member explained, family and medical leave was "good politics" that could help seize the "family values" issue from Republicans.

In 1991, however, with George Bush enjoying extraordinarily high popularity ratings in the aftermath of the Persian Gulf War and strongly

favored to win a second term, the inability of the proponents to override Bush's veto seemed to spell doom for family and medical leave. Accordingly, the proponents compromised again, raising the number of
hours an employee must work in the year preceding a leave from 1,000
to 1,250 and at that point agreeing to the exemption for key employees.

A number of alternative proposals were considered in 1991 and
1992. Some were rejected by the proponents, some by the opponents,
and some simply never generated enthusiasm from anyone. Many of
the alternatives lessened or eliminated the mandate aspect of the bill.
These included a proposal by Senator Dave Durenberger of Minnesota
restricting the enforcement mechanisms in the bill, an amendment by
Senator Orren Hatch of Utah and Representative Charles Stenholm of
Texas changing the mandate to preferential rehiring, and a proposal by
President Bush to give tax credits to businesses that provided family
and medical leave rather than requiring that they allow their employees to take leave.

A proposal by Representative Tim Penny came closest to passing.
As described by Elving and several respondents, Penny was a conservative Minnesota Democrat who was strongly opposed to family and
medical leave until 1991. In that year, however, Penny determined that
he wanted to be something of a broker on family and medical leave.
After polling the proponents and finding that they would not consider
either compromising to maternity leave only or accepting a nonman-
date bill, Penny proposed that coverage under family and medical leave
be limited to eight weeks for parental leave and six weeks for other
conditions; he also suggested weakening a number of enforcement provisions in the bill.[16] Many members of the coalition supporting family
and medical leave, including the Women's Legal Defense Fund and the
American Association of Retired Persons, supported Penny's proposal,
believing that it was their only chance to pass a bill. But legislators including Schroeder, Clay, and Roukema opposed what they viewed as a
fatal weakening of the bill. The Penny proposal failed.

The issue did not go away, however. Family and medical leave was
highlighted during the 1992 presidential campaign when Democratic
candidates Bill Clinton and Al Gore used the issue to show that George
Bush was "out of touch" with American families. Gore spoke movingly
of his family's experience when his young son, Al Jr., was critically
injured in a car accident. And in the post–Anita Hill "year of the
woman," family and medical leave was used by Democratic pollsters

and pundits as an "indicator of whether a given candidate 'got it' or not."[17] A number of respondents, including opponents of the legislation, thought in retrospect that while his opposition to family and medical leave did not cost Bush the election, it was damaging.

The Clinton Compromise

When Bill Clinton was elected president in November 1992, the passage of the Family and Medical Leave Act became a fait accompli. As the Clinton transition moved forward, however, questions arose as to which bill the new Democratic Congress would pass and which one Clinton would sign. Many of the advocates who had despaired during the compromising process felt that after so many years of trying to develop a veto-proof bill, the support of the Clinton administration meant that they had a chance to get a "real" family and medical leave bill.[18] Why not, they argued, go back and raise the number of covered employees? Why not increase the number of weeks? Why not insert a provision for paid leave? According to several outsider respondents, however, there was little interest either from the coalition or from the administration in expanding family and medical leave.

Coalition leaders argued that even with a Democratic Congress and a supportive president, there was a substantial risk to changing the family and medical leave proposal. They feared that they would confuse the more conservative members of Congress who were familiar with the "brand" of family and medical leave that had passed the 102nd Congress. If they took the time to educate legislators about the changes, the bill might lose momentum. Second, the coalition leaders felt that they had an interest in giving Clinton an easy win, which, they believed, the administration had clearly signaled that it wanted. Third, as one advocate said: "We were exhausted, just exhausted. And we knew that this was eminently do-able, it was not as though we were just occasionally seeing the light and bobbing our heads above the water, grasping at something . . . we had the votes all along, it was but for the Bush administration."

The combination of these factors made it "easier than I thought it was going to be," as one staffer recalled, to convince the advocacy groups to support the enactment of the same bill that had been passed in 1992. Family and medical leave passed in January 1993 and became the first bill signed into law by Bill Clinton. It required employers of fifty or more people working within a seventy-five-mile radius to give employees who had worked at least 1,250 hours in the previous year twelve weeks of unpaid leave for the purposes of caring for a newborn or newly adopted child, for a sick spouse or parent, or for the worker's own medical condition. It allowed businesses to exempt those in the top 10 percent of payroll from coverage. The bill covers approximately 11 percent of employers and 55 percent of employees, many of whom already had privately negotiated access to some or all of the bill's provisions. As those at the signing ceremony noted, it also represented a major step by the national government toward acknowledging that the problem of work-family balance is a public problem worthy of a legislative solution. It represented a hard-won victory for feminist and labor organizations that had supported it.

Analysis

In analyzing the decision made by the proponents about where and when to moderate, and in examining the outcome of these decisions, it is certainly appropriate to question whether a broader policy could have been achieved. This question can be divided into two periods: before and after Clinton came into office.

In interviews, all of the coalition leaders and most dissenters agreed that it would not have been possible to pass a stronger family and medical leave policy during the Reagan and Bush years. As evidence, they cited the firmness of Reagan's and Bush's resolve not to sign the bill and the resulting need to get a two-thirds majority in both houses of Congress.

However, as described above, there was considerable debate among the proponents and dissenters as to whether a stronger bill could have passed once Clinton came into office. That debate was still raging when I conducted my interviews in 1996. Looking back on the events of 1993 and 1994, when Clinton was focusing his legislative efforts on the universal health plan that ultimately failed, coalition leaders stated confidently that they had made the right choice. They argued that if they had tried to pass a stronger bill, every member of Congress and especially the Republicans who had voted to override Bush's veto in 1992, would have reconsidered his or her vote. This, they argued, would have cost time and the power associated with a bipartisan bill.

The respondents were also divided over whether attempting to pass a stronger bill would have hurt their ability to pass an incremental bill at all. Some proponents thought that waiting would have diminished momentum for family and medical leave and that it might have been impossible to get a family and medical leave bill at all. Donna Lenhoff of the Women's Legal Defense Fund said: "It would have gotten in line behind health care reform. And we would have had the [19]94 elections. That's it. Look what happened to the minimum wage. You couldn't raise the minimum wage in a Democratic Congress with a Democratic president because he wanted health care reform."[19]

Other proponents thought that a bill might still have gone through, but that it would have done so in a much more polarized and partisan atmosphere. Several advocates noted that they felt there was considerable value in passing a bipartisan family and medical leave act, even if achieving bipartisan support had to mean more compromises. One advocate even ventured to say that had a stronger family and medical leave bill passed, it might have been the subject of a repeal effort after the 1994 elections.

The supporters of family and medical leave were responding to my interview questions during a particularly low moment for Democrats in the 1990s. In mid-1996, Congress was controlled by Republicans and dominated by Newt Gingrich and his "Contract with America" reformers. President Clinton was still in a competitive reelection race, and the prospect of a unified Republican government was looming. Thus it is easy to see why advocates might feel that in retrospect, they had had a very small window in which to enact family and medical leave.[20]

These advocates' arguments still resonated in the spring of 2000, with an additional four years of hindsight. While Bill Clinton regained some of his political clout in 1997 and 1998, after his reelection but before the Monica Lewinsky scandal, he never again enjoyed the support of a Democratic majority in Congress. No one can know if Clinton would have continued to make family and medical leave a priority if it had not passed in 1993. It is thus quite possible that the coalition leaders are right: if family and medical leave had not passed in 1993, a national policy would still not be in place.

The difference between the coalition leaders and the dissenters over whether a stronger policy could have passed can be linked to different views of how the policy process works. As insiders, the coalition leadership accepted the principle of incremental change. As noted in the introductory chapter, this approach is validated by examples from recent American social policy, most notably Social Security. When Social Security was enacted in 1935, it did not cover all professions and did not cover disabilities, but over time it developed both popular and administrative support and was expanded. This is one example of a positive policy feedback, which will be discussed further in the conclusion.

The dissenters on the federal level, like those in the states, did not have the same faith that moderate policies lay the groundwork for more widespread innovation. Rather, they argued in 1996, family and medical leave has gained little momentum since the passage of the national bill in 1993, and interest in expansion has been limited to areas such as allowing parents to take time off to attend teacher conferences.[21] While the dissenters would no doubt be heartened by the efforts to pass paid family leave in a number of states, they would probably still express concern these bills are facing considerable opposition and have not yet passed.

The dissenters' concern that a moderate family and medical leave policy will not be expanded within a reasonable time horizon may be traced to the fact that while the policy benefits many members of the middle class, it does not benefit everyone, and it does not benefit people for a long period of time, as does Social Security, which provides benefits to nearly everyone in the population from the time they turn sixty-five until they die. It also may be traced to historic difficulties in developing widespread public social benefits programs. This difficulty is seen in the case of Medicare and Medicaid programs, which were accepted in the 1960s by proponents of national health insurance as a first step toward that goal. As Douglas Arnold notes, Medicaid and Medicare "eliminated the most potent argument for national health insurance."[22] Three decades later, and after two major efforts, no national health insurance program exists.

The Relationship Between State and Federal Family and Medical Leave

One question that arises in a study of both state and national public policy development is the question of how state policies affected the national political process and vice versa. As states develop policies, does it become easier or harder for advocates on the national level to pass a policy? As a national policy moves forward, how does it affect states still attempting to pass their own policies? Finally, how does the passage of family and medical leave in a group of states affect the prospects of the policy in other states? These questions are especially pertinent today, when those who believe that states are better equipped than the federal government to create effective policies are attempting to devolve control of social policy to the states.

One theory of the relationship between state and national policy innovation suggests that states serve as "laboratories" for other states and for the federal government. In this model, which was first suggested by Justice Louis Brandeis some sixty years ago, states try "novel social and economic experiments," which, if successful, can be adopted by other states and by the national government.[23] In the case of family and medical leave, the laboratories theory suggests that once a group of states passes the policy and studies shows that the policy is successful, it will be easier to pass the policy in other states and on the national level.

All respondents were asked about the relationship between state and national family and medical leave bills. To some extent, the findings from this project do validate the laboratories hypothesis. In particular, as mentioned briefly earlier, respondents mentioned a study that was conducted by the nonpartisan Families and Work Institute, examining the implementation of parental leave laws in four states: Minnesota, Wisconsin, Oregon, and Rhode Island.[24] This study strongly refuted business claims that parental leave laws would be costly or onerous to implement. It found that the vast majority of businesses had no difficulty implementing the laws, that the laws were not substantially costly for most employers, and that small businesses had no more difficulty implementing the laws than large companies did. Further, the study found that as a result of state laws, more women took at least the medically advised minimum of six weeks off after childbirth, and more new fathers took leave as well. Finally, the study found that low-income women were least likely to take off fewer than six weeks and were more likely to take longer leaves in Rhode Island, a state that provides for wage replacement of parental leaves through its Temporary Disability Insurance system. This last finding was cited by advocates of paid family and medical leave as evidence that wage replacement helps determine whether people of all classes can take advantage of the law.

In interviews, coalition leaders cited the four-state study as helpful in refuting business arguments. The study provided tangible evidence from policies already in place, in the words of one advocate, "to show that all of the horrors that the business community claimed did not in fact happen." Another advocate argued: "We could just say, we know how this works, and folks are not going under in those states. That was very helpful. And talking about those sorts of experiences, and quantifying them to the extent that they could be quantified was very helpful."

However, most respondents indicated that while the Families and Work Institute study allowed the advocates for family and medical leave to respond more effectively to business arguments, they did not think that it made a huge difference in the debate. The business opponents of the policy responded to the study in several ways. On the one hand, opponents argued, conditions in the states that had passed family and medical leave policies were substantially different from conditions on the federal level; thus applying the state experiences to the federal proposal would be like comparing apples and oranges. On the other hand, they suggested that if family and medical leave policies worked in the states, then they were not needed on the federal level. Finally, the opponents relied on their standard argument that even if the policies were not costly, they were still mandates, and as such they constituted an unreasonable intrusion of government into private affairs.

Given this response and the fact that the debate over family and medical leave was largely symbolic, most respondents thought that the Families and Work Institute study did not change many minds. It did convince some fence sitters, and it provided ammunition for those who wanted to defend their support of the policy, but it did not make a difference to most members of Congress. Referring both to the Families and Work Institute study and to a study by the Institute for Women's Policy Studies, which calculated how much money people lose when they have to leave their jobs for reasons covered by the proposed act,[25] one advocate said:

> If you didn't care about this, and I would tell you that most legislators didn't care a whit about this issue . . . and you were trying to figure out what to do and you've got [the] NFIB breathing down your neck and you've got a coalition knocking at your

door and you've got some new data that says by golly this might cost more if we don't do this for example, I think that helped people to find safe cover in the positive.

National-level respondents were asked whether they thought that representatives from states that had passed family and medical leave policies were more or less likely to support the national bill. This question tested another version of the laboratories hypothesis: that as states pass legislation, their representatives have incentives to see a policy enacted at the national level both to minimize the competitive disadvantage of having a regulatory policy that no one else has and to level the playing field for businesses with multistate operations. The hypothesis appeared to be confirmed in a study by Monroe, Garand, and Teeters of roll-call voting on family and medical leave in the House. The authors found that, even after controlling for factors such as state partisanship and ideology and a legislator's conservatism, legislators from states that pass family and medical leave are slightly, but significantly, more likely to support a national bill.[26]

Most national-level respondents felt that, anecdotally, legislators from states that had passed family and medical leave were more likely to have voted for the national bill. But most felt that this effect was not very significant, and they were not certain if it could be attributed to the fact that the states that had passed family and medical leave policies were more likely to be liberal and thus more likely to send liberal legislators to Washington. They observed that in floor debates, proponents would occasionally bring up the fact that laws were working in their home states, but that the power of this argument was often neutralized by opponents using states rights arguments to claim that what was good for one state is not necessarily good for other states or for the national government.

Another question is whether the fact that a bill was moving forward on the federal level had an effect on bills that were proposed on the state level in the years preceding 1993. Respondents on the state level were divided in their responses, with divisions coming largely along regional and ideological lines. Some respondents, particularly in Massachusetts and Connecticut, argued that the federal bill helped to create momentum, a sense that the policy was inevitable. A number of respondents in North Carolina, where family and medical leave was debated through 1993, argued that the expectation of a federal law decreased momentum on the state level because it allowed legislators to ignore the North Carolina bill, secure in the knowledge that their constituents would be covered by the federal law.

National-level respondents who had experience in the states were more equivocal, arguing that while the momentum factor was important, the sense that the national bill was going forward decreased the sense of urgency in some states. Several also stated that once the federal proposal was limited to employers of fifty or more for twelve weeks, those limits became a standard ceiling above which state advocates did not try to propose bills for fear that they would appear to be unrealistic.

Finally, many advocates argued that the experience of some states in passing successful policies did not necessarily influence other states to do the same. As with the relationship between state and national passage of family and medical leave policies, many opponents of the policy made states' rights arguments, asserting that a policy that works in Minnesota or Connecticut is not necessarily appropriate for other states. This argument was made most often by respondents from southern states, which have a history of concern for states rights and a distrust of the mostly northern states that passed family and medical leave. It was made in all four states studied, however, and it was reported by national level advocates who had also worked on state level bills. One advocate said: "When we would cite, well Oregon has this or California has [family and medical leave] they would say, no tell me about a real state. There are some states that are not as good as others, and the very progressive states don't wash in the South. Forget it."

Respondents emphasized that this type of response reflected not only an interest in states rights, but also the fact that states compete against each other and thus may not always be motivated to adopt even successful regulatory policies. This argument substantiates a hypothesis suggested by the theory of competitive federalism. Theorists of competitive federalism focus on the fact that states compete against each other to attract wealth. This creates incentives for them to engage in a race to the bottom, lowering taxes and benefits in an effort to attract wealth-producing benefits and to repel wealth-draining welfare recipients.[27] The competitive federalism argument about redistributive policies can be applied to regulatory policies like family and medical leave, which, businesses argue, hinder their ability to make profits and lead them to locate in places without those policies.

Thus, while the political processes in some states and on the national level were certainly influenced by the passage of family and medical leave in other states, it is clear that at least with regard to the case studies conducted, the effect was not very significant. This study affirms the idea that the states do act as laboratories for other states and for the federal government. The states are weak laboratories, however. Compared with having strong legislative leaders and advocates who have access to political resources and who are willing to moderate and compromise, having states pass family and medical leave was a relatively minor advantage.

These findings are not entirely surprising. The historic division between North and South and the associated distrust by southerners both of northerners and of the federal government lend credibility to the idea that state legislators, particularly in the South, would not view the passage of family and medical leave by mostly northern and historically progressive states as something to emulate. Nor are southerners likely to believe that because a policy has not led to economic losses in several northern and historically progressive states, it should be adopted on the federal level. Finally, the fact that elites in many states view even successful family and medical leave policies with suspicion underscores pervasive concerns about business friendliness. These factors, combined with the fact that no grassroots movement for family and medical leave emerged to pressure legislators to develop policies, weakened the laboratories effect.

Conclusion

Like the state case studies, this study of federal family and medical leave demonstrates the importance of operating within a supportive political opportunity structure and of having access to substantial political resources. The leaders of the national family and medical leave coalition were advantaged by their long-standing ties to the political establishment and by an interest among Democratic party leaders in using family and medical leave to recapture the family values mantra from Republicans. As in the states, the ability of the national coalition to exploit these resources was contingent on the group's willingness to propose a moderate bill, to frame it as a family values issue, and to compromise. The willingness of coalition members to moderate and compromise is associated with their status as insiders with an agenda that fit with the political opportunity structure and a belief in incremental change.

The federal case study stands out because the advocates were not willing to make *any* compromise to pass family and medical leave. While this approach ultimately relied on a supportive president as well as a supportive Congress to pass a bill, it also reflects the ability of national coalition leaders to determine priorities and stick to them even as they made every effort to pass family and medical leave. Given the political realities of the time, the advocates' goal of establishing the principle of guaranteed job protection for both men and women taking family and medical leaves, while being willing to try later to expand it, appears to be sensible.

Some of the leaders of the coalition that helped to pass the Family and Medical Leave Act are now engaged in an effort to pass a paid family leave act in order to complete the job that they started in 1993. However, the process of organizing a grassroots coalition in support of paid family and medical leave appears to be as difficult as organizing a grassroots coalition to support an unpaid policy. The proponents are mainly elite advocates like those who worked on the Family and Medical Leave Act, and business groups strongly oppose paid family and medical leave, so it may be some time before paid family and medical leave policies become law in a number of states.

6 ||| FAMILY AND MEDICAL LEAVE SINCE 1993

The passage of the Family and Medical Leave Act in February 1993 was the culmination of a long and arduous political process. Family and medical leave was first introduced at the federal level in 1985 and passed Congress twice, only to be successfully vetoed by President George Bush. It took the election of Bill Clinton, who campaigned on the promise to sign the Family and Medical Leave Act, to finally pass the bill. Like most legislation passed in our fragmented American political system, however, the law that was signed by President Clinton accomplished significantly less than its advocates had originally hoped. The Family and Medical Leave Act applies only to people who have worked 1,250 hours during the previous year for businesses with fifty or more employees working within a seventy-five mile radius. Employers are allowed to exempt those in the top 10 percent of their payroll from coverage, and, while they are required to maintain any health benefits during the leave, they are not required to pay leave-taking employees. The law covers approximately 11 percent of employers and 55 percent of employees, many of whom already had privately negotiated access to some of the bill's provisions.

The leaders of the coalition that passed the Family and Medical Leave Act in 1993 had embarked on an explicitly incremental strategy from the beginning of their attempt to pass the law. They did not introduce a paid family and medical leave bill, despite knowing that the absence of wage replacement would be particularly problematic for low- and moderate-income workers. In the interviews that I conducted, the coalition leaders argued that if they had proposed a paid family and medical leave, they would not have been taken seriously, and it would have been more difficult to get anything passed at all. The advocates for the final bill clearly viewed the Family and Medical Leave Act as a first step in a process that would eventually lead to universal coverage and wage replacement.

Other members of the coalition that worked to pass the Family and Medical Leave Act opposed the compromises, particularly the decision not to propose paid leave. They worried that an incremental bill might slow momentum for paid leave, as legislators and advocates alike might view the problem as solved and go on to other things. They also believed that, with a Democratic president and congress, 1993 represented their best chance to pass a paid family and medical leave act. In interviews conducted in 1996, they expressed concern that they had not taken advantage of the political opportunities available to them and argued that they might not have a chance to expand family and medical leave for a long time.

By 2000, the Family and Medical Leave Act had been used by millions of Americans, and it was enormously popular with the public. This suggests that the act has helped to legitimize the idea that work-family issues should be matters of public policy. While many Americans have taken advantage of family and medical leave benefits, however, many others who have needed to use the policy have not done so, either because they cannot afford the loss of pay or, according to one recent study, because they were subtly discouraged by their employers from doing so. While the Family and Medical Leave Act has changed the political climate around work-family issues, it has not yet led to more substantial protections for working families, and it has not resolved conflicts over the role that employers and public policy should play in assisting workers who need to take time off to attend to family matters.

The hopes of the coalition leaders have been realized, however, in the continuation of the movement to expand family and medical leave benefits. By 2000, paid family leave bills had been introduced in eighteen states,[1] most notably through proposals to use unemployment compensation surpluses to fund leaves for new parents. While none of these bills have passed, momentum appears to be growing. The movement to achieve paid family leave is likely to be as long and arduous as the movement for an unpaid family and medical leave, however. While paid family leave enjoys widespread public support, its advocates appear to be facing the same difficulties as the advocates for unpaid family and medical leave in organizing a grassroots movement. This is due in part to the collective action problem discussed in chapter 1: like unpaid family and medical leave, paid family leave is a public good that is needed only on an occasional basis. The collective action problem faced by organizers for paid family leave is exacerbated by the policy's being needed most by low-income workers, who are notoriously difficult to organize. Low-income workers are least likely to have privately negotiated access to paid family leave and are also least able to manage without their wages, even for a short time.

While supporters of paid family leave face an uphill battle in organizing, the business community (and particularly the small business community) is united in its opposition to the policy. The combination of weak support and strong opposition will make it difficult to enact a paid family leave in the near future.

This chapter draws on "new institutionalist" ideas of policy design and especially on the concept of a policy feedback, the idea that once a policy is enacted to respond to an issue, it can shape the politics of that issue and in turn affect the evolution of later policies.[2] As shown by Theda Skocpol and Paul Pierson, policies can affect politics in two ways. First, policies can transform state capacities, creating new administrative arrangements or expanding existing ones so that state intervention in new areas is deemed legitimate. Second, policies can affect the development and capabilities of advocates devoted to continuing and expanding that policy.[3] These advocates may be inside government, as in the case of Social Security, which enjoyed strong support both from administrators who were dedicated to expanding it incrementally and from advocates within the congressional committees that oversaw it.[4] Advocates may also come from outside government, as with the American Association of Retired Persons, whose members consistently advocate to maintain and expand Social Security and Medicare.[5]

Scholars of policy feedbacks emphasize that the way a policy is structured affects whether groups will emerge and, once they do emerge, what kind of influence they will have. Theda Skocpol uses the concept of a policy feedback to define policy success: "According to this political-process approach, a policy is 'successful' if it enhances the kinds of state capacities that can promote its future development, and especially if it stimulates groups and political alliances to defend the policy's continuation and expansion."[6]

Since 1993 state capacities with regard to work-family issues *have* been expanded, and the policy has prompted the development of a movement to enact paid family leave. It should therefore be viewed as a success by Skocpol's criteria. Nevertheless, the act must be considered a *qualified* success since no substantial expansion has yet been enacted, and dilemmas involving public policy and work-family issues have not been resolved. While it is indeed possible that the Family and Medical Leave Act will, like Social Security, evolve into a substantial protection for many people, it is not yet certain that this will be the case.

The Family and Medical Leave Act, 1993–2000

The federal Family and Medical Leave Act (FMLA) requires companies employing fifty or more people to give their employees unpaid leave of up to twelve weeks for the purposes of caring for a newborn or newly adopted child, a sick child, parent, or spouse, or for tending to their own serious illness. By the time the FMLA passed in 1993, twelve states already had family leave laws, some of which exceeded the provisions of the federal law. The states with more expansive provisions have maintained those provisions,[7] and since 1993 a few states have passed bills that go beyond the scope of the federal law. In 1998, for example, Massachusetts passed "the Small Necessities Leave Act," giving employees up to twenty-four hours of leave time to take family members to the doctor or to attend parent-teacher conferences. As of the fall of 2000, however, no state had either substantially increased the number of people covered or passed paid family leave legislation.[8]

The Family and Medical Leave Act mandated creation of a congressional commission to monitor the law. The Commission on Leave's report on the first eighteen months under Family and Medical Leave, issued in May 1996, remains the most comprehensive survey of family and medical leave use and business experience with the policy. The study estimates that before the enactment of the law, 56 percent of workers had sick leave (usually paid) available to them, while 37 percent of workers were eligible for maternity leave (usually unpaid), and 28 percent were eligible for paternity leave (also usually unpaid). The Commission on Leave concluded, "Perhaps one-quarter to one-third of full-time private and public sector employees had the kind of leave options provided by the Family and Medical Leave Act available to them before 1993."[9] Since those with privately arranged family and medical leave benefits are more likely to work in the large firms covered by the Family and Medical Leave Act, and since only 55 percent of the population is covered under the law, no more than half of those covered by the law, or a quarter of the population, obtained benefits that they had not received before.

The survey of employee use of the Family and Medical Leave Act conducted by the Commission on Leave found that some 1.2 percent of all employees took leaves under the Family and Medical Leave Act during the first eighteen months of the law's existence. The survey found that while they are not required to, many employers voluntarily pay their workers who take leaves, particularly women who take maternity leaves. Those employers are in the minority, however, and they disproportionately provide leaves to better-educated people who have higher incomes. The Commission on Leave survey found that only 27.8 percent of people with family incomes of less than $20,000 reported that they were fully paid when they took family and medical leave, compared with 64.1 percent of those with family incomes of $75,000 or more.[10] This means that those who presumably can least afford to go without their salaries during periods when they need to be away from work are also the least likely to have access to paid family leave.

The Commission on Leave survey found that while 1.2 percent of employees took leaves under the Family and Medical Leave Act, nearly three times as many, or 3.4 percent of all employees, expressed a need for leave but did not take one. Of these people, 64 percent cited their inability to live without their wages as the major reason they did not take family and medical leave. Approximately 11 percent of people turned to public assistance to fund their family and medical leaves, although with the time limits on welfare that were enacted in 1996, this "poor women's paid leave" is increasingly no longer available.[11]

Finally, the Commission on Leave found that businesses report relatively little disruption as a result of the Family and Medical Leave

Act. This is especially interesting given the strenuous opposition to the bill by the business community, which argued that requiring businesses to provide family and medical leaves would force them to lay off workers and make them less competitive. Once the law was enacted, however, the vast majority of businesses surveyed reported few if any costs associated with complying with the law, and many reported savings associated with retaining valued workers or increasing employee morale. It should be noted, however, that the survey only examined the experience of businesses that were covered by the Family and Medical Leave Act. Small businesses, which, as represented by groups such as the National Federation of Independent Businesses, claimed that they would undergo the greatest hardships if they were required to provide family and medical leaves, are exempt from the law.

Public and Elite Opinion about Family and Medical Leave

A poll taken by the *New York Times* in 1992, several months before the passage of the Family and Medical Leave Act, found strong but not overwhelming support for the measure: 57 percent of respondents thought that the bill should become law.[12] Those who opposed the legislation frequently agreed with business groups that family and medical leave should be a private matter, negotiated between an employer and an employee. Thus advocates for the policy had to fight two battles: to show that family and medical leave would benefit families and not harm businesses, and also to legitimize the issue as one in which the government should be involved.

In interviews conducted in the years following the passage of the Family and Medical Leave Act, advocates argued that one of the most important accomplishments of the legislation was to legitimize work-family issues as belonging in the public domain. They are supported in this claim by a public opinion survey conducted for the National Partnership for Women and Families (formerly the Women's Legal Defense Fund, which spearheaded the drive for the Family and Medical Leave Act) by the polling firm of Lake, Sosin, Snell, and Associates. The survey, summarized in a 1998 report by the National Partnership entitled "Family Matters," shows that 88 percent of respondents who were familiar with the Family and Medical Leave Act now have a favorable view of it. This is a significant increase from the support for family and medical leave found by the *New York Times* in 1992, and it suggests that one effect of the FMLA has been to legitimize the issue in the public's mind. In addition, the Family and Medical Leave Act is widely touted by Democratic elites as evidence of their commitment to "family values," while former Republican opponents no longer publicly advocate overturning the law. The conclusion is inescapable that family and medical leave is now widely accepted and is unlikely to be repealed soon.

The "Family Matters" survey also found widespread support for requiring employers to provide paid family leave: 82 percent of women and 75 percent of men agreed that people should be entitled to the benefit. Sixty-three percent of women and 51 percent of men said they would be more likely to support a representative who supports paid family leave.[13] The survey did not assess the strength of support for or commitment to the issue of paid family leave, for example asking whether the issue is a priority for potential voters or whether a legislator's lack of support for the policy would necessarily mean the loss of a vote. It does not reveal information about respondents' willingness not only to support paid family leave but also to organize in the effort to pass it. This book suggests that the collective action problem combined with the fact that many people already have access to paid family leave will make it hard to organize a movement for it.[14] The movement for paid family leave thus far appears to be largely elite driven, just like the movement for unpaid family and medical leave.

The finding that family and medical leave is widely supported by the public should be qualified in two other ways. While the public overwhelmingly supports family and medical leave on a *theoretical* level, recent research suggests that less tangible factors prevent individuals from taking needed family and medical leaves, even when they can afford to do so. A study of the use of parental leave policies in a large company in Boston, Massachusetts, conducted by sociologist Mindy Fried, found that many managers discourage their employees from taking family and medical leaves by doing such things as giving workers who have taken leaves lower performance ratings. Fried argues that policies like family and medical leave conflict with the corporate "overtime culture," which assumes that employees who work the longest hours are the most dedicated to their jobs.[15] Fried's work is supported by that of Juliet Schor, whose now-classic *The Overworked*

American documents how the average American in 1987 worked 163 hours a year—approximately one month at the full-time rate of 40 hours a week—more than the average worker did in 1969.[16] Anecdotal evidence by the journalist Sue Shellenbarger, the author of the *Wall Street Journal*'s "Work and Family" column,[17] also supports Fried's contention that in a tenuous economy, workers are pressured to put in extra hours at the office in order to fuel their managers' perceptions that they are committed to their job.[18] Pressured workers are less likely to take the family leaves to which they are entitled.

Second, there is some evidence that workers who take time off to attend to family matters, especially parents of young children, may be subject to resentment from colleagues who do not have children. A survey by the Heldrich Center for Workforce Development and the Center for Survey Research found that 35 percent of respondents who were unmarried or childless thought it was "'unfair' to offer 'family-friendly' benefits without offering other benefits to employees without dependents."[19] These arguments are also reflected in a new book by journalist Elinor Burkett, who charges that childless workers are frequently asked to work extra hours so that workers with children can take extra time off. She also argues that family-friendly benefits such as subsidized child care and family leave violate equal-pay-for-equal-work provisions.[20] While it is unclear how strongly these views are supported by workers who are childless (who *do* benefit from coverage by the Family and Medical Leave Act, which as noted earlier also allows people to take time off to attend to nonparental needs), it is certainly worth considering that workers who take family and medical leave may incur hostility from coworkers in addition to discouragement from employers.

Starting with the States: The Effort to Pass a Paid Family Leave

In contrast to the movement for an unpaid family and medical leave, which was started largely at the national level and was picked up by advocates on the state level, the movement for paid family leave is starting entirely in the states. According to Donna Lenhoff, the general counsel and director of Work-Family Programs at the National Partnership for Women and Families (formerly the Women's Legal Defense Fund), this is due to the advocates' belief that a federal bill would be "premature," and that the best approach is to let the states pass policies that could potentially be emulated elsewhere after they have proved themselves successful.[21]

The effort to establish paid family leave began in New Jersey in 1997. New Jersey is one of five states (the others are California, Hawaii, New York, and Rhode Island) that have a temporary disability insurance (TDI) law providing partial income replacement for workers who become disabled for nonjob-related reasons. TDIs are funded by taxes on employers, employees, or both (depending on the states). State TDI laws are one of the major reasons that people have access to wage replacement for reasons of maternity and health disability, in part because many companies that do business in these five states provide uniform benefits to all of their employees, regardless of where they live. Temporary disability laws do not cover leave to care for newborn or sick children or parents, however.

New Jersey's TDI system has been running a surplus for a number of years, and in 1996 Governor Christine Todd Whitman diverted $250 million from it to general revenues. In response, a coalition led by the state AFL-CIO got a bill introduced in the legislature to require that when returned, the $250 million should be used to extend TDI to cover workers taking up to twelve weeks of family leave.[22] The bill was strongly opposed by business groups, including the New Jersey Business and Industry Association, which argued that employer TDI rates would be raised as a result. The bill did not progress after Whitman was reelected, but, as the first effort to pass a paid family leave since 1993, it attracted attention from national advocates interested in expanding the Family and Medical Leave Act. In an interview, Donna Lenhoff of the National Partnership for Women and Families said that the New Jersey effort "made us sit up and say now it's time" to try to pass paid family leaves.[23]

Two states that promptly followed New Jersey were Massachusetts and Vermont. Advocates in these states chose a different mechanism for funding paid family leaves, however. Neither state has a TDI system, but both states are in the pleasant situation of having a substantial surplus in their unemployment compensation fund. Massachusetts' surplus stood at approximately $1.8 billion in June 1999; in December of that year, the legislature approved a cut in the taxes that employers pay into the fund. Advocates therefore proposed amending the state's unemployment compensation laws to allow people to receive unemployment compensation while they take family leaves. In addition to their unemployment compensation bill, the advocates in Massachusetts introduced a TDI bill.

The advocates in Massachusetts and Vermont were soon advised that the U.S. Department of Labor would argue that any attempt to use unemployment surpluses to fund paid family leaves would violate the provision that recipients of unemployment funds must be constantly available for new work.[24] They contacted Senators Edward Kennedy of Massachusetts, Christopher Dodd of Connecticut (long-time supporters of family and medical leave), and Patrick Leahy of Vermont to lobby President Clinton to direct the Department of Labor to waive the rule. In interviews, advocates remembered that Kennedy was particularly helpful, especially once he was encouraged by leaders of the Massachusetts AFL-CIO, in convincing Clinton to support paid family leave. In May 1999, Clinton issued a directive that the Department of Labor allow states to use unemployment surpluses to provide wage replacement for parents taking family leaves to care for newborn or newly adopted children. While the directive was clearly a victory for proponents of paid family leave, the victory was tempered somewhat by its exclusion of those who wish to take leaves for other reasons covered by the Family and Medical Leave Act, such as caring for sick or elderly relatives.

In the year since the introduction of paid family leave bills in Massachusetts and Vermont, bills have been introduced in sixteen other states. Most of these bills would allow parents of newborn and newly adopted children to draw unemployment compensation as the Clinton directive suggests. By the fall of 2000, however, none of these bills had been enacted. As with the unpaid Family and Medical Leave Act, the business community mobilized to fight paid family leave, opposing the state bills and organizing a letter-writing campaign to the Department of Labor in an attempt to limit the effects of the Clinton directive. There is no indication that they will cease in their efforts, and in addition there is always the possibility that a Republican congress or president might overturn the Clinton directive and forbid states to change unemployment compensation rules to fund family leaves. In interviews, many of the advocates for paid family leave on both the state and national levels indicated that they viewed their movement as a multiyear effort.

The fact that a movement for paid family leave has started only six years after the passage of the Family and Medical Leave Act indicates that the advocates have not allowed the existence of unpaid leave to lull them into complacency, as the dissenters feared it would. An examination of the burgeoning movements for paid family leave in Massachusetts and Washington provides preliminary insights into efforts to expand incremental policies and into the dilemmas facing advocates. In both of these states, advocates are making decisions to moderate, believing that such a strategy will most likely lead to success. The research is based on interviews with advocates and on participant observation of the paid family leave coalition meetings in Massachusetts.

The coalition to pass a paid family leave act in Massachusetts is led by two groups. The first is the Women's Statewide Legislative Network, a feminist advocacy group. The second is the Massachusetts AFL-CIO. These two groups are supported by the work of Monica Halas, the senior attorney at Greater Boston Legal Services, who works on unemployment law. The coalition for paid family leave has been meeting monthly since April 1998. Attendees at coalition meetings include representatives from the above groups and from the Massachusetts Catholic Conference, local labor unions, and women's organizations and staff members of the legislators supporting the bills.

The Massachusetts effort is both notable and representative of other states in that it is strongly supported by organized labor. In an interview Kathleen Casavant, secretary-treasurer of the Massachusetts AFL-CIO, said that paid family leave is "one of our top four issues."[25] Casavant claimed credit on behalf of her organization for Clinton's directive to the Department of Labor, remembering that the president of the Massachusetts AFL-CIO had contacted Senator Edward Kennedy, who had then telephoned the president (other advocates confirmed her recollection). She said that the Massachusetts AFL-CIO is hoping to use its advocacy for paid family leave as a way to increase its membership, observing that young people whom the AFL-CIO wants to recruit frequently change jobs, and that while some jobs come with paid leave, many do not. She argued, "If it were legislated, then everyone would get the same benefit."

The early interest by organized labor in paid family leave is especially notable in contrast with the time it took for organized labor to become involved in the effort to pass the unpaid Family and Medical Leave Act. While labor ultimately became an important part of the coalition to pass the FMLA, it did not get involved until late in the political process, once its leaders realized that the issue would be an important Democratic weapon. In part this was because labor had less of a direct stake in unpaid family and medical leave, which was already provided for in many union contracts.

As Casavant's comments indicate, the situation is different for paid family leave. Organized labor's interest in paid family leave is particularly strong because labor sees the issue as a potential tool for attracting new members at a time when it is actively seeking to expand. Two recent surveys sponsored by the national AFL-CIO support the idea that paid family leave could be an effective tool. A survey of young workers (ages eighteen to thirty-four) released in September 1999 found that "lacking time for family responsibilities" was one of their top three concerns, and a survey of working women released in March 2000 found that "many women [feel] stretched and overstretched"; 83 percent of those surveyed supported expanding the Family and Medical Leave Act to provide paid family leave.[26]

The effort to pass a paid family leave in Massachusetts is also interesting because the draft legislation included proposals for both a TDI bill ("The Family and Employment Security Act," or FESA) and a bill to provide unemployment compensation to those taking family leaves. FESA would have created a temporary disability insurance fund, which would have provided wage replacement to those taking either disability or family leave. (It would have been a broader bill than the TDIs in other states, which cover only disability leaves.) The unemployment insurance bill would have simply extended unemployment benefits to any person taking family leave. These bills were introduced in part because President Clinton's directive to the Department of Labor specified that unemployment funds be used only to cover parents taking leave to care for newborn or newly adopted children. The coalition in Massachusetts wanted to pass a broader bill covering families, and it hoped to achieve a compromise covering new parents under unemployment compensation funds and everyone else under a temporary disability model. By the spring of 2000, however, it became clear that both bills could not be achieved in the same legislative session, so the advocates for paid family leave in Massachusetts faced another moderation dilemma. If they agreed to focus on what they term Baby UI (the unemployment compensation bill, which provided for leaves only for new parents), they risked fragmenting their coalition. If they tried to push both bills simultaneously in an effort to achieve comprehensive paid family leave benefits in Massachusetts, they risked losing both bills.

In the spring of 2000, the Massachusetts advocates resolved their moderation dilemma in favor of pragmatism. Discussion at the March 2000 coalition meeting focused on efforts to stimulate interest in the Baby UI bill, and the minutes of that coalition meeting sent out to activists asked: "What can we realistically get passed in this legislative session? Baby UI!" The minutes went on: "While it would only help new parents for now . . . it would be a major victory in legitimizing the need for job-protected, paid family leave for all working people. Passing Baby UI this year will lay the foundation for getting the bigger program passed in the next legislative session."[27]

More than a decade after the coalition for paid family leave in Massachusetts rejected moderation in an effort to pass the first paid family leave bill in the country, its heirs embraced the principle of incremental reform. In the summer of 2000, their willingness to moderate nearly paid off. Despite opposition from the business community and from the conservative speaker of the Massachusetts House of Representatives, Baby UI passed both houses as an amendment to the state budget. It was vetoed, however, by Governor Paul Cellucci, who proposed offering tax credits to businesses offering paid family leave instead.

The coalition to pass paid family leave in Massachusetts plans to reintroduce its bill in the 2001 legislative session. It is strongly supported by the feminist community and by organized labor, although no strong grassroots movement has yet been organized to support the policy. It will be most interesting to see whether the moderates continue to dominate the coalition, and with what result.

In contrast to the advocates in Massachusetts, advocates for paid family leave in the state of Washington did not have to struggle to determine whether their bill would conform to President Clinton's directive or if they would try to achieve more widespread benefits. A bill introduced in 1999 and reintroduced in 2000 provides workers with five weeks of unemployment insurance to care for a newborn or newly adopted child. In an interview, sponsor Senator Lisa Brown argued that there had not been much debate over the question of what to introduce.

She said, "I think that's partly the old 'camel's nose under the tent' argument. You start narrow, see what happens."[28] John Burbank, the executive director of the Economic Policy Institute, a leading member of the coalition supporting paid family leave, argued that "caring for a newborn is completely understandable" to the public.[29] Brown noted that a commission is currently being formed to develop public policies in response to new research showing that crucial brain development happens in early childhood, and she stated that she is hoping that this commission will support her bill.

The sponsors of paid family leave in Washington are motivated by their commitment to passing legislation that "targets within universalism" by providing economic support to both poor and middle-class families. Brown said her interest in paid family leave stems directly from her interest in welfare reform; in 1998 she attempted to extend the work exemption for new mothers from three months to a year, but was rebuffed by legislators who told her stories of middle-class women having to go back to work earlier than they wanted, and who argued that welfare recipients should not have a luxury that is denied to middle-class women. Brown argued that if everyone could have paid family leave, then work exemptions for welfare recipients would not be an issue.[30]

The issue of welfare reform reflects a general dilemma faced by organizers about responding to the fact that paid family leaves would disproportionately help low-income families. A recent study by Jody Heymann and Alison Earle of the Harvard School of Public Health found that only 21.4 percent of employed mothers who had been on AFDC for two years or more had jobs with sick leave, compared with 51.3 percent of employed mothers who had never been on AFDC. However, former welfare recipients were found to be significantly more likely to have a child with asthma or another chronic condition for which they would, presumably, need to take time off from work to care.[31] But in interviews, organizers in both Washington and Massachusetts argued that they did not want to frame paid family leave as a way to help welfare reform succeed, for fear of having paid family leave stigmatized as "just another welfare issue." They agreed with Brown that it is important to emphasize that paid family leave would help people of all classes, in an attempt to build as broad a coalition as possible.

Part of the advocates' reasoning may be associated with the fact that there are considerable obstacles to organizing a movement for paid family leave largely among low-income people. Numerous studies have examined the differences in the rates of political participation among low-income and high-income people. They conclude that poor people participate less because they have fewer resources to do so and, furthermore, feel their participation counts for less.[32] This difficulty was reflected in a conversation with one advocate in Massachusetts, who stated that the former welfare recipients she works with are so glad to have jobs that they do not even consider the idea that they should be asking for benefits and rights.

Without strong support from the low-income people who stand to benefit the most, the advocates for paid family leave lack an important source of organizing strength. As noted earlier, high-income people are far more likely than low-income people to have privately negotiated access to paid family leave; they are thus likely to be less motivated to get something that will not benefit them personally. Without a strong grassroots constituency, elite advocates may be more likely to compromise away important benefits (this is the converse of the moderation dilemma). For example, the sponsors of paid family leave in Washington said that they are placing their effort within the context of a broader effort to reform unemployment compensation laws. In an interview, John Burbank of the Economic Policy Institute noted that he hoped that paid family leave would be part of a package including such issues as training subsidies for unemployed lumber workers, which he stated is his "highest priority."[33] He admitted, however, that within that context, paid family leave might get bargained away.

The Washington effort to pass paid family leave contrasts with that in Massachusetts in ways that mirror the strategic dilemmas faced by advocates for unpaid family and medical leave. The Massachusetts coalition leaders appear to have a broader base of support, but their coalition demanded the introduction of two bills rather than one, which threatened to complicate the process and make it harder to pass anything. Their decision in the spring of 2000 to take the pragmatic approach and focus on one bill represents a step away from the decisions of their predecessors and may ultimately help them to get something passed.

In Washington, a smaller group of policy activists and legislators introduced paid parental leave as part of a larger effort to overhaul the unemployment compensation system. Not needing to please a broad constituency, the group was able to craft a narrow bill. While the bill had only advanced to the hearing stage by the fall of 2000, it appears to have considerable potential. However, the fact that this effort is part of a package means that paid family leave may be bargained away.

Prospects for Paid Family Leave

Predicting whether a policy will pass is a tricky business. As any student of public policy knows, many factors can influence the path of legislation, and with few exceptions most bills take a long time to pass. The few that pass quickly often do so in response to what John Kingdon has labeled a "focusing event: . . . a crisis or disaster that comes along to call attention to a problem, a powerful symbol that catches on, or the personal experience of a policy maker."[34] It is certainly possible that paid family leave might be the subject of a focusing event: a child, left alone because of the lack of paid family leave, might suffer injury or death, or a legislator with a family member needing paid leave might embark on a personal crusade. As has been shown in earlier chapters, family and medical leave certainly has the capacity to become a family values issue, and paid family leave might be the right cause at the right time for someone seeking to adopt that mantra.

But the experience of the unpaid Family and Medical Leave Act serves as a reminder that it is not inevitable that the family values frame will succeed in helping to enact controversial legislation like paid family leave. Business groups are opposing paid family leave on both the federal and the state levels, arguing that using unemployment insurance as a way to fund paid family leaves jeopardizes the unemployment insurance funds and will ultimately harm workers.[35]

The arguments made by business groups that paid family leave policies will be too costly echo arguments made in opposition to unpaid family and medical leave policies as well as to numerous social protections throughout the twentieth century, ranging from minimum wage and maximum working hours legislation to health and safety requirements. In general, business groups have lost these arguments when legislators and the public have come to believe that the costs they claimed were exaggerated, or that the benefits of such legislation outweighed any costs. The Congressional Commission on Leave survey suggests that businesses (at least large businesses) did exaggerate the costs of mandating unpaid family and medical leave, and the public opinion surveys cited above suggest that the public, at least, clearly believes that providing paid family leave should be a social responsibility.

As noted earlier, however, it is unclear whether the public is willing to fight for this principle. One final reason why it may be difficult to mobilize people on behalf of paid family leave is that, while public opinion may be moving in the direction of endorsing a "politics of family care,"[36] there is not yet the kind of consensus that supports the widespread family policies enjoyed in much of the industrialized world and particularly in western Europe. One reason for this may be continued disagreement over the status of mothers in the workplace. Recent public opinion polls show that despite the fact that the percentage of women in the workforce is at historic highs, nearly half of respondents think that women with children under school age should stay at home, and more than 40 percent think that more mothers working outside the home is a "bad thing for our society."[37] It follows that even if some of these people are included in the 80 percent of the public that supports paid family leave, they are probably doing so with some ambivalence, since mothers of young children are so closely identified with family and medical leave.

As was the case with unpaid family and medical leave, the New Right does not appear to be making its opposition to paid family leave a major priority; at present business groups seem to be the major opponents of paid family leave. Some opponents, however, are emphasizing that the policy would further endorse the principle of working mothers. For example, an op-ed in the *New York Times* in the summer of 1999 by the conservative social critic Danielle Crittenden charged that paid family leave would "set a new norm" that all women would go back to work after their leaves had expired.[38]

Probably a greater obstacle to developing paid family leave is that, as Mona Harrington argues, there has never been a "clear challenge" to the "long-prevailing assumption that, beyond poverty, care was a strictly family matter, a private responsibility."[39] Instead, issues such as family leave have long been relegated to the status of "women's issues" and largely ignored. While Harrington shows that this may be changing due to politicians' awareness of the gender gap in voting, the acknowledgment of a comprehensive public role in providing family support is probably a long way off. This will inevitably affect any movement for paid family leave, because as long as the public and legislators do not wholeheartedly endorse the idea that support for working families should be a public responsibility,[40] business arguments that the policies are too costly or too risky will be more likely to fall on receptive ears.

Conclusion

Given the criteria laid out by Skocpol, the Family and Medical Leave Act should be considered a qualified success. Judging from public opinion surveys and legislative behavior, the policy is firmly entrenched in the American political system, so that state involvement in work-family issues is now largely legitimized. It is thus unlikely that the legislation will be repealed. But it must also be remembered that the Family and Medical Leave Act was limited in scope, leaving 45 percent of the population without coverage and not providing wage replacement. Critics might argue that state capacities should not be considered to have been "expanded" through the enactment of such a minor and symbolic piece of legislation.

I argue, however, that the Family and Medical Leave Act should be considered a success for two reasons. The first reason is that the enactment of family and medical leave has been an important part of a movement toward the recognition that work-family issues are public problems worthy of public solutions and toward the development of a national sense that there is a social responsibility to help families balance their work and family lives. While this national sense has clearly not been fully developed in the seven years since the enactment of the Family and Medical Leave Act, overwhelming public support of the act suggests that progress has been made. Nor would it have been realistic to expect such a massive cultural change in a mere seven years. Major changes in public ideas about such major institutions as work and the family (to say nothing of gender roles) take decades, if not generations, to make their way into legislation. What is important is that the Family and Medical Leave Act is part of this process.

The second major reason that family and medical leave should be considered a success is that it has energized a movement for its own expansion. Admittedly, this movement is still in the infant stage, but again, this is not entirely unexpected, given normal patterns of social change. As I argued earlier, it is of the utmost importance that the advocates for family and medical leave, in the words of one observer, saw the legislation as "the twenty-yard line instead of as the end goal."[41] The fact that advocates continue to view the legislation as an incremental reform needing improvement and the fact that they are willing to work slowly and deliberately toward achieving that goal suggest that even if the current effort to enact paid family leave does not succeed, the issue will continue to come up until one such effort does.

7 ‖ CONCLUSION

This project has examined why family and medical leave passed in some states but not others, and why certain states and the federal government passed the policies they did. It identified four types of variables that facilitate policy innovation: a favorable political context, a favorable political opportunity structure, substantial resources available to supporters, and a willingness by supporters to make use of resources by framing their proposals in a culturally appropriate way and fitting their strategies to the political context. It drew together literature on resource mobilization and group strategy to develop a new model of policy innovation.

The project identified a "moderation dilemma" for groups determining what to propose, how to frame and lobby their bills, and when to compromise. Moderation during the agenda-setting stage was crucial for achieving credibility for family and medical leave, a contested policy innovation that enjoyed public support, but for which there was no public outcry. Moderation helped to attract powerful sponsors, to win the support of legislative and executive leaders, and to blunt the power of the opposition. For some of the groups most likely to support family and medical leave, however, moderation and compromise involved sacrificing the very goals around which they were organized and required a new acceptance of the principle of incremental change.

A Model of Policy Innovation

As noted above, this study identified four types of variables that facilitate the passage of policy innovations like family and medical leave.
First, I confirm the well-known idea that innovations are more likely
to pass in places where the political and cultural context is favorable.
The quantitative study conducted by Garand and Monroe and described
in chapter 1 suggests that family and medical leave policies are more
likely to pass in liberal states where the public is more supportive of
feminism. The political climate in Massachusetts and Connecticut was
advantageous for family and medical leave. Conversely, the conservative political climate in Tennessee and North Carolina served as a
hurdle.

Second, like other scholars of social change, I find that the political
opportunity structure may hinder or facilitate possibilities for policy
innovation. In the case of family and medical leave, facilitating structures included a unified leadership, the presence of political goals that
could be linked with the achievement of the bill, and the lack of dis-
tracting issues. In Connecticut, the movement for family and medical
leave was led by the president of the state senate, who was convinced
that he could use the issue to launch a run for higher office. On the national level, the belief by leading Democrats that the issue could help
defeat President George Bush provided incentives that helped to advance the bill. In contrast, the political climate in North Carolina was
chaotic, and in Massachusetts the legislative leadership was fragmented and a proposal for universal health insurance made it more difficult to focus on the issue of family and medical leave.

Third, this study shows that the resources available to individual
coalitions matter: advocates who are credible and who have access to
decision makers are more likely to succeed. In Connecticut, the president of the senate used his power to persuade others to support the bill
and created a committee specifically to process work-family bills. In
Tennessee, the maternity leave coalition was led by a group with strong
ties to legislative leaders and experience passing moderate, profamily
legislation. On the federal level, family and medical leave benefited
from the support of groups with well-established ties to Congress and
reputations for being reasonable.

All of the above variables are best characterized as resource variables, providing broad political opportunities and constraints. Nevertheless, while resources were necessary to pass family and medical leave policies, they were not sufficient: strategy mattered as well. Advocates who proposed less-wide-ranging bills and who framed their proposals as "family" rather than as "women's" or "labor" bills were far more likely to see their bills move past the agenda-setting stage. The supporters of family and medical leave in successful states and on the national level did not propose the paid family leave policies they wanted, and they exempted the smallest businesses from the beginning of the policy process. The coalition in Tennessee proposed a maternity leave only and defined it as a "bonding bill," and advocates in Connecticut situated family and medical leave within a group of family-oriented proposals. These decisions were crucial to their ability to gain early credibility for their bills, which in turn was crucial to their ability to move forward.

After family and medical leave bills had moved forward in the policy process, advocates found it necessary to compromise again in order to pass legislation. During later stages of negotiation, the advocates in Connecticut exempted businesses with fewer than seventy-five employees from family and medical leave coverage, while the national coalition limited its proposal to twelve weeks of coverage and agreed to exempt the top 10 percent of employees in any firm. These compromises were seen as essential to securing the final votes needed.

Despite the importance accorded to moderation and compromise by this project, the fact remains that some policy advocates will *not* make the kinds of compromises that are necessary to achieve credibility, to bargain successfully, and ultimately to pass legislation. Groups of insiders (generally elite, professional groups with foundation or government funding) are more likely than groups of outsiders (generally mass-based, amateur groups with few institutional ties) to make use of available resources, to adopt strategies of moderation and compromise, and to frame family and medical leave in culturally appropriate ways. Groups of insiders are subject to a different set of incentives than groups of outsiders: they are more likely to need to claim credit even for an incremental bill, and they are more likely to share the values of those in power, which often include moderation and compromise. In contrast, groups of outsiders are less likely to view an incremental bill as a win and are more likely to be skeptical of moderation.

The distinction between insider and outsider approaches can be seen in the case studies of the family and medical leave policy process. The coalition leaders for the policy were in power in Connecticut, while the Tennessee and national coalitions included people with long-standing relationships with those in power. The advocates were professional elites who saw themselves as working to establish the principle of government support for working families, which they saw as the first step in a long process. In contrast, the leader of the movement for family and medical leave in North Carolina was seen as unusually weak, and the Massachusetts family and medical leave coalition was dominated by groups with weaker ties to the establishment and with an agenda that deemphasized the importance of incremental change. Some advocates in Massachusetts (and some dissenters elsewhere) felt that it was just as important to *introduce* paid family and medical leave legislation as it was to *pass* unpaid family and medical leave bills.

Generalizability of Cases

Are the experiences documented in the five case studies unique, or can they be generalized to other states considering family and medical leave? Can the model of policy innovation developed above be applied to other issues? How pervasive is the moderation dilemma, both in other areas of social policy and in American politics generally? The evidence from this study suggests that the model is generalizable to both other states and other issues.

The evidence on generalizability to other states comes from interviews conducted for the five case studies used in this project. A number of respondents had experience with family and medical leave in states other than the one about which they were being interviewed. Once they indicated this, they were asked to offer observations about the other state as well. While the data from these interviews show some variation between states that were and were not included in the case studies (as it does between the case studies themselves), many findings persist. The first is the importance of framing family and medical leave as a family values issue rather than as a woman's or a feminist issue. This finding was emphasized by respondents familiar with three other successful states (California, New Jersey, and Wisconsin). One advocate who had had experience in both Connecticut and California remembered that the advocates in California also situated their movement within an agenda for children and families to avoid having family and medical leave marginalized as a women's issue even though it was, from her perspective, part of a "comprehensive women's economic agenda."

Respondents also emphasized the importance of finding credible sponsors who could transcend stereotypes of the groups often associated with lobbying for women's and labor issues. One of the best examples of this can be seen in New Jersey, where the movement for family and medical leave was led by the Junior League. As a quintessential insider group with a history of working on children's rather than feminist issues, the Junior League was able to reach people whom feminist and labor advocates could not, and succeeded in framing the bill as a family values bill. One advocate who worked on family and medical leave in Connecticut and then helped to organize a coalition to support the policy in New Jersey remembered that on Thanksgiving of the year family and medical leave came up for a vote in the New Jersey legislature, members of the Junior League delivered carrot cakes to every legislator at his or her home, with a note attached that read, "In this special time for family, please remember that we all need time for family." With the support of moderate Republican governor Thomas Kean, the bill passed overwhelmingly.

Finally, people familiar with the process in other states indicated that proposing moderate bills and being willing to compromise was an essential part of a successful strategy there also. Paid family and medical leave was not introduced in any of the successful states mentioned, despite statements by advocates that they would have liked to propose it and still hoped to do so. Bills that passed in these states nearly always ended up exempting small businesses and limiting the number of weeks of coverage. Like the compromises made in Connecticut and Tennessee, these compromises were made to broaden coalitions and to attract the support of moderate legislators. In Wisconsin, for example, one advocate remembered that the bill there was compromised from twenty-six weeks of coverage down to six to attract the support of "moderate Republican women" and to "keep it a bipartisan bill."

Respondents discussing family and medical leave made frequent references to other social policy issues. They most frequently likened family and medical leave to other mandates on business such as health

insurance and environmental regulations, but they also mentioned issues like abortion and civil rights. They mentioned similar dilemmas
involved in framing bills, choosing sponsors, and determining when to
compromise, and they emphasized that the lessons of moderating and
framing to fit the cultural context can be applied to a variety of issues.

Respondents overwhelmingly argued that advocates for business
mandates need to frame their proposals in emotionally compelling
ways. They affirmed that it is very difficult to enact such mandates,
both because of the power of business lobbies devoted to opposing
them and because of generalized support for capitalism, distaste for
government intervention, and the fear that regulation would have a
negative impact on the economy. And they argued that the example of
family and medical leave coalitions that successfully transformed the
policy from a business mandate with an unfortunate association with
feminism to an issue of family values[1] offers insight into how such
mandates can be won, against what most scholars recognize as tremendous odds.[2]

One example cited by many respondents was regulations on HMOs,
such as recently enacted laws to require HMOs to cover mammograms
or to allow women who have just given birth to remain in the hospital
for specified amounts of time. Respondents noted that proponents of
these laws had been able to frame them successfully as motherhood
and apple pie issues instead of as regulations on business. As with family and medical leave, proponents of state legislation to require HMOs
to allow women to remain in the hospital for forty-eight hours after
birth told personal stories (in North Carolina, the sponsor of the bill
gave the example of her daughter, who had been discharged from a hospital soon after a complicated birth) and argued that the issue was one
of conscience and health rather than business regulation.

Other examples included environmental regulation and health and
safety regulations. As with family and medical leave, respondents cited
the importance of credible sponsors who could legitimate a story and
of Kingdonian focusing events that would help to make a story more
credible.[3] Also in North Carolina, respondents told me of a factory fire
that killed twenty-five people and sparked the passage of a number of
worker safety regulations that, they said, would ordinarily have been
rejected as too onerous on business.

The respondents indicated, however, that it is difficult to frame some issues in ways that will resonate in the political culture. The most prominent example, which was mentioned by a number of respondents, was that of welfare reform. Respondents frequently compared welfare reform with family and medical leave, noting that while advocates for expanded welfare benefits often try to frame their issue as one of children's rights or health care,[4] they have great difficulty changing the long-dominant image of welfare as one of government support for the undeserving.[5] These comments are reflected in the debate over what ultimately became the Personal Responsibility and Work Opportunity Reconciliation Act of 1996, which was raging during the time that I conducted the interviews for this book.

Additionally, some advocates do not have enough credibility for decision makers to believe that they truly stand for mainstream, culturally acceptable values, regardless of how strenuously they work to frame the issues they are working on in those terms. A recent survey of state legislative leaders, many of whom are moderates and conservatives, found widespread distrust of advocates for children's and family issues. Advocates are seen as oblivious of the realities of politics and blindly liberal.[6]

Finally, advocates for a variety of issues may not want to engage in the compromise that may be required for framing policies in ways that are likely to help them to pass. This project affirms the idea that strategy is a "nested game" situated within the incentives that advocates have for their activism and the needs of the group to survive. Advocates may prefer to lose in committee or on the legislative floor rather than lose their belief that they are doing the right thing.[7] This may be especially true of issues involving rights, such as abortion. A number of respondents indicated that it is virtually impossible for advocates to compromise on abortion and still maintain the integrity of their position.

Generalizability of the Moderation Dilemma

The question of when to compromise in order to achieve political goals is perennial in democratic systems where winning a majority often requires building a coalition. While the moderation dilemma is felt by advocates in any democratic system, it may be especially acute in systems where power is dispersed among opposing parties. In the

United States the moderation dilemma is exacerbated by the fragmentation of political power among the three branches of national government and among federal, state, and local governments. The need to compromise is intensified during periods of divided government, when it is especially difficult to fashion policies acceptable to both the president and majorities in an opposing Congress.[8] But as is pointed out by Fiorina and by Laver and Shepsle, the fragmentation of political power is not unique to the United States: coalition governments in European democracies (with the exception of Britain) usually require the sharing of political power by opposing political parties.[9]

The Moderation Dilemma Reconsidered

As noted above, those who dissented from the compromises made by coalition leaders in Connecticut, Tennessee, and on the national level made powerful arguments to explain their opposition to the compromises made. They argued that because the family and medical leave bills passed cover less than half the population and are unpaid, they represent symbolic rather than substantial reform. Further, dissenters argued that incremental bills, rather than being steps toward a larger goal, could decrease momentum and detract attention from more widespread policies. In cases where compromise involved accepting a stereotype of beneficiaries (as with maternity leave in Tennessee), dissenters argued that the costs associated with perpetuating such stereotypes outweighed the immediate benefits available to those with access to the law.

My review of the history of family and medical leave since 1993 in chapter 6 shows, however, that contrary to the dissenters' fears, the leaders of the coalition that enacted the Family and Medical Leave Act have continued in their fight to extend the bill. However, by 2000, no significant expansion of family and medical leave had been achieved on either the state or the national level. While I argue that public support for the idea of government support for work-family balance makes it likely that further policies will be enacted, it is possible that this will not happen, and that the Family and Medical Leave Act will have to be evaluated on its own merits alone, rather than as the first bill enacted as part of a process leading up to the establishment of widespread supports for working families.

Even if this is the case, family and medical leave should still be considered an important policy achievement. Family and medical leave policies have made a difference in the lives of many people, both practically and symbolically. While incremental bills certainly come with the risk that they will preclude the enactment of more substantial bills, it is not at all clear that the beneficiaries of these bills (in the case of family and medical leave, working families) are better off with nothing at all.

There is no doubt that family and medical leave benefits many people: some one-and-a-half to three million people took advantage of the policy in the first eighteen months of coverage.[10] Thus, while certainly the bill could cover far more people than it does, and it could certainly cover them better, its accomplishment in covering the people it does should not be understated.[11] Second, and as pointed out by numerous coalition leaders, family and medical leave has a symbolic value beyond the people and issues it covers. By enacting family and medical leave legislation, both federal and state governments aligned themselves in support of policies to help members of working families balance their lives. This message has not been lost on the public, or on businesses not covered by the act. It is reflected in the proliferation of voluntary policies, many of which exceed the requirements of the act itself,[12] that businesses have adopted in efforts to show that they are family friendly. While employees may be discouraged from making use of these policies, their existence is an important first step.

Even if passing an unpaid family and medical leave has slowed momentum for a more widespread policy, it is far from clear that waiting would have produced the desired result. Politics is an unpredictable business, and advocates can never know if the next political cycle will bring new opportunities or new constraints. While acknowledging that the decision to accept Medicaid and Medicare stalled momentum for national health insurance, John Gilmour cites the example of Nixon's 1974 health care proposals, which were dismissed by Democrats confident that they would be able to do better in the next Congress. While the Democrats increased their congressional majority in 1975, new economic crises made "the adoption of a major new program . . . unfeasible."[13]

Similarly, the advocates for family and medical leave could not have predicted that Bill Clinton's first term in office would be dominated by the health care debacle. As national coalition leaders now attest with 20/20 hindsight, it is highly unlikely that a more widespread bill would have passed after 1993, and it is possible that no bill at all would have passed if the advocates had waited. The example of family and medical leave in Massachusetts lends credibility to this argument. When advocates decided to propose paid leave in 1985, they did so in a strong political and economic climate. However, their proposal for paid family and medical leave stalled, and by the time an unpaid family and medical leave policy was proposed, the climate had changed.

The dissenters' argument that there are costs associated with introducing bills that stereotype beneficiaries (as happened with the Tennessee maternity-leave only bill) requires consideration as well. As described in chapter 2, policies that accord women special treatment have long been criticized by feminists concerned that they would compromise the viability of women's equality in the long run. The Tennessee maternity leave bill, which as amended in 1988 covers only bonding between mothers and their children, falls into this special treatment category and is thus immediately suspect. The question to be answered, then, is whether or not these costs outweigh the benefits available to the women who can take advantage of the law.

This question is a difficult one. As noted in chapter 4, no respondents could imagine a situation in which a stronger bill could have passed in Tennessee. Thus the dilemma facing the advocates in Tennessee truly was whether to pass a maternity-only bill or not to pass a bill at all. On the one hand, as with the national family and medical leave bill and most other incremental legislation, the Tennessee maternity leave law did benefit some people, albeit fewer than those who would have benefited from a gender-neutral bill. On the other hand, the law encoded the principle that women but not men need time to care for new babies.

Given the fact that laws add the weight of government legitimacy behind social arrangements, a credible argument can be made that the advocates in Tennessee should have introduced a gender-neutral bill that would not pass rather than encoding the principle of special treatment for women. The fact that the advocates in Tennessee were insiders (in contrast to the advocates in Massachusetts) is especially important here: even if the bill did not pass, it would certainly have received attention. As it was, the bill that passed made a difference for a very small percentage of people but at the cost of furthering stereotypes of women as caretakers of children, something that has historically been associated with women's inability to achieve equality in the workforce. In addition, it should also be noted that in contrast to Connecticut and to other states that passed gender-neutral bills, the Tennessee law did not provide an example to help the federal bill pass.

This last point serves as a further reminder that strategic decisions may also be "nested within" knowledge about strategies that are being adopted by advocates for the same policy in other arenas. Normative conclusions about the rightness of strategy need to take this into account. As described in chapter 3, there was little value in introducing paid leave in Massachusetts simply to get it considered by elites and the public because the advocates had so little credibility that scant attention was paid to their proposal. Several national-level respondents suggested, however, that the Massachusetts experience contributed to the national debate by providing a vision of what *could* be proposed and reminding people on both sides of what was possible. In contrast, the decision to propose maternity leave in Tennessee cannot be considered strategic in the context of the national movement for family and medical leave.

In comparison, the decision by federal advocates to refuse to propose maternity leave only should be seen as courageous. The advocates on the federal level made compromises, but they made these compromises consciously, after considerable debate, and while keeping in mind their ultimate goal. In striking a balance between their desire to pass *something* and their desire to pass an important piece of legislation, they maintained their principles and they set the stage to achieve a better bill. One proponent said: "A successful model would be, you start there [with a modest bill] because you use the culture, you start where you are, so to speak, and you have incremental success, but you know you are headed for something else."

It should be noted that not everyone agrees that if the advocates on the national level were going to compromise, they should have made the compromises they did. A 1991 article by feminist legal theorist Christine Littleton, published after the first Bush veto of the Family and Medical Leave Act, took issue with the national advocates' decision to compromise on pay and on the number of people covered as opposed to gender. Emphasizing the fact that a maternity-only policy probably could have passed before 1993 (which was confirmed by a number of respondents), Littleton argues that since far more women than men make use of family and medical leave, it would have been better to pass a more substantial bill even if it covered women only.[14] Littleton aligns herself with the "difference" feminists described in chapter 2, who argued that maternity-only policies do not provide special protection for women, but instead enable them to be in the workforce in the first place. She extends their argument by downplaying the costs associated with providing women with maternity-based protections and asserts that it is more important to pass a broad maternity-leave bill than to pass a gender-neutral family and medical leave bill.

While Littleton's argument certainly has merits (in large part because women *do* take family and medical leaves more often than men),[15] I must respectfully disagree with it. The history of gender-specific protection in the United States, which as shown in chapter 2 has made it more difficult for women to achieve equality in the workforce, indicates that while there might be short-term benefits associated with providing women with broader maternity leave benefits, in the long run these benefits would come at a significant cost. If the movement for family and medical leave is to be seen as part of a long-term movement aimed at helping women and men to achieve true equality, then even incremental legislation should not compromise this goal. To paraphrase Littleton, "heading for something else" needs to involve more than a short-term calculation of immediate benefits.

The major normative conclusion of this project is that moderation and compromise may not always be the right approach, but they can be valuable tools for advocates attempting to pass contested policy innovations. Moderation and compromise should be undertaken only after a careful consideration of both short-term and long-term costs and benefits. An incremental bill should lay the groundwork for a more extensive policy and at the very least should not hinder the advocates' chances of passing more substantial legislation in the future. Furthermore, incremental change should not be accepted as an end in itself but within the context of a movement for broad social change. Even as they behave pragmatically, doing what is necessary to achieve progress within a system that is set up to make widespread change difficult, advocates can maintain their passion for comprehensive reforms and should be constantly on the lookout for ways to achieve their goals. As noted previously, policy windows may open unexpectedly, through elections, disasters, or other focusing events. Advocates must be ready to take advantage of opportunities that present themselves.

This approach to resolving the moderation dilemma reflects an approach to politics suggested by Max Weber in his well-known essay, "Politics as a Vocation." While obviously understanding the desire to pursue "an ethic of absolute ends," Weber warns that such an ethic is potentially dangerous and "cannot stand up under the . . . irrationality of the world."[16] He argues that passionate commitment to right must be supplemented by an ethic of responsibility, "in which one has to give an account of the foreseeable results of one's action" and be, to a great extent, pragmatic. Applied to the moderation dilemma, Weber's conclusion that "politics takes both passion and perspective"[17] serves as a reminder to advocates to find a balance between the two.

Advice for Advocates

Advocates for policy innovations like family and medical leave can apply the lessons of this study to their decisions. They can use the model of how policy innovation occurs, the philosophical approach above, and the emerging literature on "policy feedbacks" described in chapters 1 and 6. This literature shows that policies can expand the administrative capacity of the state and can change ideas about the role of government in public life, thus setting the stage for their own expansion. Part of this, as Hugh Heclo points out, involves "policy learning" by experts and decision makers, who rely on their experience with existing policies as they formulate new ones and who may be prompted to expand modest policies that are proven successful.[18] Policies can also facilitate or hinder the development of interest groups, which in turn can serve as powerful forces to lobby for expansion if they are given the right incentives. Advocates should design policies so as to take maximum advantage of these effects.

In the three cases studied where the insiders won and moderate family leave bills were passed, advocates on both sides did not in retrospect view the moderation dilemma as destructive. Donna Lenhoff, the chief architect of the federal Family and Medical Leave Act, said, "It's always good to have a left flank,"[19] and she and other coalition leaders noted that they had used the National Organization for Women's withdrawal from the federal coalition to respond to opposition, claiming that the bill was so moderate that even NOW would not support it! From the other side of the divide, Fund for a Feminist Majority president (and former NOW president) Eleanor Smeal labeled the moderation dilemma a "creative tension" and said, "We're still allies."[20] However, these warm sentiments were expressed within the context of serious disagreements over strategy and moderates' clear domination of the federal debate. The example of Massachusetts, where outsiders dominated the debate, illustrates the degree to which proposing a more widespread bill can make it more difficult to accomplish anything. Advocates must carefully weigh the value of having a left flank against the threat that that left flank will dominate their coalition and prevent any bill from passing.

Suggestions for Further Research

This project presents a model of policy innovation that incorporates the resources available to advocates and explanations for the strategic decisions they make. It leaves a number of questions unanswered, however. Two questions in particular concern how advocates make strategic decisions. This study has shown that organizational structure is associated with group strategy, but it has not explained exactly how strategy is fashioned. The successful coalitions examined in this study had agendas that fit with the political opportunity structure *and* they made more accurate calculations about what they can achieve. Conversely, coalition leaders for the failed attempt to pass a paid family and medical leave in Massachusetts described in chapter 3 had more radical agendas *and also* underestimated the costs of introducing paid leave. It is difficult to separate these causal factors and to determine the degree to which strategic decisions result from having a different agenda or from calculations about what is possible to pass at a particular time.

My examination of the current efforts to enact paid family leave in Massachusetts and Washington described in chapter 6 suggests that coalitions may weigh ideological and practical considerations in different ways. In my observations of Massachusetts coalition meetings over a period of six months during the fall of 1999 and the spring of 2000, I found that members wanted to actively lobby for both the narrow Baby

UI bill covering only parents of newborn or newly adopted children and for the broader temporary disability insurance bill that would cover people taking leave to care for spouses and for extended family members. Over time, however, coalition leaders determined that they did not have the resources to achieve both bills, and they decided that they would focus on the first proposal for Baby UI. While they continued to believe strongly in the importance of a broader bill, the advocates in Massachusetts decided to moderate based on their calculations about the size of their policy window.[21]

In contrast, the lead advocates in Washington appear to have developed their proposal to provide paid family leave only to parents of newborn or newly adopted children from ideological as well as practical considerations. While they, too, expressed the desire to have a broader bill, they expressed far fewer reservations about the value of passing incremental reforms. This may reflect the fact that the coalition for paid family leave in Washington has been dominated by legislators, while the coalition in Massachusetts is dominated by outside activists. As explained earlier, insider activists are more likely to accept values of moderation and compromise, which are emphasized to such a great extent in the American political system.

More research is needed, however, to understand the process by which activists determine what they will propose and when they will compromise and to explain how ideology and strategic calculations are weighed out against each other. This would involve studying more than two examples of coalitions in the process of making strategic decisions, potentially observing a large number of coalitions determining strategy on a variety of issues.

A second unanswered question is why in places where the policy process is dominated by outsiders, insiders did not attempt to wrest control over family and medical leave proposals away by offering counter-proposals. This question applies especially well to North Carolina, where many respondents linked the failure of family and medical leave to its sponsorship by a particularly uninfluential legislator. Given the weakness of the political opportunity structure in North Carolina, it is probable that no insider advocate saw an advantage to proposing family and medical leave. Unless it can be linked to other goals such as the furthering of a political career or the chance to claim a political symbol, advocates have few incentives to make the issue a priority.

This in turn is unlikely to happen in places where there are particularly few political resources, as in North Carolina in the late 1980s and early 1990s.

It is also possible that the norms of state legislatures are such that advocates feel bound to respect their colleagues' jurisdiction. In Massachusetts, where the lead advocate was the majority whip in the house of representatives, advocates who disagreed with the strategy of proposing paid family and medical leave were nonetheless unwilling to launch a counter-effort that would presumably have alienated the sponsor and her coalition. This may be associated with the fact that family and medical leave provides few tangible benefits and is unlikely to attract enough support for two coalitions, or it may simply reflect an unwritten rule that legislators do not generally interfere with their colleagues' bills.

More research is needed to explain the process by which a bill becomes identified with a particular legislator or advocacy group and the process by which this identification sticks. It is clear that the association that is formed between a bill and its sponsor at an early point is crucial to the fate of the bill, but it is not clear why one association forms while another does not.

Conclusion

This study has shown that in order to pass family and medical leave policies, advocates needed to have substantial resources and also needed to have an agenda that fit with the political opportunity structure. Successful advocates were those who viewed policy making as a long-term process, in which incremental change could be continued over time. The advocates' views of the policy process were shaped by the structure of the organization they were involved with: insiders with relationships with legislators and with a stake in achieving *an* outcome were more likely than outsiders to moderate and accept compromise.

Seven years after the passage of the federal Family and Medical Leave Act, the policy should be viewed as a success. It is popular both with the public and with Democratic politicians, who like to claim credit for it as evidence of their commitment to families. It has set the stage for its own expansion, prompting the continued efforts of interest groups on the local and national levels to begin developing a movement for more substantial paid family leave policies. While it remains to be seen whether these movements will ultimately be successful, their very formation is a significant development.

While some advocates feel that the need to moderate and accept compromise is lamentable, moderation was necessary to pass family and medical leave policies. Advocates considering proposing legislation like family and medical leave need to be able to understand and respond to the moderation dilemma. Incremental bills must be understood as first steps rather than as substantial change, but they can be important first steps, as long as they are developed in ways that are congruent with advocates' long-term goals.

SELECTION OF INTERVIEW SUBJECTS

In the process of researching the debates over family and medical leave in the four states and the federal government, I conducted 128 interviews between April 1995 and June 1996 [see appendix 2 for list of respondents]. Ninety-one of these interviews, or 71 percent, were conducted in person. Thirty-seven interviews, or 29 percent, were conducted by telephone. I also conducted an additional ten interviews between June and September 1999, on the subject of state efforts to pass paid family leave. Seven of these interviews were conducted by telephone, and three were conducted in person.

Interview respondents were selected on the basis of three criteria. First, a review of bill drafts, news articles, and hearing transcripts provided a list of sponsors and cosponsors as well as those who had publicly supported and opposed family and medical leave bills in debate. All the main sponsors of the state bills and many of the chief staff members for the main sponsors of the federal bill were interviewed, and a second group of supporters and opponents was selected for interviews. A sample of staff members who were mentioned in these hearings was also interviewed. Once preliminary contacts were made, respondents were asked to provide names of other important figures in the debate over family and medical leave.[1] All respondents were asked to identify both supporters and opponents of the bill. These figures included staff members, legislators, and members of interest groups. Finally, local representatives from labor and from two national organizations, the National Organization for Women (a major feminist group) and the National Federation of Independent Businesses (which led the fight to oppose family and medical leave) were contacted in each state and on the federal level, whether or not they had been mentioned previously.

Respondents were contacted by telephone and asked to participate in an interview ranging in length from thirty to forty-five minutes. The original 1995–96 project was defined as a study of legislative decisions to regulate business, focusing on the experience of legislators deciding whether or not to pass family and medical leave policies. The 1999 paid leave project was defined as a study of the effort to pass paid family leave policies. All but six of those contacted agreed to participate.[2] Respondents were offered confidentiality to any degree they chose: they could either not be identified by name, in which case they would be identified categorically (as "legislators" or "staffers") or they could choose to be identified as interview subjects but select quotes that they did not want attributed to them. In the original project, two respondents in the states (one in each of two states) and three respondents on the national level (all congressional staff members) requested complete anonymity. In the follow-up project, two state staff members requested complete anonymity. All requests are respectfully heeded throughout the project.

In the process of writing this book, I provided additional protection to my research subjects by attributing quotes only when absolutely necessary (when it is clear who the respondent is from the content or context of the quote). I recontacted those subjects whom I needed to cite and received their written permission to use the material.

All except six of the original interviews and three of the follow-up interviews were tape-recorded, by permission of the respondents.[3] The interviews lasted from twenty minutes to three hours; the median length was about forty-five minutes. The interviews were open-ended, but were based on a common set of questions developed for state and national respondents. To avoid bias, questions tailored to specific hypotheses were asked toward the end of the interviews. Respondents were asked to provide information about the debate over family and medical leave, to describe their participation in the debate, to speculate about why the proposal passed or failed, and to discuss the resources available and strategies chosen by the participants. They were also asked questions about the relationships between state and national family and medical leave initiatives. A number of respondents provided access to their personal files or offered other documents relating to their participation in the debate. Some of these were offered only after promises of confidentiality. Due to time constraints, three respondents had to be interviewed over more than one day.

INTERVIEW SUBJECTS

CONNECTICUT

Adamo, Joseph; former representative, chair of the Committee on Labor and Public Employees in 1989. Interview by author, Wethersfield, Conn., June 19, 1995.

Cocco, Jacqueline; representative; chair of Family and Workplace Committee in 1989. Interview by author, Hartford, Conn., June 21, 1995.

Donovan, Chris; representative, representative of the Service Employees International Union to the Task Force on Work and Family Roles. Interview by author, Meriden, Conn., July 13, 1995.

Farr, Robert; representative, member of Family and Workplace Committee in 1989. Interview by author, Hartford, Conn., June 20, 1995.

Fatone, Toni; staff of the Family and Workplace Committee. Interview by author, Hartford, Conn., July 12, 1995.

Finn-Stevenson, Dr. Matia; Bush Center in Child Development and Social Policy, Yale University. Telephone interview by author, August 1, 1995.

Frank, Meryl; Bush Center in Child Development and Social Policy, Yale University, and coordinator, New Jersey Family Leave Coalition. Telephone interview by author, July 26, 1995.

Freedman, Judith; senator, member of Task Force on Work and Family Roles. Interview by author, Westport, Conn., July 14, 1995.

Gelsi, Frederick; representative, member of Task Force on Work and Family Roles and chair of Family and Workplace Committee in 1987. Telephone interview by author, August 2, 1995.

Gray, Fredrica; former executive director of the Permanent Commission on the Status of Women. Interview by author, Enfield, Conn., June 26, 1995.

Harper, Joe; former representative. Interview by author, New Britain, Conn., July 13, 1995.

Hopley, Carolyn; former vice president for legislation at the National Organization for Women, Connecticut. Telephone interview by author, July 19, 1995.

Jaeckle, Robert; representative, member of Family and Workplace Committee. Interview by author, Hartford, Conn., June 20, 1995.

Koprowski, Pamela; director of Government Affairs at Champion International. Interview by author, Stanford, Conn., July 14, 1995.

Larson, John; former senator. Interview by author, Hartford, Conn., June 26, 1995.

Magnan, Maureen; staff to the Task Force on Work and Family Roles. Interview by author, Hartford, Conn., July 12, 1995.

Moody, Lisa; staff to Senate Republicans. Telephone interview by author, August 1, 1995.

Moser, Jeanne Kardos; former director of employee benefits at the Southern New England Telephone Company. Telephone interview by author, July 19, 1995.

Orlowski, Diane; JFD Tube and Coil Company, and representative of the National Federation of Independent Businesses to the Task Force on Work and Parenting Roles. Interview by author, Hamden, Conn., June 15, 1995.

Reimer, Annemarie; former director of research at the Connecticut Business and Industry Association. Interview by author, Hartford, Conn., July 12, 1995.

Robertson, Phillip, former senator; member of the Family and the Workplace Committee. Interview by author, Cheshire, Conn., June 19, 1995.

Smith, Reginald J., former senator. Interview by author, New Britain, Conn., August 3, 1995.

Stewart, Bonnie; lobbyist for the Connecticut Business and Industry Association. Interview by author, Hartford, Conn., August 3, 1995.

Woods, Cecilia; director of research for senate Democrats. Interview by author, Hartford, Conn., June 21, 1995.

Zalinskis, Jane Grenon; director of employee benefits at the Southern New England Telephone Company. Interview by author, New Haven, Conn., June 19, 1995.

Ziegler, Dr. Edward; director of the Bush Center on Social Policy at Yale University. Interview by author, New Haven, Conn., August 2, 1995.

Zimmerman, Diane; executive director of the Connecticut Commission on Children. Interview by author, Hartford, Conn., July 14, 1995.

MASSACHUSETTS

Balser, Diane; founding director of the Women's Statewide Legislative Network. Interview by author, Cambridge, Mass., June 22, 1995.

Bookman, Ann. Telephone interview by author, June 13, 1995.

Bosley, Daniel; representative, chair of the House Committee on Commerce and Labor. Interview by author, Boston, Mass., May 16, 1995.

Boviard, Carolyn; Massachusetts State Director of the National Federation of Independent Businesses. Interview by author, Boston, Mass., May 12, 1995.

Brazelton, Dr. T. Berry. Interview by author, Cambridge, Mass., May 5, 1995.

Bump, Suzanne; former representative. Interview by author, Boston, Mass., May 23, 1995.

Businger, John; representative. Interview by author, Boston, Mass., May 8, 1995.

Campbell, Elizabeth; lobbyist for the American Association of Retired Persons. Interview by author, Boston, Mass., May 2, 1995.

Cellucci, Elizabeth; staff to the Commerce and Labor Committee. Interview by author, Boston, Mass., April 10, 1995.

Gibson, Mary Jane; former representative. Interview by author, Eastham, Mass., May 13, 1995.

Gray, Barbara; representative. Interview by author, Boston, Mass., May 2, 1995.

Harrigan, Loretta; representative of the Associated Industries of Massachusetts to the Task Force on Parenting Leave and the Task Force on Temporary Disability Insurance. Interview by author, Cambridge, Mass., May 19, 1995.

Hoyt, Sally; vice president of the Massachusetts Federation of Business and Professional Women. Interview by author, Reading, Mass., May 6, 1995.

Hudner, Karen; former lobbyist for the American Civil Liberties Union. Interview by author, Cambridge, Mass., June 1, 1995.

Jones, Tom. Staff to the Commerce and Labor Committee. Interview by author, Boston, Mass., April 25, 1995.

Larkin, Peter; representative. Interview by author, Boston, Mass., June 7, 1995.

Lemanski, Kenneth; former representative, chair of Commerce and Labor Committee in 1985 and 1986. Interview by author, Boston, Mass., May 19, 1995.

Li, Vivien; women's advisor to the Dukakis administration. Interview by author, Boston, Mass., May 30, 1995.

Lord, Richard; executive vice president for legislative policy for Associated Industries of Massachusetts; and Lynda Slevoski, lobbyist. Interview by author, Boston, Mass., June 7, 1995.

Magnani, David; senator. Interview by author, Boston, Mass., June 13, 1995.

Morris, Haidee; former counsel for the Massachusetts Secretary of Labor. Interview by author, Cambridge, Mass., May 5, 1995.

Parker, Joanie; former lobbyist for the Coalition of Labor Union Women. Telephone interview by author, May 17, 1995.

Pines, Lois; senator. Interview by author, Boston, Mass., May 8, 1995.

Segal, Phyllis; former legal director of the National Organization for Women's Legal Defense and Education Fund. Telephone interview by author, June 9, 1995.

Travinski, Marilyn; former representative, chair of the Commerce and Labor Committee, 1987–1989. Telephone interview by author, June 12, 1995.

Wolf, Betsy; former lobbyist for the National Organization of Women. Telephone interview by author, July 5, 1995.

Zuckerman, Mark; former attorney for Commerce and Labor committee. Telephone interview by author, April 15, 1995.

NORTH CAROLINA

Ballance, Frank; senator, former cochair of the North Carolina Commission on the Family. Interview by author, Warrenton, N.C., March 25, 1996.

Barnes, Ann; representative. Telephone interview by author, April 24, 1996.

Blue, Dan; representative, former speaker of the North Carolina House of Representatives. Interview by author, Raleigh, N.C., March 27, 1996.

Davis, Robin; president of the National Organization for Women, North Carolina. Interview by author, Raleigh, N.C., March 25, 1996.

Fitzsimon, Chris; former press secretary to Speaker Dan Blue. Interview by author, Raleigh, N.C., March 25, 1996.

Follmer, Don; special assistant for policy and communications to Harold Brubaker, speaker of the North Carolina House of Representatives. Interview by author, Raleigh, N.C., March 27, 1996.

Glasser, Florry; director of work-family programs, North Carolina Equity. Interview by author, Raleigh, N.C., March 26, 1996.

Gray, Lyons; representative. Interview by author, Winston-Salem, N.C., March 28, 1996.

Holt, Bertha "B."; former chair of the North Carolina Caucus of Women Legislators. Interview by author, Burlington, N.C., March 29, 1996.

Kennedy, Annie Brown; former representative. Interview by author, Winston-Salem, N.C., March 29, 1996.

Kirk, Phil; president of North Carolina Citizens for Business and Industry. Interview by author, Raleigh, N.C., March 26, 1996.

Legislative aide one, North Carolina House of Representatives. Interview by author, Raleigh, N.C., March 28, 1996.

Marshbanks, Lynn; staff attorney to the North Carolina Commission on the Family. Interview by author, Raleigh, N.C., March 28, 1996.

Payne, Harry; commissioner of labor for the State of North Carolina. Interview by author, Raleigh, N.C., March 28, 1996.

Plexico, Clark; senator, member of the North Carolina Commission on the Family. Telephone interview by author, April 29, 1996.

Preston, Fran; North Carolina Retail Merchants Association. Telephone interview by author, April 12, 1996.

Russell, Carolyn; representative. Interview by author, Raleigh, N.C., March 27, 1996.

Schoonmaker, Meyrissa; president of the North Carolina Center for Laws Affecting Women. Interview by author, Winston-Salem, N.C., March 29, 1996.

Scott, Chris; president of the North Carolina AFL-CIO. Interview by author, Raleigh, N.C., March 27, 1996.

Summers, Brenda; director of North Carolina Equity. Interview by author, Raleigh, N.C., March 26, 1996.

Valuri, Susan; former state director of the North Carolina National Federation of Independent Businesses. Telephone interview by author, May 9, 1996.

TENNESSEE

Anderson, Betty; former staff to Governor Ned McWherter. Interview by author, Nashville, Tennessee, January 11, 1996.

Atchley, Ben; senator. Interview by author, Nashville, Tennessee, January 10, 1996.

Austin, Cathy; former president of the Tennessee chapter of the National Organization for Women. Telephone interview by author, June 3, 1996.

Cushing, Lynn; former president of the Tennessee chapter of the National Organization for Women. Interview by author, Nashville, Tennessee, January 9, 1996.

Fentress, Charles; state director of the Tennessee National Federation of Independent Business. Interview by author, Nashville, Tennessee, January 11, 1996.

Ford, John; senator. Interview by author, Nashville, Tennessee, January 9, 1996.

Former representative one, telephone interview by author, February 1, 1996.

Garrett, Tim; representative. Interview by author, Nashville, Tennessee, January 10, 1996.

Gaskill, Robert; vice president of the Tennessee Business and Industry Association. Interview by author, Nashville, Tennessee, January 5, 1996.

Goetz, Dave; executive director of the Tennessee Business Roundtable. Interview by author, Nashville, Tennessee, January 8, 1996.

Grunou, Bob; former commissioner of Human Services, State of Tennessee. Interview by author, Nashville, Tennessee, January 11, 1996.

Haynes, Betty; former staff to Governor Ned McWherter. Telephone interview by author, January 8, 1996.

Haynes, Joe; senator. Interview by author, Nashville, Tennessee, January 9, 1996.

Koella, Carl; senator. Interview by author, Nashville, Tennessee, January 10, 1996.

Lewelling, Martha; former president of the Memphis chapter of the Older Women's League. Interview by author, Memphis, Tennessee, February 22, 1996.

Lyle, Mary Frances; lobbyist for the Tennessee Women's Political Caucus. Interview by author, Nashville, Tennessee, January 8, 1996; telephone interview by author, June 12, 1996.

McWherter, Ned; former governor of Tennessee. Telephone interview by author, February 2, 1996.

Naifeh, Jimmy; former majority leader and current speaker of the Tennessee House of Representatives. Telephone interview by author, January 30, 1996.

Neeley, Jim; president of the Tennessee chapter of the AFL-CIO. Interview by author, Nashville, Tennessee, January 8, 1996.

O'Brien, Anna Belle; senator. Interview by author, Nashville, Tennessee, January 10, 1996.

Petray, Bobbie; lobbyist for the Tennessee chapter of the Eagle Forum. Telephone interview by author, January 14, 1996.

Purcell, Bill; representative, majority leader of the Tennessee House of Representatives. Telephone interview by author, March 21, 1996.

Rochelle, Robert; senator. Interview by author, Nashville, Tennessee, January 5, 1996.

Weinberg, Hedy; director of the Tennessee ACLU. Telephone interview by author, March 18, 1996.

Williams, Karen; former representative. Interview by author, Nashville, Tennessee, January 9, 1996.

Wood, Yvonne; president of the Tennessee Women's Political Caucus. Telephone interview by author, February 4, 1996.

NATIONAL

Bravo, Ellen; director of 9-5, the National Association of Working Women. Telephone interview by author, May 23, 1996.

Dalton, Anne; National Association of Junior Leagues. Telephone interview by author, May 28, 1996.

Feinstein, Fred; former chief counsel and staff director for the Subcommittee on Labor-Management Relations of the House Committee on Education and Labor.

Interview by author, Washington, D.C., May 13, 1996; telephone interview by author, July 1, 1996.

Galinsky, Ellen; codirector of the Families and Work Institute. Telephone interview by author, June 4, 1996.

Gandy, Kim; vice president of the National Organization for Women. Interview by author, Washington, D.C., May 13, 1996.

Humphrey, Anne Radigan; former director of the Congressional Caucus for Women's Issues. Interview by author, New Bedford, Mass., June 8, 1996.

Kolker, Ann; National Women's Law Center. Telephone interview by author, June 4, 1996.

Legislative staff one, Telephone interview by author, May 21, 1996.

Legislative staff two, Interview by author, Washington, D.C., May 14, 1996

Legislative staff three, Interview by author, Washington, D.C., May 15, 1996

Lenhoff, Donna; general counsel and director of Work-Family Programs, Women's Legal Defense Fund, now the National Partnership for Women and Families. Interview by author, Washington, D.C., May 14, 1996.

Motley, John; former lobbyist for the National Federation of Independent Business. Interview by author, Washington, D.C., May 14, 1996.

Murphey, Patrick; chief of staff for Representative Cass Ballinger. Telephone interview by author, June 10, 1996.

Norton, Helen; staff attorney for the Women's Legal Defense Fund. Interview by author, May 16, 1996.

O'Grady, Jane; lobbyist for the AFL-CIO. Interview by author, Washington, D.C., May 17, 1996.

Reuss, Pat; former legislative director of the Women's Equity Action League. Telephone interview by author, June 11, 1996.

Ruff, Jackie; former staff to Senate Committee on Education and Labor. Telephone interview by author, May 29, 1996.

Schlafly, Phyllis. Telephone interview by author, May 28, 1996.

Sementilli-Dann, Lisa; former staff for the Center for Policy Alternatives. Telephone interview by author, June 6, 1996.

Shellabarger, Thomas; lobbyist for the United States Catholic Conference. Interview by author, Washington, D.C., May 17, 1996.

Smeal, Eleanor; former president of NOW and current president of the Fund for a Feminist Majority. Telephone interview by author, June 21, 1996.

Spalter-Roth, Roberta; Institute for Women's Policy Research. Interview by author, May 15, 1996.

Steinschneider, Janice; former attorney for the Center for Policy Alternatives. Interview by author, Washington, D.C., May 16, 1996.

Tarplin, Rich; former staff to the Senate Committee on Children, Youth, and Families. Interview by author, Washington, D.C., May 13, 1996; telephone interview by author, June 5, 1996.

Tarr-Whelan, Linda; director, Center for Policy Alternatives. Telephone interview by author, May 28, 1996.

Tavenner, Mary; former lobbyist for the National Association of Wholesalers and founder of the Concerned Alliance of Responsible Employers. Interview by author, Washington, D.C., May 17, 1996.

Wilson, Steve; chief of staff to Representative Marge Roukema. Interview by author, Washington, D.C., May 15, 1996.

FAMILY AND MEDICAL LEAVE SINCE 1993

Brown, Lisa; senator. Interview by author, September 28, 1999.

Burbank, John; executive director of the Economic Opportunity Institute, Seattle, Washington. Telephone Interview by author, July 13, 1999.

Casavant, Kathleen; secretary/treasurer of the Massachusetts AFL-CIO. Interview by author, Boston, Mass., September 10, 1999.

Emsellem, Maurice; National Employment Law Project. Telephone interview by author, August 4, 1999.

Halas, Monica; senior employment attorney for Greater Boston Legal Services. Interview by author, Boston, Mass., July 29, 1999.

Jelen, Patricia; representative. Interview by author, Boston, Mass., August 9, 1999.

Johnson, Linda; director of the Women's Statewide Legislative Network. Telephone interview by author, July 6, 1999.

Legislative Staff one, New York State Assembly. Telephone Interview by author, June 29, 1999.

Legislative Staff two, New Jersey Legislature. Telephone Interview by author, June 22, 1999.

Lenhoff, Donna. Telephone interview by author, June 23, 1999.

NOTES

CHAPTER ONE

1. For institutionalist arguments about American exceptionalism, see Margaret Weir, Ann Shola Orloff, and Theda Skocpol, eds., *The Politics of Social Policy in the United States* (Princeton, N.J.: Princeton University Press, 1988); Theda Skocpol, *Protecting Soldiers and Mothers: The Political Origins of Social Policy in the United States* (Cambridge, Mass.: Belknap Press of Harvard University Press, 1992); Paul Pierson, *Dismantling the Welfare State? Reagan, Thatcher, and the Politics of Retrenchment* (New York: Cambridge University Press, 1994), especially 31–39; and Sven Steinmo, "American Exceptionalism Reconsidered: Culture or Institutions?" in *The Dynamics of American Politics: Approaches and Interpretations*, ed. Lawrence C. Dodd and Calvin Jillson (Boulder, Col.: Westview Press, 1994), 106–31.

2. There is some disagreement as to whether divided government itself prevents the enactment of significant legislation. Divided government certainly does, however, make it easier for the parties controlling each branch to block each other's proposals and probably necessitates a heightened willingness to compromise. See James Sundquist, "Needed: A Political Theory for the New Era of Coalition Government in the United States," *Political Science Quarterly* 103 (1988): 613–35; David Mayhew, *Divided We Govern: Party Control, Lawmaking, and Investigations, 1946–1990* (New Haven, Conn.: Yale University Press, 1991); Morris Fiorina, *Divided Government* (New York: Macmillan, 1992).

3. See John B. Gilmour, *Strategic Disagreement: Stalemate in American Politics* (Pittsburgh, Pa.: University of Pittsburgh Press, 1995), especially introduction. The best example of an exception, also known as a "big bang," is the New Deal.

4. John Kingdon, *Agendas, Alternatives, and Public Policies*, 2nd ed. (New York: Harper Collins, 1995), 191–92.

5. R. Douglas Arnold, *The Logic of Congressional Action* (New Haven, Conn.: Yale University Press, 1990), 110.

6. Gilmour, *Strategic Disagreement*, 38.

7. *A Workable Balance: Report to Congress on Family and Medical Leave Policies* (Washington, D.C.: The Women's Bureau of the U.S. Department of Labor, 1996).

8. "Family and Medical Leave Policy," *Congressional Digest* 67, no. 3 (May 1988): 131.

9. Kirsten Wever, *The Family and Medical Leave Act* (Cambridge, Mass.: The Radcliffe Public Policy Institute, 1996). Wever cites as the source of her data Christopher J. Ruhm and Jackqueline L. Teague, "Parental Leave Policies in Europe and North America," NBER Working Paper no. 5065, Cambridge, Mass., March 1995.

10. Wever argues that the lack of a strong parental leave results from the fact that "work and family policy in the U.S. has not tended to concern itself explicitly with the needs of the majority of American families—people not in total poverty but still needing to balance personal health and health of family members against the need to work." *The Family and Medical Leave Act*, 7–8.

11. For example, see Christine L. Day, *What Older Americans Think: Interest Groups and Aging Policy* (Princeton, N.J.: Princeton University Press, 1990).

12. Claudia Goldin, *Understanding the Gender Gap: An Economic History of American Women* (New York: Oxford University Press, 1990).

13. This argument is made by Theda Skocpol in her discussion of mothers' pensions in *Protecting Soldiers and Mothers*.

14. This term was coined by Pierson, *Dismantling the Welfare State*.

15. See James Davison Hunter, *Culture Wars: The Struggle to Define America* (New York: Basic Books, 1991).

16. James C. Garand and Pamela A. Monroe, "Family Leave Legislation in the American States: Toward a Model of State Policy Adoption," *Journal of Family and Economic Issues* 16, no. 4 (Winter 1995): 341–63.

17. Competitive federalism is the idea that states and localities compete against each other to attract revenue-producing taxpayers and businesses. Some scholars argue that competitive federalism may lead to a "race to the bottom," where states and localities lower taxes and limit regulations. See Paul Peterson and Mark Rom, *Welfare Magnets: The Case for a National Standard* (Washington, D.C.: Brookings Institution, 1989); and Paul Peterson, *The Price of Federalism* (Washington, D.C.: Brookings Institution, 1995).

18. See Herbert McCloskey and John Zaller, *The American Ethos: Public Attitudes toward Capitalism and Democracy* (Cambridge, Mass.: Harvard University Press, 1994). For a discussion of the "fit" between group approaches and cultural and institutional constraints, see Skocpol, *Protecting Soldiers and Mothers*, introduction.

19. Lindblom explains, "Because public functions in the market system rest in the hands of businessmen, it follows that jobs, prices, production, growth, the standard of living, and the economic security of everyone else all rest in their hands." Charles Lindblom, *Politics and Markets: The World's Political-Economic Systems* (New York: Basic Books, 1977), 172; also Lindblom, "The Market as Prison," *Journal of Politics* 44 (1982): 324–36.

20. See E. E. Schattschneider, *The Semi-Sovereign People: A Realist's View of Democracy in America*, reissued with an introduction by David Andamany (New York: Harcourt Brace Jovanovich, 1975); C. Wright Mills, *The Power Elite* (New York: Oxford University Press, 1956). Contemporary works include Kay Lehman Schlozman and John Tierney, *Organized Interests and American Democracy* (New York: Harper Collins, 1986).

21. David Vogel, "The Political Power of Business in America: A Reappraisal," *British Journal of Political Science* 13 (1983): 19–43. See also Vogel, *Fluctuating Fortunes: The Political Power of Business in America* (New York: Basic Books, 1989).

22. Paul Pierson, "The Scope and Nature of Business Power: Employers and the American Welfare State, 1900–1935," paper presented at the Annual Meeting of the American Political Science Association, Chicago, Ill., September 1995.

23. Cathie Jo Martin, *Stuck in Neutral: Business and the Politics of Human Capital Investment Policy* (Princeton, N.J.: Princeton University Press, 2000). Martin's discussion of small business opposition to family and medical leave is in chapter 7.

24. See Mancur Olson, *The Logic of Collective Action* (Cambridge, Mass.: Harvard University Press, 1965).

25. The *Workable Balance* employee survey covering the first eighteen months after the enactment of the Family and Medical Leave Act (FMLA) found that nearly 17 percent of employees had taken leave for a reason covered by the FMLA, and that nearly 90 percent of leaves had lasted twelve weeks or less. Note that only 7 percent of these workers, or 1.2 percent of the total workforce, designated their leaves as "Family and Medical Leave Act" leaves. Commission on Family and Medical Leave, *A Workable Balance*, xix–xx.

26. A *New York Times* survey taken in October 1992, just before the passage of the Family and Medical Leave Act, found that it was supported by 57 percent of respondents. See Felicity Barringer, "In Family-Leave Debate, a Profound Ambivalence," *New York Times*, October 7, 1992.

27. See "Parental Leave—A Windfall for Yuppies." *Phyllis Schlafly Report* 20, no. 4 (November 1986), section 1.

28. See Richard E. Dawson and James A. Robinson, "Interparty Competition, Economic Variables, and Welfare Policies in the American States," *Journal of Politics* 25 (May 1963): 265–89; Thomas Dye, *Politics, Economics, and the Public: Policy Outcomes in the American States* (Chicago: Rand McNally, 1966); Richard I. Hofferbert, "The Relation between Public Policy and Some Structural and Environmental Variables in the American States," *American Political Science Review* 60 (March 1966): 73–82.

29. See V. O. Key, *Southern Politics in State and Nation* (New York: Alfred A. Knopf, 1949); Charles F. Cnudde and Donald J. McCrone, "Party Competition and Welfare Policies in the American States," *American Political Science Review* 63 (September 1969): 858–66; Ira Sharkansky and Richard I. Hofferbert, "Dimensions of State Politics, Economics, and Public Policy," *American Political Science Review* 63 (September 1969): 867–79.

30. See Daniel Elazar, *American Federalism: A View from the States*, 3rd ed. (New York: Harper and Row, 1984); Robert S. Erikson, Gerald C. Wright, and John C. McIver, *Statehouse Democracy: Public Opinion and Policy in the American States* (New York: Cambridge University Press, 1993).

31. Hugh Heclo, *Modern Social Policies in Britain and Sweden* (New Haven, Conn.: Yale University Press, 1974), chapter 6.

32. Jeffrey M. Stonecash, "The State Politics Literature: Moving beyond Covariation Studies and Pursuing Politics," *Polity* 28 (Summer 1994): 559–79.

33. See John D. McCarthy and Mayer Zald, *The Trend of Social Movements in America: Professionalism and Resource Mobilization* (Morristown, N.J.: General Learning Press, 1973); McCarthy and Zald, "Resource Mobilization and Social Movements: A Partial Theory," *American Journal of Sociology* 82 (1977): 1212–41; William Gamson, *The Strategy of Social Protest* (Homewood, Ill.: Dorsey Press, 1975); Charles Tilly, *From Mobilization to Revolution* (Reading, Mass.: Addison-Wesley, 1978); J. Craig Jenkins, "Resource Mobilization Theory and the Study of Social Movements," *American Review of Sociology* 9 (1983): 527–53.

34. See Doug McAdam, *Political Process and the Development of Black Insurgency, 1930–1970* (Chicago: University of Chicago Press, 1982).

35. Lee Ann Banaszak, *Why Movements Succeed or Fail: Opportunity, Culture, and the Struggle for Woman Suffrage* (Princeton, N.J.: Princeton University Press, 1996), esp. 29–30. See also Hanspeter Kreisi, "The Political Opportunity Structure of New Social Movements: Its Impact on Their Mobilization," in *The Politics of Social Protest,* ed. J. Craig Jenkins and Bert Klandermans (Minneapolis: University of Minnesota Press, 1995); Sidney Tarrow, *Power in Movement: Social Movements, Collective Action, and Politics* (New York: Cambridge University Press, 1994).

36. See also Skocpol, *Protecting Soldiers and Mothers.*

37. Schattschneider, *Semi-Sovereign People,* 102.

38. Peter Bachrach and Morton S. Baratz, "The Two Faces of Power," *American Political Science Review* 56 (1962): 947–52.

39. Steven Lukes, *Power: A Radical View* (New York: Macmillan, 1974).

40. Roger W. Cobb and Charles D. Elder, *Participation in American Politics: The Dynamics of Agenda-Building* (Boston: Allyn and Bacon, 1972).

41. Nelson Polsby, *Political Innovation in America: The Politics of Policy Initiation* (New Haven, Conn.: Yale University Press, 1984), 166.

42. Barbara Nelson, *Making an Issue of Child Abuse: Political Agenda-Setting for Social Problems* (Chicago: University of Chicago Press, 1984).

43. Kingdon, *Agendas, Alternatives, and Public Policies,* chapter 8.

44. Deborah Stone, "Causal Stories and the Formation of Policy Agendas," *Political Science Quarterly* 104 (1989): 281–300.

45. Frank Baumgartner and Bryan D. Jones, *Agendas and Instability in American Politics* (Chicago: University of Chicago Press, 1993). See also their article and others in *The Politics of Problem Definition: Shaping the Policy Agenda,* ed. David A. Rochefort and Roger W. Cobb (Lawrence, Kans.: University Press of Kansas, 1994).

46. Arnold, *The Logic of Congressional Action.* On credit claiming, see David Mayhew, *Congress: The Electoral Connection* (New Haven, Conn.: Yale University Press, 1974); and Morris Fiorina, *Congress: Keystone of the Washington Establishment* (New Haven, Conn.: Yale University Press, 1977). On blame avoidance, see R. Kent Weaver, "The Politics of Blame Avoidance," *Journal of Public Policy* 6 (1986): 371–98.

47. Theda Skocpol, "Targeting within Universalism: Politically Viable Policies to Combat Poverty in the United States," in *Social Policy in the United States: Fu-*

ture Possibilities in Historical Perspective, ed. Theda Skocpol (Princeton, N.J.: Princeton University Press, 1995). Skocpol's argument is rebutted by Robert Greenstein in "Universal and Targeted Approaches to Relieving Poverty: An Alternative View," in Christopher Jencks and Paul Peterson, eds., *The Urban Underclass* (Washington, D.C.: Brookings Institution, 1991).

48. Joyce Gelb and Marian Lief Palley, *Women and Public Policies,* rev. and exp. ed. (Princeton, N.J.: Princeton University Press, 1987), introduction.

49. David A. Snow and others, "Frame Alignment Processes, Micromobilization, and Movement Participation," *American Sociological Review* 51 (1986): 464–81. See also David A. Snow and Robert D. Benford, "Ideology, Frame Resonance, and Participant Mobilization," in *From Structure to Action: Comparing Social Movement Research Across Cultures,* ed. Bert Klandermans, Hanspeter Kriesi, and Sidney Tarrow (Greenwich, Conn.: JAI Press, 1988), 197–217; and David Snow, "Master Frames and Cycles of Protest," in *Frontiers in Social Movement Theory,* ed. Aldon Morris and Carol McClurg Mueller (New Haven and London: Yale University Press, 1992).

50. Sidney Tarrow, *Power in Movement: Social Movements, Collective Action, and Politics* (New York: Cambridge University Press, 1994), 129–30.

51. Skocpol, *Protecting Soldiers and Mothers,* 54–57.

52. Olson, *The Logic of Collective Action.*

53. Tarrow, *Power in Movement,* 15.

54. James Q. Wilson, *Political Organizations,* 2nd ed., rev., (Princeton, N.J.: Princeton University Press, 1995), 33–34.

55. Ibid., 282.

56. Ibid., 286–87.

57. Jane Mansbridge, *Why We Lost the ERA* (Chicago: University of Chicago Press, 1986).

58. Thomas Gais and Jack L. Walker Jr., "Pathways to Influence in American Politics," in *Mobilizing Interest Groups in America: Patrons, Professions, and Social Movements,* ed. Jack L. Walker Jr. (Ann Arbor, Mich.: University of Michigan Press, 1991).

59. See also Roberta Spalter-Roth and Ronnee Schreiber, "Outsider Issues and Insider Tactics: Strategic Tensions in the Women's Policy Network during the 1980s," in *Feminist Organizations: Harvest of the New Women's Movement,* ed. Myra Marx Ferree and Patricia Yancey Martin (Philadelphia: Temple University Press, 1995).

60. Ibid., 113.

61. Wilson, *Political Organizations,* 285.

62. While Gais and Walker find that "patrons" encourage nonprofit and citizen groups to pursue insider strategies, they also find that they encourage for-profit groups to engage in outsider strategies.

63. Also see Gilmour, *Strategic Disagreement,* 28–29.

64. See Margaret Weir, Ann Shola Orloff, and Theda Skocpol, eds., *The Politics of Social Policy in the United States* (Princeton, N.J.: Princeton University Press, 1988); Paul Pierson, "'Policy Feedbacks' and Political Change: Contrasting Reagan

and Thatcher's Pension-Reform Initiatives," *Studies in American Political Development* 6 (Fall 1992): 359–90; Pierson, "When Effect Becomes Cause: 'Policy Feedback' and Political Change," *World Politics* (1993): 595–628; Skocpol, *Protecting Soldiers and Mothers*; Pierson, *Dismantling the Welfare State*.

65. Skocpol, *Protecting Soldiers and Mothers*, 58–59.

66. Martha Derthick, *Policymaking for Social Security* (Washington: Brookings Institution, 1979). Also Edward Berkowitz, *Social Security after Fifty: Successes and Failures* (Westport, Conn.: Greenwood Press, 1987); Berkowitz, *Mr. Social Security: The Life of Wilbur J. Cohen* (Lawrence, Kans.: University Press of Kansas, 1995).

67. Charles Lindblom, "The Science of Muddling Through," *Public Administration Review* 19 (1959): 79–88.

68. The source of my data is The United States Department of Labor, *State Maternity/Family Leave Law* (Washington, D.C.: Women's Bureau of the U.S. Department of Labor, 1993).

69. See Garand and Monroe, "Family Leave Legislation," 344–45. For a discussion of the Pregnancy Discrimination Act of 1978, see chapter 2.

70. Garand and Monroe, "Family Leave Legislation," 345.

71. See Key, *Southern Politics in State and Nation*; Daniel Elazar, *American Federalism*; Earl Black and Merle Black, *Politics and Society in the South* (Cambridge, Mass.: Harvard University Press, 1987).

72. In coding states as "liberal" or "conservative," I relied on Erikson, Wright, and McIver's coding of states according to aggregated *New York Times* public opinion polls over ten years. Connecticut and Massachusetts were coded among the one-third most "liberal" states, while Tennessee and North Carolina were coded among the one-third most "conservative" states. See Erikson, Wright, and McIver, *Statehouse Democracy: Public Opinion and Policy in the American States* (New York: Cambridge University Press, 1993).

73. See Donald G. Mathews and Jane Sherron DeHart, *Sex, Gender, and the Politics of the ERA: A State and the Nation* (New York: Oxford University Press, 1990).

CHAPTER TWO

1. Theda Skocpol, *Protecting Soldiers and Mothers: The Political Origins of Social Policy in the United States* (Cambridge, Mass.: Belknap Press of Harvard University Press, 1992), 254–56.

2. *Lochner v. New York*, 198 U.S. 45 (1905).

3. Skocpol, *Protecting Soldiers and Mothers*, 258.

4. See Nancy Cott, *The Bonds of Womanhood: "Women's Sphere" in New England, 1780–1835* (New Haven, Conn.: Yale University Press, 1977); Cott, *The Grounding of Modern Feminism* (New Haven, Conn.: Yale University Press, 1987); Carl Degler, *At Odds: Women and the Family in America from the Revolution to the Present* (New York: Oxford University Press, 1980).

5. The Lowell "Mill Girls" are often cited as examples of this trend: the families of these girls were assured that, rather than destroying their characters, "a few years of hard labor in the mills would make them into better wives and mothers." See Alice Kessler-Harris, *Out to Work: A History of Wage-Earning Women in the United States* (New York: Oxford University Press, 1982), xxx.

6. According to the Bureau of the Census, in 1900, 14.6 percent of white, native-born women with two native-born parents worked, while 25.4 percent of women with one or more foreign born parents worked, and 43.2 percent of black women worked. The Bureau of the Census, *Statistics on Women at Work, Based on Unpublished Information Derived from Schedules of the Twelfth Census, 1900* (Washington, D.C.: Government Printing Office, 1907).

7. See Kessler-Harris, *Out to Work*; and Kessler-Harris, *A Women's Wage: Historical Meanings and Social Consequences* (Lexington, Ky.: University of Kentucky Press, 1990).

8. Kessler-Harris, *Out to Work*, 81.

9. In the 1872 Supreme Court case *Bradwell v. Illinois* (83 U.S. 130), Justice Bradley stated, "The paramount destiny and mission of women is to fulfill the noble and benign offices of wife and mother." See Eleanor Flexner, *A Century of Struggle: The Women's Rights Movement in the United States*, rev. ed. (Cambridge, Mass.: Belknap Press of Harvard University Press, 1975).

10. Paula Baker, "The Domestication of Politics: Women and American Political Society, 1780–1920" in *Women, the State, and Welfare*, ed. Linda Gordon (Madison, Wis.: University of Wisconsin Press, 1990), 58.

11. Skocpol, *Protecting Soldiers and Mothers*, 333–40.

12. *Mueller v. Oregon*, 208 U.S. 412 (1908). From the decision by Justice Brewer.

13. Ibid.

14. Skocpol, *Protecting Soldiers and Mothers*, 408.

15. Kessler-Harris, *Out to Work*, 187.

16. Ida M. VanEtten, "The Condition of Women Workers under the Present Industrial System," Address to the National Convention of the American Federation of Labor, Detroit, Mich., 1890.

17. See Lise Vogel, *Mothers on the Job: Maternity Policy in the U.S. Workplace* (New Brunswick, N.J.: Rutgers University Press, 1993). See also discussions in Cott, *The Grounding of Modern Feminism*; and Kessler-Harris, *Out to Work*.

18. 1921 Letter from Alice Paul to Jane Norman Smith, quoted in Cott, *The Grounding of Modern Feminism*, 122.

19. As noted in the introductory chapter, this distrust arose over the more radical tactics adopted by the NWP during the suffrage era. Members of the League of Women Voter's parent, the National American Woman Suffrage Association, had been horrified when the NWP picketed President Woodrow Wilson during World War I, accusing him of "denying to the women of his country the democratic rights he claimed to uphold abroad." See Cott, *The Grounding of Modern Feminism*, 59.

20. Quoted in Kessler-Harris, *Out to Work*, xxx.

21. Ibid., 211.

22. Roger Biles, *A New Deal for the American People* (De Kalb, Ill.: Northern Illinois University Press, 1991), 194. See also Lois Scharf, *To Work and to Wed: Female Employment, Feminism, and the Great Depression* (Westport, Conn.: Greenwood Press, 1980), 40.

23. Kessler-Harris, *Out to Work*, 256. See also Scharf, *To Work and to Wed*, 40.

24. Biles, *A New Deal for the American People*, 202.

25. Ruth Milkman, *Gender at Work: The Dynamics of Job Segregation by Sex during World War II* (Chicago: University of Illinois Press, 1987), 28.

26. Quoted in Kessler-Harris, *Out to Work*, 258.

27. Ibid., 256.

28. See Mary Elizabeth Pidgeon, *Women in the Economy of the United States of America: Employed Women under NRA Codes* (Washington, D.C.: Government Printing Office, 1937), 99.

29. Biles, *A New Deal for the American People*, 203.

30. Milkman, *Gender at Work*, 31.

31. Pidgeon, *Women in the Economy of the United States of America*, 8.

32. See Alan Brinkley, "The Idea of the State," in *The Rise and Fall of the New Deal Order: 1930–1980*, ed. Steve Fraser and Gary Gerstle (Princeton, N.J.: Princeton University Press, 1989).

33. *NLRB v. Jones & Laughlin*, 301 U.S. 1 (1937).

34. Sherna Berger Gluck, *Rosie the Riveter Revisited: Women, the War, and Social Change* (Boston, Twayne Publishers, 1987), 10.

35. "Family and Medical Leave Legislation," *Congressional Digest* 72: 1 (January 1993), 3.

36. See Claudia Goldin, "The Role of World War II in the Rise of Women's Employment," *American Economic Review* 81 (September, 1991), 741–42.

37. Kessler-Harris, *Out to Work*, 276.

38. Gluck, *Rosie the Riveter Revisited*, 12.

39. Kessler-Harris, *Out to Work*, 278.

40. Karen Anderson, *Wartime Women: Sex Roles, Family Relations, and the Status of Women during World War II* (Westport, Conn.: Greenwood Press, 1981), 4. Anderson attributes 72.2 percent of the increase in working women between 1940 and 1944 to married women. Several scholars also note that it was during World War II that married women's labor force participation outnumbered single women's for the first time.

41. Displayed in Maureen Honey, *Creating Rosie the Riveter: Class, Gender, and Propaganda during World War II* (Amherst, Mass.: University of Massachusetts Press, 1984), 125.

42. Kessler-Harris, *Out to Work*, 288.

43. Anderson, *Wartime Women*, 59.

44. Sherri Kossoudji and Laura J. Dresser, "End of a Riveting Experience: Occupational Shifts at Ford after World War II," *American Economic Review* 82 (May 1992), 520.

45. See Benjamin Spock, *Baby and Child Care* (New York: Pocket Books, 1957), 569–70. See also description in Anderson, *Wartime Women*, 177.

46. Milkman, *Gender at Work*, 49–50.

47. Kossoudji and Dresser, "End of a Riveting Experience," 519; Anderson, *Wartime Women*, 166.

48. Koussoudji and Dresser, "End of a Riveting Experience," 525.

49. Anderson, *Wartime Women*, 146.

50. "Standards for Maternity Care and Employment of Mothers in Industry,"

(Washington, D.C.: United States Department of Labor, Women's and Children's Bureau, July 1942).

51. Charlotte Silverman, "Maternity Policies in Industry," *Child* 8, no. 2 (August 1943): 20–24. *Child* magazine was published by the Children's Bureau of the U.S. Department of Labor.

52. Frank Levy, *Dollars and Dreams: The Changing American Income Distribution* (New York: W.W. Norton, 1988), 47.

53. Stephanie Coontz, *The Way We Never Were: American Families and the Nostalgia Trap* (New York: Basic Books, 1992), 25.

54. Ibid., 43.

55. See Elaine Tyler May, "Cold-War, Warm Hearth: Politics and the Family in Post-War America," in *The Rise and Fall of the New Deal Order: 1930–1980*, ed. Steve Fraser and Gary Gerstle (Princeton, N.J.: Princeton University Press, 1989).

56. Coontz, *The Way We Never Were*, 38; Levy, *Dollars and Dreams*, 49.

57. Betty Friedan, *The Feminine Mystique* (New York: W.W. Norton, 1963).

58. See, for example, The National Organization for Women, "Statement of Purpose," reprinted in *Feminism in Our Time: The Essential Historical Writings, World War II to the Present*, ed. Miriam Schneir (New York: Vintage Books, 1994), 95–102.

59. *Statistical Abstract of the United States* 1993, table 633.

60. Felicity Barringer, "In Family-Leave Debate, A Profound Ambivalence," *New York Times*, October 7, 1992.

61. Levy, *Dollars and Dreams*, 100.

62. Juliet Schor, *The Overworked American: The Unexpected Decline of Leisure* (New York: Basic Books, 1992), 29. Schor estimates that between 1969 and 1987, men increased their paid work time by an average of 98 hours per year, while women increased their work time by 305 hours.

63. *Statistical Abstract of the United States* 1993, table 633.

64. "Report of the President's Commission on the Status of Women," in Schneir, *Feminism in Our Time*, 38–47.

65. Barbara Ryan, *Feminism and the Women's Movement: Dynamics of Change in Social Movement, Ideology, and Activism* (New York: Routledge, 1992), 42–44.

66. Meryl Frank and Robyn Lipner, "History of Maternity Leave in Europe and the United States," in *The Parental Leave Crisis: Toward a National Policy*, ed. Edward Ziegler and Meryl Frank (New Haven, Conn.: Yale University Press, 1988), 17.

67. "Prohibition of Sex Discrimination Based on Pregnancy," H. Rept. 95-948, together with Dissenting Views, to Accompany H.R. 6075, March 13, 1978.

68. *Geduldig v. Aiello*, 417 U.S. 484 (1974), at 496–497.

69. *Gilbert v. G.E.*, 429 U.S. 125 (1976).

70. See Jane Mansbridge, *Why We Lost the ERA* (Chicago: University of Chicago Press, 1986).

71. Joyce Gelb and Marian Lief Palley, "The Pregnancy Discrimination Act," in *Women and Public Policies*, ed. Joyce Gelb and Marian Lief Palley (Princeton, N.J.: Princeton University Press, rev. and exp. ed.,1987), 167–68.

72. Samuel Issacharoff and Elyse Rosenblum, "Women and the Workplace: Accommodating the Demands of Pregnancy," *Columbia Law Review* 94, no. 7 (November 1994): 2181.

73. "New Pregnancy Benefits and Discrimination Rules, with Explanation and State Survey" (Chicago, Ill.: Commerce Clearing House, 1978).

74. Vogel, *Mothers on the Job*, 55. See also Wendy Williams, "Equality's Riddle: Pregnancy and the Equal Treatment/Special Treatment Debate," *N.Y.U. Journal of Law and Social Change* 13 (1984–85): 325–80.

75. Quoted in Vogel, *Mothers on the Job*, 75. See also Williams, "Equality's Riddle"; and Herma Hill Kay, "Equality and Difference: The Case of Pregnancy," *Berkeley Women's Law Journal* 1, no. 1 (Fall 1985): 1–38.

76. Quoted in Vogel, *Mothers on the Job*, 85. Also see Ronald Elving, *Conflict and Compromise: How Congress Makes the Law* (New York: Simon and Schuster, 1995). This debate will be more fully explicated in the chapter on the federal process.

77. Vogel, *Mothers on the Job*, 81. Also Elving, *Conflict and Compromise*; and Issacharoff and Rosenblum, "Women and the Workplace."

78. See Vogel, *Mothers on the Job*, 55. Key works in this genre include Nancy Chodorow, *The Reproduction of Mothering: Psychoanalysis and the Sociology of Gender* (Berkeley, Cal.: University of California Press, 1978) (cited by Williams, "Equality's Riddle," 355); Simone DeBeauvoir, *The Second Sex* (New York: Alfred A. Knopf, 1952), especially chaps. 1, 27; Shulamith Firestone, *The Dialectic of Sex* (New York: William Morrow, 1970).

79. Quoted in Williams, *Equality's Riddle*, 359.

80. Vogel, *Mothers on the Job*, 108–09. See also Williams, *Equality's Riddle*.

81. *California Federal Savings and Loan Association v. Guerra*, 479 U.S. 272 (1987),

82. Gelb and Palley, *Women and Public Policies*, 8.

CHAPTER THREE

1. Larson ran for governor of Connecticut in 1994. He lost in the primary, and interestingly, several respondents believed that he lost because he was not attractive to the left wing of the Connecticut Democratic party. But four years later, in 1998, Larson made a successful run for Congress; his campaign literature highlighted his success in passing Connecticut's Family and Medical Leave Act.

2. Cecilia Woods, interview by author, Hartford, Conn., June 21, 1995.

3. See R. Douglas Arnold, *The Logic of Congressional Action* (New Haven, Conn.: Yale University Press, 1990).

4. Frank Baumgartner and Bryan D. Jones, "Agenda Dynamics and Policy Subsystems," *Journal of Politics* 53 (1991): 1044–74.

5. See Roberta Spalter-Roth and Ronnee Schreiber, "Outsider Issues and Insider Tactics: Strategic Tensions in the Women's Policy Network during the 1980s," in *Feminist Organizations: Harvest of the New Women's Movement*, ed. Myra Marx Ferree and Patricia Yancey Martin (Philadelphia: Temple University Press, 1990); Joan Hulse Thompson, "The Family and Medical Leave Act: A Policy for Families," in *Women and Politics: Have Outsiders Become Insiders?* ed. Lois Duke (New York: Prentice Hall, 1993).

6. The three businesses represented in this category were the Aetna Insurance Company, Champion International Paper Company, and the Southern New England Telephone Company.

7. Woods interview.

8. John Larson, interview by author, Hartford, Conn., June 26, 1995.

9. Mary Jane Gibson, interview by author, Eastham, Mass., May 13, 1995.

10. Several participants noted to me that by its nature as a committee that traditionally comprised half business supporters and half labor supporters, Commerce and Labor was going to be hostile to bills like paid family and medical leave. One suggested that Gibson should have tried to word the bill in such a way that it would have been received first by another committee.

11. There were many such companies in Massachusetts even as early as the mid-1980s. My respondents most commonly mentioned Stride Rite, Polaroid, and Raytheon. Discussions with human resource and public relations directors in these companies during the summer of 1995 revealed that some were approached about testifying, but did not.

12. A number of proponents ascribed this to the fact that most unions are still dominated by men and also noted that unions have fewer incentives to support family and medical leave because these policies can often be won through collective bargaining. However, as described in chapter 5, the national AFL-CIO became a strong supporter of family and medical leave once it realized that the bill could be a powerful weapon in the Democrats' arsenal. The current effort to pass a paid family leave act in Massachusetts is supported by the state AFL-CIO, which views the effort as one way to build its credibility among young workers. This will be described in chapter 6.

13. Kingdon, *Agendas, Alternatives, and Public Policies*, 139–43.

14. Ibid., 127–31.

15. See Skocpol, *Protecting Soldiers and Mothers*.

16. The states that preceded Connecticut in the enactment of private-sector family and medical leave (as opposed to maternity leave) laws were as follows: Minnesota, covering employers of twenty-one or more for six weeks; Maine, covering employers of twenty-five or more for eight weeks (later expanded to eighteen weeks); Oregon, covering employers of twenty-five or more for twelve weeks; Washington, covering employers of 100 or more for twelve weeks; and Wisconsin, covering employers of fifty or more for eight weeks (all within a one-year period).

17. Admittedly, the passage of the national Family and Medical Leave Act, which occurred in 1993, covers employers of fifty or more people in Connecticut as well as elsewhere. And since the passage of the FMLA, no state has lowered its business-size threshold.

18. Sara Evans discusses the role of the women's movement in transforming formerly personal issues into public ones in *Personal Politics: The Roots of Women's Liberation in the Civil Rights Movement and the New Left* (New York: Vintage Books, 1984).

19. See Barbara Nelson's discussion of the transformation of child abuse from a private to a public issue in *Making an Issue of Child Abuse* (Chicago: University of Chicago Press, 1984).

20. For a discussion of policy feedbacks, see chapter 1.

21. Mansbridge, *Why We Lost the ERA*, 188.

Chapter Four

1. See V. O. Key, *Southern Politics in State and Nation* (New York: Alfred A. Knopf, 1949); Daniel J. Elazar, *American Federalism: The View from the States*, 3rd ed. (New York: Harper and Row, 1984); Earl Black and Merle Black, *Politics and Society in the South* (Cambridge, Mass.: Harvard University Press, 1987).

2. I code Tennessee's law as a family and medical leave law because it goes beyond maternity disability to cover leave for "bonding" between a mother and child.

3. As noted earlier, when asked to compare Tennessee with North Carolina, most respondents who rated Tennessee as progressive also thought that North Carolina had a progressive tradition. They made frequent references to the recent refusal of both Tennessee and North Carolina to provide massive subsidies to companies to relocate to their state even as neighboring South Carolina and Alabama had done so.

4. See discussion in Vogel, *Mothers on the Job*, 88. Vogel quotes Justice Marshall: "Congress intended the PDA to be a 'floor beneath which pregnancy disability benefits may not drop—not a ceiling above which they may not rise.'"

5. See, for example, comments by Senator Hicks, Tennessee House of Representatives, Commerce Committee Hearing, April 21, 1987.

6. Mary Frances Lyle, interview by author, Nashville, Tenn., January 8, 1996. After passing the "bonding bill" in 1987, the advocates went back in 1988 and successfully changed the language of the bill to define it as leave for giving birth and nursing.

7. Betty Anderson, interview by author, Nashville, Tenn., January 11, 1996.

8. Ned McWherter, telephone interview by author, February 2, 1996.

9. See text of H.B. 1182, "The Tennessee Job Protection Act," 1987.

10. Lyle, telephone interview by author, June 12, 1996.

11. Debate in the House Committee on Calendar and Rules, Tennessee House of Representatives, April 14, 1987.

12. This is another example of Skocpol's concept of "fit" between group capacities and political opportunities.

13. See Key, *Southern Politics*; and Paul Luebke, *Tar Heel Politics: Myths and Realities* (Chapel Hill, N.C.: University of North Carolina Press, 1990). Luebke argues that North Carolina politics is characterized by tension between "modernizers," who see change as an opportunity for prosperity, and "traditionalists," who fear the disruption that accompanies change. He observes that issues like day care are affected by this tension; it follows that the debate over family and medical leave is as well.

14. See Donald Mathews and Jane Sherron DeHart, *Sex, Gender, and the Politics of the ERA: A State and a Nation* (New York: Oxford University Press, 1990).

15. Also see Luebke, *Tar Heel Politics*, chapter 6.

16. Chris Scott, president of the North Carolina AFL-CIO, interview by author, Raleigh, North Carolina, March 27, 1996.

17. Family and Medical Leave Coalition, North Carolina. Minutes of meeting, December 3, 1992.

18. Chris Fitzsimon, former press secretary to Speaker Dan Blue, interview by author, Raleigh, North Carolina, March 25, 1996.

19. Annie Brown Kennedy, interview by author, Winston-Salem, N.C., March 29, 1996.

20. Ibid.

21. These are what James Q. Wilson labels distributed benefits and concentrated costs. See *Political Organizations*, 2nd ed., rev. (Princeton: Princeton University Press, 1995), chapter 16.

22. At the time I was conducting interviews in Tennessee, the legislature there was debating its own "drive-through-deliveries" legislation. Respondents in Tennessee repeatedly made analogies between the Tennessee maternity leave bill and the drive-through-deliveries legislation.

23. See James Q. Wilson, *The Politics of Regulation* (New York: Basic Books, 1980), chapter 10.

24. Kennedy interview.

25. Kingdon, *Agendas, Alternatives, and Public Policies*.

26. Ibid.

CHAPTER FIVE

1. *Geduldig v. Aiello* 417 U.S. 484 (1974); *Gilbert v. G.E.*, 429 U.S. 125 (1976).

2. See Vogel, *Mothers on the Job*.

3. Ronald Elving notes that Donna Lenhoff of the Women's Legal Defense Fund, who eventually became the leader of the coalition that supported the passage of the Family and Medical Leave Act, periodically convened "the PDA [Pregnancy Discrimination Act] alumni association." Discussions held by these groups eventually led to the movement for family and medical leave. See Ronald Elving, *Conflict and Compromise: How Congress Makes the Law* (New York: Touchstone Books, 1995), 20.

4. Ibid. Elving's excellent history of the passage of the Family and Medical Leave Act serves as a basis for much of the following description. In the process of interviewing many of the same participants in order to develop an explanation for the role of interest group resources and strategy, I have corroborated many of his findings and filled in gaps left by his analysis.

5. Ibid., 51–52.

6. It should be noted, however, that the Children's Defense Fund was primarily concerned that family and medical leave would detract from efforts to pass the ABC (Act for Better Child Care Services) child care bill, which was introduced in Congress in 1987. The fact that the Family and Medical Leave Act was not a strong bill was of secondary importance. See Mary Frances Berry, *The Politics of Parenthood: Child Care, Women's Rights, and the Myth of the Good Mother* (New York: Viking, 1993), chapter 8.

7. See Jane Mansbridge, *Why We Lost the ERA* (Chicago: University of Chicago Press, 1986); Thomas Gais and Jack L. Walker Jr., "Pathways to Influence in American Politics," in *Mobilizing Interest Groups in America: Patrons, Professions, and Social Movements*, ed. Jack L. Walker Jr. (Ann Arbor, Mich.: University of Michigan Press, 1991).

8. Thomas Shellabarger, interview by author, Washington, D.C., May 17, 1996.

9. Donna Lenhoff, interview by author, Washington, D.C., May 14, 1996.

10. Quoted in Elving, *Conflict and Compromise,* 178.

11. Lenhoff interview.

12. See discussion in Elving, *Conflict and Compromise,* 194–95.

13. See James T. Bond and others, *Beyond the Parental Leave Debate: The Impact of Laws in Four States* (New York: The Families and Work Institute, 1991).

14. John Motley, interview by author, Washington, D.C., May 14, 1996.

15. *Congressional Quarterly Almanac* 1989: 348.

16. Elving, *Conflict and Compromise,* 222–26; Lenhoff interview.

17. Quote from Democratic pollster Celinda Lake, cited in Elving, *Conflict and Compromise,* 257.

18. Kim Gandy, interview by author, Washington, D.C., May 13, 1996.

19. Lenhoff interview.

20. Kingdon, *Agendas, Alternatives, and Public Policies.*

21. See "Clinton Is Asking Congress to Expand the Family Leave Law," *New York Times,* February 2, 1997.

22. R. Douglas Arnold, *The Logic of Congressional Action* (New Haven: Yale University Press, 1990), 110.

23. *New State Ice Company v. Liebmann,* 285 U.S. 262 (1937). Quoted in Eileen Lorenzi McDonagh, "Representative Democracy and State Building in the Progressive Era," *American Political Science Review* 86 (December 1992): 946.

24. Bond and others, *Beyond the Parental Leave Debate.*

25. Roberta Spalter-Roth and Heidi Hartmann, *Unnecessary Losses: Costs to Americans of the Lack of Family and Medical Leave* (Washington, D.C.: The Institute for Women's Policy Research, 1990).

26. Pamela A. Monroe, James C. Garand, and Holly Teeters, "Family Leave Legislation in the U.S. House: Voting on the Family and Medical Leave Act of 1990," *Family Relations* 44 (1995): 46–55.

27. See Peterson and Rom, *Welfare Magnets;* Peterson, *The Price of Federalism.*

Chapter Six

1. Because far more people have access to paid medical leave through their employers than have paid family leave, most of the proposed state legislation specifically provides paid "family" rather than "family and medical" leave.

2. See, for example, Weir, Orloff, and Skocpol, eds., *The Politics of Social Policy in the United States;* Skocpol, *Protecting Soldiers and Mothers;* Pierson, "'Policy Feedbacks' and Political Change"; Pierson, *Dismantling the Welfare State?*

3. Skocpol, *Protecting Soldiers and Mothers,* introduction.

4. See discussions in Martha Derthick, *Policymaking for Social Security* (Washington, D.C.: Brookings Institution, 1979); Edward Berkowitz, *Social Security after Fifty: Successes and Failures* (Westport, Conn.: Greenwood Press, 1987).

5. See, for example, Day, *What Older Americans Think.*

6. Skocpol, *Protecting Soldiers and Mothers,* 59.

7. For example, Maine's law covers employers of twenty-five or more people,

while Vermont's law covers employers of ten or more people. No states mandate paid family leave.

8. The only exception to this is Minnesota, which provides a small subsidy to parents who stay home with their young children. This subsidy is provided through the tax code, however, and bears little relationship to any of the proposed paid family and medical leaves.

9. Commission on Family and Medical Leave, *A Workable Balance*.

10. Ibid., table 5a.

11. Monica Halas, Testimony before the Joint Committee on Commerce and Labor, Massachusetts State House, April 7, 1999.

12. Felicity Barringer, "In Family-Leave Debate, a Profound Ambivalence," *New York Times*, October 7, 1992.

13. "Family Matters: A National Survey of Women and Men," conducted for the National Partnership for Women and Families by Lake, Sosin, Snell, Perry, and Associates, January 28–February 1, 1998. These statistics are also reflected in a poll of working families conducted by the AFL-CIO in the summer of 1999. See Steven Greenhouse, "Asking Its Views, Labor Woos the Young," *New York Times*, September 1, 1999.

14. It is worth noting that this is similar to the situation experienced by advocates for national health insurance in 1994. At the time, while many Americans lacked health insurance or feared that they would lose it, most people were satisfied with their coverage. These people were susceptible to charges made by opponents of the Clinton health plan that they stood to lose more than they might gain from any new plan. See Skocpol, "Targeting within Universalism."

15. Mindy Fried, *Taking Time: Parental Leave Policy and Corporate Culture* (Philadelphia: Temple University Press, 1998). Fried's discussion of the "overtime culture" is on 33–39.

16. Juliet Schor, *The Overworked American: The Unexpected Decline of Leisure* (New York: Basic Books, 1991).

17. Sue Shellenbarger, *Work and Family: Essays from the "Work and Family" Column of the Wall Street Journal* (New York: Ballentine Books, 1999).

18. Fried, *Taking Time*, 184.

19. Reported in *The National Report on Work and Family*, 12, no. 6 (March 23, 1999), 43.

20. Elinor Burkett, *The Baby Boon: How Family-Friendly America Cheats the Childless* (New York: The Free Press, 2000).

21. Donna Lenhoff, telephone interview by author, June 23, 1999.

22. Melody Petersen, "Bill Is Introduced to Provide Paid Time Off for Family Leave," *New York Times*, May 23, 1997.

23. Lenhoff interview, June 23, 1999.

24. The unemployment surplus bills would label a worker "unemployed" during the time that he or she was out of work, but, unlike other unemployment situations, the worker would not be able to come back for a specified period of time.

25. Kathleen Casavant, secretary-treasurer of the Massachusetts AFL-CIO, interview by author, Boston, Mass., September 10, 1999.

26. See Greenhouse, "Asking Its Views"; and Steven Greenhouse, "Poll of Working Women Finds Them Stressed," *New York Times*, March 10, 2000.

27. Family Leave Coalition, March 3, 2000, Meeting Minutes and Action Steps Needed. Document prepared by the Women's Statewide Legislative Network, March 2000.

28. State senator Lisa Brown, telephone interview by author, September 28, 1999.

29. John Burbank, executive director of the Economic Policy Institute, telephone interview by author, July 13, 1999.

30. Brown interview.

31. Jody Heymann and Alison Earle, "The Impact of Welfare Reform on Parents' Ability to Care for Their Children's Health," *American Journal of Public Health* 89, no. 4 (April 1999): 502–05.

32. See, for example, Sidney Verba, Kay Lehman Schlozman, and Henry Brady, *Voice and Equality: Civic Voluntarism in American Politics* (Cambridge, Mass.: Harvard University Press, 1995).

33. Burbank interview.

34. Kingdon, *Agendas, Alternatives, and Public Policies*, 94–100.

35. See Jerry Jasinowski [president, National Association of Manufacturers], "How Not to Help New Parents," *New York Times*, November 10, 1999. Also testimony by Richard Lord, executive vice president for legislative policy at Associated Industries of Massachusetts, and Kenneth T. Gear, vice president and counsel, Retailers Association of Massachusetts, before the Joint Committee on Commerce and Labor, Massachusetts Statehouse, April 7, 1999.

36. Mona Harrington, *Care and Equality: Inventing a New Family Politics* (New York: Alfred A. Knopf, 1999), p. 44.

37. First survey by the National Opinion Research Center-General Social Survey, 1994. Second by the Princeton Survey Research Associates for the Pew Research Center, March 14–26, 1997. Cited in *Public Perspective* 9, no. 2 February–March 1998).

38. Danielle Crittenden, "A Mother's Place Is . . ." *New York Times*, July 21, 1999.

39. Harrington, *Care and Equality*, p. 45.

40. See also discussion in Paula Rayman and Ann Bookman, "Creating a Research and Public Policy Agenda for Work, Family, and Community," *Annals of the American Association of Political and Social Science* 562 (March 1999), 191–211.

41. Conversation with Paula Rayman, director of the Radcliffe Public Policy Center, Cambridge, Mass., May 25, 1999.

CHAPTER SEVEN

1. See Deborah Stone, "Causal Stories and the Formation of Policy Agendas," *Political Science Quarterly* 104 (1989): 281–300. Also see Murray Edelman, *The Symbolic Uses of Politics* (Urbana, Ill.: University of Illinois Press, 1964).

2. See David Plotke, "The Political Mobilization of Business," in *The Politics of Interests: Interest Groups Transformed*, ed. Mark Petracca (Boulder, Col.: Westview

Press, 1992).

3. See John Kingdon, *Agendas, Alternatives, and Public Policies*, 2nd ed. (New York: Harper Collins, 1995), 94–100.

4. See, for example, Robert Pear, "Thousands to Rally in Capital on Children's Behalf," *New York Times*, May 31, 1996; and Pear, "Who Stands for Children," *New York Times*, June 1, 1996.

5. See Michael B. Katz, *In the Shadow of the Poorhouse: A Social History of Welfare in America* (New York: Basic Books, 1986); Linda Gordon, *Pitied but Not Entitled: Single Mothers and the History of Welfare* (New York: Free Press, 1994); Theda Skocpol, "Brother, Can You Spare a Job? Work and Welfare in the United States," in *Social Policy in the United States: Future Possibilities in Historical Perspective*, ed. Theda Skocpol (Princeton, N.J.: Princeton University Press, 1995).

6. Margaret Blood, "State Legislative Leaders: Keys to Effective Legislation for Children and Families" (Centerville, Mass.: State Legislative Leaders Foundation, 1995).

7. See Gilmour, *Strategic Disagreement*. Also see George Tsebelis, *Nested Games: Rational Choice in Comparative Politics* (Berkeley, Cal.: University of California Press, 1990), quoted in Gilmour.

8. See James Sundquist, "Needed: A Political Theory for the New Era of Coalition Government in the United States," *Political Science Quarterly* 10 (1988): 613–35; David Mayhew, *Divided We Govern: Party Control, Lawmaking, and Investigations 1946–1990* (New Haven: Yale University Press, 1991); Fiorina, *Divided Government*.

9. Michael Laver and Kenneth A. Shepsle, "Divided Government: America Is Not Exceptional," *Governance* 4 (1991): 250–69, quoted in Fiorina, *Divided Government*. The difference, of course, is that each party controls one branch of a divided government while all the parties in a coalition together control the entire government. Fiorina states: "The contrast is real, but the larger similarity is important: in both cases each party needs the acquiescence of others in order to govern." Ibid., 113.

10. Commission on Family and Medical Leave, *A Workable Balance*.

11. *A Workable Balance* included numerous examples of people whose lives were improved as a result of their access to family and medical leave. And in a recent case that shows that not all of the benefits of family and medical leave have gone to working women, a Maryland state trooper was awarded $375,000 after being denied a leave to care for his newborn daughter because he is male. See Tamar Lewin, "Father Awarded $375,000 in Parental Leave Case," *New York Times*, February 5, 1999.

12. Commission on Family and Medical Leave, *A Workable Balance*, chapter 3.

13. Gilmour, *Strategic Disagreement*, 170.

14. Christine Littleton, "Does It Still Make Sense to Talk about 'Women?'" *UCLA Women's Law Journal* 15 (1991).

15. The Congressional Leave study found that women take 58.2 percent of all family and medical leaves. Commission on Family and Medical Leave, *A Workable Balance*, table 5a.

16. Max Weber, "Politics as a Vocation," in *From Max Weber: Essays in Sociol-*

ogy, trans. and ed. H. H. Gerth and C. Wright Mills (New York: Oxford University Press, 1946), esp. 120–28.

17. Ibid., 128.

18. Hugh Heclo, "Social Policy and Policy Learning," in *Modern Social Policies in Britain and Sweden*, ed. Hugh Heclo (New Haven: Yale University Press, 1974). See also Pierson, *Dismantling the Welfare State?* 40–42.

19. Donna Lenhoff, interview by author, Washington, D.C., May 14, 1996.

20. Eleanor Smeal, telephone interview by author, June 21, 1996.

21. One possible explanation for this is that the advocates for paid family leave in Massachusetts learned from the experience of their predecessors who had failed in the 1980s. However, none of the advocates from that first effort are involved in the current effort, and in interviews, the leaders of the current coalition expressed little knowledge of the 1980s effort.

Appendix One

1. This technique is called "snowballing." See Robert S. Weiss, *Learning from Strangers: The Art and Method of Qualitative Interview Studies* (New York: Macmillan, 1994).

2. Several potential respondents could not be reached. For example, one key state staff member had passed away, while another had moved out of the country. Several people were incapacitated at the time they were contacted.

3. The six original interviews were not taped because of technical difficulties such as the presence of too much background noise. Due to technical difficulties, none of the follow-up interviews could be taped.

SUGGESTIONS FOR FURTHER READING

Amenta, Edwin, Elisabeth S. Clemens, Jefren Olsen, Sunita Parikh, and Theda Skocpol. "The Political Origins of Unemployment Insurance in Five American States." *Studies in American Political Development* 2 (1987): 137–82.

Anderson, Karen. *Wartime Women: Sex Roles, Family Relations, and the Status of Women during World War II*. Westport, Conn.: Greenwood Press, 1981.

Arnold, R. Douglas. *The Logic of Congressional Action*. New Haven, Conn.: Yale University Press, 1990.

Bachrach, Peter, and Morton Baratz. "The Two Faces of Power." *American Political Science Review* 56 (1962): 947–52.

Baker, Paula. "The Domestication of Politics: Women and American Political Society, 1780–1920." *American Historical Review* 89 (June 1984): 620–47. Also in *Women, the State, and Welfare*, edited by Linda Gordon. Madison, Wis.: University of Wisconsin Press, 1990.

Banaszak, Lee Ann. *Why Movements Succeed or Fail: Opportunity, Culture, and the Struggle for Woman Suffrage*. Princeton, N.J.: Princeton University Press, 1996.

Barnett, W. Steven, and Gerald L. Musgrave. "The Economic Impact of Mandated Family Leave on Small Businesses and Their Employees." Washington: NFIB Foundation, 1991.

Barringer, Felicity. "In Family-Leave Debate, a Profound Ambivalence." *New York Times*, October 7, 1992.

Bauer, Gary. "Little Time, No Money, and Few Options: The Empty Symbolism of the Family and Medical Leave Act." Testimony before the Education and Labor Committee, U.S. House of Representatives, Washington, D.C., February 28, 1991.

Baumgartner, Frank R., and Bryan D. Jones. "Agenda Dynamics and Policy Subsystems." *Journal of Politics* 53 (1991): 1044–74.

———. *Agendas and Instability in American Politics*. Chicago: University of Chicago Press, 1993.

Berkowitz, Edward. *Social Security after Fifty: Successes and Failures*. Westport, Conn.: Greenwood Press, 1987.

———. *Mr. Social Security: The Life of Wilbur J. Cohen*. Lawrence, Kans.: University Press of Kansas, 1995.

Berman, Congressman Howard L. "Author of California Pregnancy Law Declares Support for National Family and Medical Leave Act." Press Release. Washington, D.C., February 25, 1987.

Bernardin, Joseph Cardinal. Testimony on S. 249, The Parental and Medical Leave Act of 1987, before the Subcommittee on Children, Family, Drugs, and Alcoholism, Committee on Labor and Human Resources, United States Senate, Chicago, Ill., September 14, 1987.

Berry, Mary Frances. *The Politics of Parenthood: Child Care, Women's Rights, and the Myth of the Good Mother.* New York: Viking, 1993.

Biles, Roger. *A New Deal For the American People.* DeKalb, Ill.: Northern Illinois University Press, 1991.

"Bill Would Require Granting Leave to Employees." *Memphis Business Journal,* January 21, 1991.

Black, Earl, and Merle Black. *Politics and Society in the South.* Cambridge, Mass.: Harvard University Press, 1987.

Blood, Margaret. *State Legislative Leaders: Keys to Effective Legislation for Children and Families.* Centerville, Mass.: State Legislative Leaders Foundation, 1995.

Bond, James T., Ellen Galinsky, Michele Lord, Graham L. Staines, and Karen R. Brown. *Beyond the Parental Leave Debate: The Impact of Laws in Four States.* New York: The Families and Work Institute, 1991.

Bond, James T., Ellen Galinsky, and Jennifer E. Swanberg., *The 1997 National Study of the Changing Workforce.* New York: The Families and Work Institute, 1997.

Bookman, Ann. "Parenting without Poverty: The Case for Funded Parental Leave." In *Parental Leave and Child Care: Setting A Research and Policy Agenda,* edited by Janet Shibley Hyde and Marilyn J. Essex. Philadelphia: Temple University Press, 1991.

Brinkley, Alan. "The Idea of the State." In *The Rise and Fall of the New Deal Order: 1930-1980,* edited by Steve Fraser and Gary Gerstle. Princeton, N.J.: Princeton University Press, 1989.

Broder, John M. "Clinton Proposes Using Surpluses to Extend Family Leave Benefits." *New York Times,* May 24, 1999.

Bureau of the Census. *Statistics of Women at Work, Based on Unpublished Information Derived from the Schedules of the Twelfth Census, 1900.* Washington, D.C.: U.S. Government Printing Office, 1907.

Burkett, Elinor. *The Baby Boon: How Family-Friendly America Cheats the Childless.* New York: The Free Press, 2000.

Bush Center in Child Development and Social Policy, Yale University. *Issues of Parental Leave: Its Practice, Availability, and Future Feasibility in the State of Connecticut.* Report to the Connecticut Task Force to Study Work and Family Roles, 1988.

California Federal Savings and Loan Association v. Guerra, 479 U.S. 272 (1987).

Chira, Susan. "New Realities Fight Old Images of Mother." *New York Times,* October 4, 1992.

Chodorow, Nancy. *The Reproduction of Mothering: Psychoanalysis and the Sociology of Gender.* Berkeley, Cal.: University of California Press, 1978.

"Clinton Is Asking Congress to Expand the Family Leave Law." *New York Times,* February 2, 1997.

Cnudde, Charles F., and Donald J. McCrone. "Party Competition and Welfare Policies in the American States." *American Political Science Review* 63 (September 1969): 858–66.

Cobb, Roger W., and Charles D. Elder. *Participation in America: The Dynamics of Agenda-Building.* Boston: Allyn and Bacon, 1972.

Commerce Committee Hearing Transcript, Tennessee House of Representatives, April 21, 1987.

Commission on the Family, State of North Carolina. "Report to the 1991 General Assembly of North Carolina." Raleigh, N.C.: January 31, 1991.

———. "Report to the 1993 General Assembly of North Carolina." Raleigh, N.C.: January 27, 1993.

Committee on Calendar and Rules, Tennessee House of Representatives. Debate on HB 1002, April 14, 1987.

Committee on Education and Labor, United States House of Representatives. "The Family and Medical Leave Act of 1989." Report together with Minority, Supplemental, Additional, and Individual Views. 101st Congress, 1st session, 1989. Report 101-28, Part I.

Congressional Caucus for Women's Issues. *The Family and Medical Leave Act.* Washington, D.C.: CCWis., October 1992.

Congressional Quarterly Almanac 1989.

Connecticut General Assembly. The Task Force to Study Work and Family Roles and Parental and Medical Leave in the Private Sector. Minutes of meetings, Hartford, Conn.: October 29, 1987, November 30, 1987, January 5, 1988, February 1, 1988, March 1, 1988.

Connecticut House of Representatives, Transcript of Floor Debate, June 6, 1989.

Connecticut Senate. Transcript of Floor Debate, April 19, 1989.

"Connecticut Legislature Reviews Law Requiring Employers to Grant Family Leave." *Bureau of National Affairs, Pension and Benefits Reporter,* February 6, 1989.

Coonz, Stephanie. *The Way We Never Were: American Families and the Nostalgia Trap.* New York: Basic Books, 1992.

Cott, Nancy. *The Bonds of Womanhood: "Women's Sphere" in New England, 1780–1835.* New Haven, Conn.: Yale University Press, 1977.

———. *The Grounding of Modern Feminism.* New Haven, Conn.: Yale University Press, 1987.

Crittenden, Danielle. "A Mother's Place Is . . ." *New York Times,* July 21, 1999.

Daily Labor Report, August 3, 1989.

Dawson, Richard E., and James A. Robinson. "Interparty Competition, Economic Variables, and Welfare Policies in the American States." *Journal of Politics* 25 (May 1963): 265–89.

Day, Christine. *What Older Americans Think: Interest Groups and Aging Policy.* Princeton, N.J.: Princeton University Press, 1990.

DeBeauvoir, Simone. *The Second Sex.* New York: Alfred A. Knopf, 1952.

Degler, Carl. *At Odds: Women and the Family in America from the Revolution to the Present*. New York: Oxford University Press, 1980.

Democratic National Committee. "President Bill Clinton and Democrats: Standing up for Children and Families." Washington, D.C.: DNC, 1996.

Derthick, Martha. *Policymaking for Social Security*. Washington, D.C.: Brookings Institution, 1979.

Dervarics, Chris. "Family Leave: Is It Good for Business?" *State Legislatures*, August 1991.

Dodson, Debra L., Susan J. Carroll, Ruth B. Mandel, Katherine E. Kleeman, Ronnee Schreiber, and Debra Liebowitz. *Voices, Views, and Votes: The Impact of Women in the 103rd Congress*. New Brunswick, N.J.: Center for the American Woman and Politics, Eagleton Institute of Politics, Rutgers University, 1995.

Dye, Thomas. *Politics, Economics, and the Public: Policy Outcomes In the American States*. Chicago: Rand McNally, 1966.

———. *American Federalism: Competition among Governments*. Lexington, Mass.: D.C. Heath, 1990.

Edelman, Murray. *The Symbolic Uses of Politics*. Urbana, Ill.: University of Illinois Press, 1964.

Elving, Ronald D. *Conflict and Compromise: How Congress Makes the Law*. New York: Simon and Schuster, 1995.

Epstein, Barbara Leslie. *The Politics of Domesticity: Women, Evangelism, and Temperance in Nineteenth Century America*. Middletown, Conn.: Wesleyan University Press, 1981.

Erikson, Robert S., Gerald C. Wright, and John P. McIver. *Statehouse Democracy: Public Opinion and Policy in the American States*. New York: Cambridge University Press, 1993.

Evans, Sara M. *Personal Politics: The Roots of Women's Liberation in the Civil Rights Movement and the New Left*. New York: Vintage Books, 1984.

Family and Medical Leave Coalition, North Carolina. Minutes of Meeting, September 24, 1992.

———. Minutes of Meeting, December 3, 1992.

"Family and Medical Leave Policy." *Congressional Digest* 67:3, May 1988.

"Family and Medical Leave Legislation." *Congressional Digest* 72:1, January 1993.

Family and Workplace Committee, State of Connecticut. Hearing, March 12, 1987.

Family Leave Coalition, Massachusetts. March 3, 2000. Meeting Minutes and Action Steps Needed.

Family Leave Coalition, Massachusetts. June 4, 1999. Meeting Minutes.

Family Matters: A New Survey of Women and Men. Conducted for the National Partnership for Women and Families by Lake, Sosin, Snell, Perry, and Associates, January 28–February 1, 1998.

Finn-Stevenson, Matia, and Eileen Trzcinski. "Mandated Leave: An Analysis of Federal and State Legislation." *American Journal of Orthopsychiatry* 61 (October 1991): 567–75.

Fiorina, Morris. *Congress: Keystone of the Washington Establishment*. New Haven, Conn.: Yale University Press, 1977.

———. *Divided Government*. New York: Macmillan, 1992.

Firestone, Shulamith. *The Dialectic of Sex*. New York: William Morrow, 1970.

Flexner, Eleanor. *A Century of Struggle: The Women's Rights Movement in the United States*, rev. ed. Cambridge, Mass.: The Belknap Press of Harvard University Press, 1975.

FMLA Coalition. "Grassroots Activities: 'Adopt a State' Campaign." Memo to Family and Medical Leave Activists. Washington, D.C.: Women's Legal Defense Fund, December 13, 1990.

Fried, Mindy. *Taking Time: Parental Leave Policy and Corporate Culture*. Philadelphia: Temple University Press, 1998.

Friedan, Betty. *The Feminine Mystique*. New York: W. W. Norton, 1963.

Gais, Thomas, and Jack L. Walker Jr. "Pathways to Influence in American Politics." In *Mobilizing Interest Groups in America: Patrons, Professions, and Social Movements*, edited by Jack L. Walker Jr. Ann Arbor, Mich.: University of Michigan Press, 1991.

Galinsky, Ellen, and James T. Bond. *The 1998 Business Work-Life Study: A Sourcebook*. New York: The Families and Work Institute, 1998.

Gamson, William. *The Strategy of Social Protest*. Homewood, Ill.: Dorsey Press, 1975.

Garand, James C., and Pamela A. Monroe. "Family Leave Legislation in the American States: Toward a Model of State Policy Adoption." *Journal of Family and Economic Issues* 16, no. 4 (Winter 1995): 341–63.

Gaventa, John. *Power and Powerlessness: Quiescence and Rebellion in an Appalachian Valley*. Chicago: University of Chicago Press, 1980.

Gear, Kenneth T. Testimony before the Joint Committee on Commerce and Labor, Massachusetts Statehouse, April 7, 1999.

Geduldig v. Aiello, 417 U.S. 484 (1974).

Gelb, Joyce, and Marian Lief Palley. *Women and Public Policies*. Revised and expanded edition. Princeton, N.J.: Princeton University Press, 1987.

Gibson, Mary Jane. "Employment Leave: Foundation for Family Policy." *New England Journal of Public Policy* 6 (1990): 209–16.

———. Testimony on H. 2191, Employment Leave Insurance. Commerce and Labor Committee, Massachusetts House of Representatives, April 8, 1991.

General Electric Company v. Gilbert 429 U.S. 125 (1976).

Gilman, Charlotte Perkins. *Women and Economics*. New York: Harper and Row, 1966.

Gilmour, John B. *Strategic Disagreement: Stalemate in American Politics*. Pittsburgh, Pa.: University of Pittsburgh Press, 1995.

Gladstone, Leslie W. "Family and Medical Leave Legislation." Congressional Research Service Issue Brief. Washington, D.C.: Congressional Research Service, 1993.

Gluck, Sherna Berger. *Rosie the Riveter Revisited: Women, the War, and Social Change*. Boston: Twayne Publishers, 1987.

Goldin, Claudia. *Understanding the Gender Gap: An Economic History of American Women*. New York: Oxford University Press, 1990.

————. "The Role of World War II in the Rise in Women's Employment." *American Economic Review* 81 (September 1991): 741–56.

Gordon, Linda. *Pitied but Not Entitled: Single Mothers and the History of Welfare.* New York: Free Press, 1994.

"Governor Signs Bill Broadening Leave Policy for State Workers." *Hartford Courant,* May 21, 1987.

Greater Boston Legal Services and the National Employment Law Project. "Memorandum in Support of Massachusetts Bill Amending Its Unemployment Compensation Law to Include Eligibility for Family and Medical Leave." March 15, 1999.

————. "An Analysis of Federal Law, State Precedents, and Public Policy Considerations Supporting the Use of the Unemployment Insurance System for Partial Wage Replacement During Family and Medical Leave." July 16, 1999.

Greenhouse, Steven. "Asking Its Views, Labor Woos the Young." *New York Times,* September 1, 1999.

————. "Poll of Working Women Finds Them Stressed." *New York Times,* March 10, 2000.

Greenstein, Robert. "Universal and Targeted Approaches to Relieving Poverty: An Alternative View." In *The Urban Underclass,* edited by Christopher Jencks and Paul Peterson. Washington, D.C.: Brookings Institution, 1991.

Halas, Monica. Testimony before the Joint Committee on Commerce and Labor, Massachusetts Statehouse, April 7, 1999.

Harrington, Mona. *Care and Equality: Inventing a New Family Politics.* New York: Alfred A. Knopf, 1999.

Hartmann, Heidi I. "Costs to Women and Their Families of Childbirth and Lack of Parental Leave." Testimony before the Subcommittee on Children, Families, Drugs, and Alcoholism, Committee on Labor and Human Resources, U.S. Senate, Washington, D.C., October 29, 1987.

Hartmann, Heidi I., and Roberta M. Spalter-Roth. "Family and Medical Leave: Who Pays for the Lack of It?" Washington, D.C.: The Women's Research and Education Institute, 1989.

Hartmann, Susan M. *From Margin to Mainstream: American Women and Politics since 1960.* Philadelphia: Temple University Press, 1989.

Heclo, Hugh. *Modern Social Policies in Britain and Sweden.* New Haven, Conn.: Yale University Press, 1974.

Heymann, Jody, and Alison Earle. "The Impact of Welfare Reform on Parents' Ability to Care for Their Children's Health." *American Journal of Public Health* 89, no. 4 (April 1999): 502–05.

Hofferbert, Richard I. "The Relation between Public Policy and Some Structural and Environmental Variables in the American States." *American Political Science Review* 60 (March 1966): 73–82.

Honey, Maureen. *Creating Rosie the Riveter: Class, Gender, and Propaganda during World War II.* Amherst, Mass.: University of Massachusetts Press, 1984.

House Committee on Calendar and Rules, Tennessee House of Representatives. Debate, April 14, 1987.

Hunter, James Davison. *Culture Wars: The Struggle to Define America*. New York: Basic Books, 1991.

Issacharoff, Samuel, and Elyse Rosenblum. "Women and the Workplace: Accommodating the Demands of Pregnancy." *Columbia Law Review* 94, no. 7 (November 1994): 2154–221.

Jasinowski, Jerry. "How Not to Help New Parents." *New York Times*, November 10, 1999.

Jenkins, J. Craig. "Resource Mobilization Theory and the Study of Social Movements." *American Review of Sociology* 9 (1983): 527–53.

Johnson, Kirk. "Family Leave Is Advancing in Connecticut." *New York Times*, February 20, 1989.

Kammerman, Sheila B., Alfred J. Kahn, and Paul Kingston. *Maternity Policies and Working Women*. New York: Columbia University Press, 1983.

Katz, Michael. *In the Shadow of the Poorhouse: A Social History of Welfare in America*. New York: Basic Books, 1986.

Kay, Herma Hill. "Equality and Difference: The Case of Pregnancy." *Berkeley Women's Law Journal* 1, no 1 (Fall 1985): 1–38.

Kessler-Harris, Alice. *Out to Work: A History of Wage-Earning Women in the United States*. New York: Oxford University Press, 1982.

———. *A Woman's Wage: Historical Meanings and Social Consequence*. Lexington, Ky: University Press of Kentucky, 1990.

Key, V. O. *Southern Politics in State and Nation*. New York: Alfred A. Knopf, 1949.

Kingdon, John. *Agendas, Alternatives and Public Policies*. 2nd ed. New York: Harper Collins, 1995.

Kitschelt, Herbert P. "Political Opportunity Structures and Political Protest: Anti-Nuclear Movements in Four Democracies." *British Journal of Political Science* 16 (1986): 57–85.

Knox, Richard A. "Massachusetts Enacts Health Bill: Care-for-All Act Is First in Nation." *Boston Globe*, April 14, 1988.

Kossoudji, Sherrie, and Laura J. Dresser. "End of a Riveting Experience: Occupational Shifts at Ford after World War II." *American Economic Review* 82 (May 1992): 519–25.

Kreisi, Hanspeter. "The Political Opportunity Structure of New Social Movements: Its Impact on Their Mobilization." In *The Politics of Social Protest*, edited by J. Craig Jenkins and Bert Klandermans. Minneapolis. Minn.: University of Minnesota Press, 1995.

Krieger, Linda J., and Patricia N. Cooney. "The Miller-Wohl Controversy: Equal Treatment, Positive Action, and the Meaning of Women's Equality." *Golden Gate University Law Review* 13 (Summer 1983): 513–72.

Laver, Michael, and Kenneth A. Shepsle. "Divided Government: America Is Not Exceptional." *Governance* 4 (1991): 250–69.

"Legislative Priorities: 1995 Massachusetts Legislative Session." National Federation of Independent Businesses, Massachusetts chapter. Boston, Mass.: 1995.

Lenhoff, Donna. "Grassroots Call to Action." Memo to Family and Medical Leave Supporters. Washington, D.C.: Women's Legal Defense Fund, July 23, 1992.

———. "What It Took to Pass the Family and Medical Leave Act: A Nine-Year Campaign Pays Off." Pamphlet. Washington, D.C.: Women's Legal Defense Fund, August 18, 1994.

Levy, Frank. *Dollars and Dreams: The Changing American Income Distribution.* New York: W. W. Norton, 1988.

Lewin, Tamar. "Father Awarded $375,000 in Parental Leave Case." *New York Times,* February 5, 1999.

Lewis, Bill. "Family, Medical Leave Proposal Filed." *Nashville Business Journal,* January 21, 1991.

Lindblom, Charles. "The Science of Muddling Through." *Public Administration Review* 19 (1959): 79–88.

———. *Politics and Markets: The World's Political-Economic Systems.* New York: Basic Books, 1977.

———. "The Market as Prison." *Journal of Politics* 44 (1982): 324–36.

Littleton, Christine. "Does It Still Make Sense to Talk about Women?" *UCLA Women's Law Journal* 15 (1991).

Lochner v. New York, 198 U.S. 45 (1905).

Lord, Richard. Testimony before the Joint Committee on Commerce and Labor, Massachusetts Statehouse, April 7, 1999.

Loth, Renee. "From 'Women's' Issues to People's Issues." *Boston Globe,* February 21, 1988.

———. "Paid Leave Proposal Gains Friends, Foes." *Boston Globe,* April 11, 1989.

Luebke, Paul. *Tar Heel Politics: Myths and Realities.* Chapel Hill, N.C.: University of North Carolina Press, 1990.

Lukes, Steven. *Power: A Radical View.* New York: Macmillan, 1974.

Mansbridge, Jane. *Why We Lost the ERA.* Chicago: University of Chicago Press, 1986.

Mathews, Donald G., and Jane Sherron DeHart. *Sex Gender, and the Politics of ERA: A State and the Nation.* New York: Oxford University Press, 1990.

May, Elaine Tyler. "Cold War–Warm Hearth: Politics and the Family in Postwar America." In *The Rise and Fall of the New Deal Order, 1930–1990,* edited by Steve Fraser and Gary Gerstle. Princeton, N.J.: Princeton University Press, 1989.

Mayhew, David. *Congress: The Electoral Connection.* New Haven, Conn.: Yale University Press, 1974.

———. *Divided We Govern: Party Control, Lawmaking, and Investigations, 1946–1990.* New Haven, Conn.: Yale University Press, 1991.

McAdam, Doug. *Political Process and the Development of Black Insurgency, 1930–1970.* Chicago: University of Chicago Press, 1982.

McCain, Nina. "Activist in the House: Rep. Mary Jane Gibson Works to Make Parental Leave an Option for Working Parents." *Boston Globe,* October 28, 1986.

McCarthy, John D., and Mayer N. Zald. *The Trend of Social Movements in America: Professionalism and Resource Mobilization.* Morristown, N.J.: General Learning Press, 1973.

———. "Resource Mobilization Theory and Social Movements: A Partial Theory."

American Journal of Sociology 82 (1977): 1212–41.

McCloskey, Herbert, and John Zaller. *The American Ethos: Public Attitudes toward Capitalism and Democracy.* Cambridge, Mass.: Harvard University Press, 1984.

McDonagh, Eileen Lorenzi. "Representative Democracy and State Building in the Progressive Era." *American Political Science Review* 86 (December, 1992): 938–48.

Milkman, Ruth. *Gender at Work: The Dynamics of Job Segregation by Sex during World War II.* Chicago: University of Illinois Press, 1987.

Mills, C. Wright. *The Power Elite.* New York: Oxford University Press, 1956.

Mitchell, Alison. "Banking on Family Issues, Clinton Seeks Parents' Votes." *New York Times,* June 25, 1996.

Mohl, Bruce. "Massachusetts Fiscal Fall Is Seen as Sharpest in Northeast." *Boston Globe,* July 30, 1989.

Monroe, Pamela, and James C. Garand. "Parental Leave Legislation in the U.S. Senate: Toward a Model of Roll-Call Voting." *Family Relations* 40 (April, 1991): 208–18.

Monroe, Pamela, James C. Garand., and Holly Teeters. "Family Leave Legislation in the U.S. House: Explaining Roll-Call Voting on the Family and Medical Leave Act of 1990." *Family Relations* 44 (January, 1995): 46–55.

Mueller v. Oregon, 208 U.S. 412 (1908).

NLRB v. Jones & Laughlin, 301 U.S. 1 (1937).

Nelson, Barbara. *Making an Issue of Child Abuse.* Chicago: University of Chicago Press, 1984.

New State Ice Company v. Liebmann, 285 U.S. 262 (1932).

"New Pregnancy Benefits and Discrimination Rules, with Explanation and State Survey." Chicago: Commerce Clearing House, 1978.

Nichols, Nancy. "What Ever Happened to Rosie the Riveter?" *Harvard Business Review* 71: 4 (July-August 1993): 54–62.

North Carolina Equity. *Women's Agenda, 1993–94.* Raleigh, N.C.: NC Equity Women's Agenda Program, February, 1993.

Olson, Mancur. *The Logic of Collective Action: Public Goods and the Theory of Groups.* Cambridge, Mass.: Harvard University Press, 1965.

Orlowski, Diane. *Minority Report of the Task Force to Study Work and Family Roles and Parental and Medical Leaves of Absence in the Private Sector.* Submitted to the Connecticut General Assembly, February 21, 1989.

Orr, Sally, and George Haskett. *Parental Leave: Options for Working Parents.* A Report of a Conference Sponsored by the Association of Junior Leagues. New York: Association of Junior Leagues, Inc., 1985.

"Paid Leave for Parents." *New York Times,* December 1, 1999.

"Parental Leave—A Windfall for Yuppies." *The Phyllis Schlafly Report* 20, no. 4, section 1, November 1986.

Parental Leave and Productivity. Study by the Families and Work Institute, New York, 1990.

"Parental Leave Distracts from the Real Problem, the High Cost of Living." Manchester Connecticut *Journal Inquirer,* February 24, 1989.

Parker, Joanie. Testimony in Support of H 2191, An Act Establishing Employment Insurance. Commerce and Labor Committee, Massachusetts House of Representatives, April 8, 1991.

Pazniokas, Mark. "State House Passes Bill Mandating Time Off for New Parents." *Hartford Courant*, June 7, 1989.

Pear, Robert. "Thousands to Rally in Capital on Children's Behalf." *New York Times*, May 31, 1996.

———. "Dispute over Plan to Use Jobless Aid for Parental Leave." *New York Times*, November 8, 1999.

Permanent Commission on the Status of Women. "Briefing Paper: Family and Medical Leave, S.B. 315." Hartford, Conn.: April 15, 1989.

Petersen, Melody. "Bill Is Introduced to Provide Paid Time Off for Family Leave." *New York Times*, May 23, 1997.

Peterson, Paul. *The Price of Federalism*. Washington, D.C: Brookings Institution, 1995.

Peterson, Paul, and Mark C. Rom. *Welfare Magnets: The Case for a National Standard*. Washington, D.C.: Brookings Institution, 1990.

Pidgeon, Mary Elizabeth. *Women in the Economy of the United States of America: Employed Women under the NRA Codes*. Washington, D.C..: U.S. Government Printing Office, 1937.

Pierson, Paul. "'Policy Feedbacks' and Political Change: Contrasting Reagan and Thatcher's Pension-Reform Initiatives." *Studies in American Political Development* 6 (Fall 1992): 359–90.

———. "When Effect Becomes Cause: 'Policy Feedback' and Political Change." *World Politics* (1993): 595–628.

———. *Dismantling the Welfare State? Reagan, Thatcher, and the Politics of Retrenchment*. New York: Cambridge University Press, 1994.

———. "Fragmented Welfare States: Federal Institutions and the Development of Social Policy." *Governance* 8 (1995): 449–78.

———. "The Scope and Nature of Business Power: Employers and the American Welfare State, 1900–1935." Paper presented at the Annual Meeting of the American Political Science Association, Chicago, Ill., September 1995.

Plotke, David. "The Political Mobilization of Business." In *The Politics of Interests*, edited by Mark Petracca. Boulder, Col.: Westview Press, 1992.

Polsby, Nelson. *Political Innovation in America: The Politics of Policy Initiation*. New Haven, Conn.: Yale University Press, 1984.

"Presidential Debate between Bill Clinton and Former Senator Bob Dole," *New York Times*, October 18, 1996.

"Prohibition of Sex Discrimination Based on Pregnancy." House Report 95-948, 95th Cong., 2d Sess. Washington: U.S. Government Printing Office, 1978.

Public Perspective 9 (2): February-March, 1998.

Purdum, Todd S. "Clinton Talks of Welfare and Family Leave." *New York Times*, September 11, 1996.

Radigan, Anne L. *Concept and Compromise: The Evolution of Family Leave Legislation in the U.S. Congress*. Washington, D.C.: Women's Research and Education Institute, 1988.

Rayman, Paula, and Ann Bookman. "Creating a Research and Public Policy Agenda for Work, Family, and Community." *Annals of the American Association of Political and Social Science* 562 (March 1999): 191–211.

Rochefort, David A., and Roger W. Cobb, eds. *The Politics of Problem Definition: Shaping the Policy Agenda.* Lawrence, Kans.: University Press of Kansas, 1994.

Rodensky, Lisa. *"California Savings and Loan Association v. Guerra:* Preferential Treatment and the Pregnancy Discrimination Act." *Harvard Women's Law Journal* 10 (1987): 225–51.

Ryan, Barbara. *Feminism and the Women's Movement: Dynamics of Change in Social Movement, Ideology, and Activism.* New York: Routledge, 1992.

Salomon, Alan. "Law Requires Jobs to Be Held Open Four Months for New Mothers." *Memphis Business Journal,* July 6, 1987.

Scharf, Lois. *To Work and to Wed: Female Employment, Feminism, and the Great Depression.* Westport, Conn.: Greenwood Press, 1980.

Schattschneider, E. E. *The Semi-Sovereign People: A Realist's View of Democracy in America,* reissued with an introduction by David Adamany. New York: Harcourt, Brace, Jovanovich, 1975.

Schlozman, Kay Lehman. "What Accent the Heavenly Chorus? Political Equality and the American Pressure System." *Journal of Politics* 46 (1984): 1006–32.

Schlozman, Kay Lehman, and John Tierney. *Organized Interests and American Democracy.* New York: Harper Collins, 1986.

Schlozman, Kay Lehman, and Sidney Verba. *Injury to Insult: Unemployment, Class, and Political Response.* Cambridge, Mass.: Harvard University Press, 1979.

Schneir, Miriam. *Feminism in Our Time.* New York: Vintage Books, 1994.

Schoonmaker, Meyressa. Letter to Marian Franklin, unpublished. December 10, 1990.

———. Telephone Conference with Rep. Annie Brown Kennedy. Memo to Family and Medical Leave Coalition Nucleus, undated.

Schoonmaker, Meyressa, and Sandra D. Hildebolt. Memo to members of the Family and Medical Leave Coalition, March 5, 1993.

Schor, Juliet. *The Overworked American: The Unexpected Decline of Leisure.* New York: Basic Books, 1992.

Sementilli-Dann, Lisa, Eva Gasser-Sanz, Alison Lown, Stephen T. Middlebrook, Glenn Northern, Janice Steinschneider, and Sharon Stoneback. *Family and Medical Leave: Strategies for Success.* Washington, D.C.: Center for Policy Alternatives, 1991.

Sharkansky, Ira. "The Utility of Elazar's Political Culture." *Polity* 2 (1969): 66–83.

Sharkansky, Ira, and Richard I. Hofferbert. "Dimensions of State Politics, Economics, and Public Policy." *American Political Science Review* 63 (September 1969): 867–79.

Shellenbarger, Sue. *Work and Family: Essays from the "Work and Family" Column of the Wall Street Journal.* New York: Ballentine Books, 1999.

Silverman, Charlotte, M.D. "Maternity Policies in Industry." *Child* Magazine (U.S. Department of Labor, Children's Bureau) 8:12 (August 1943): 20–24.

Skocpol, Theda. *Protecting Soldiers and Mothers: The Political Origins of Social Pol-*

icy in the United States. Cambridge, Mass.: Belknap Press of Harvard University Press, 1992.

———. *Social Policy in the United States: Future Possibilities in Historical Perspective.* Princeton, N.J.: Princeton University Press, 1995.

Skocpol, Theda, Marjorie Abend-Wein, Susan Goodrich-Lehman, and Christopher Howard. "Women's Associations and the Enactment of Mother's Pensions in the United States." *American Political Science Review* 87 (1993): 686–701.

Snow, David A., E. Burke Rochford Jr., Steven K. Worden, and Robert D. Benford. "Frame Alignment Processes, Micromobilization, and Movement Participation." *American Sociological Review* 51 (1986): 464–81.

Snow, David A., and Robert D. Benford. "Ideology, Frame Resonance, and Participant Mobilization." In *From Structure to Action: Comparing Social Movement Research across Cultures,* edited by Bert Klandermans, Hanspeter Kreisi, and Sidney Tarrow. Greenwich, Conn.: JAI Press, 1988: 197–217.

Snow, David. "Master Frames and Cycles of Protest." In *Frontiers in Social Movement Theory,* edited by Aldon Morris and Carol McClurg Mueller. New Haven, Conn.: Yale University Press, 1992.

Spalter-Roth, Roberta, and Heidi Hartmann. *Unnecessary Losses: The Costs to Americans of the Lack of Family and Medical Leave.* Washington: Institute for Women's Policy Research, 1990.

Spalter-Roth, Roberta, and Ronnee Schreiber. "Outsider Issues and Insider Tactics: Strategic Tensions in the Women's Policy Network during the 1980s." In *Feminist Organizations: Harvest of the New Women's Movement,* edited by Myra Marx Ferree and Patricia Yancey Martin. Philadelphia: Temple University Press, 1995.

Spock, Benjamin. *Baby and Child Care.* New York: Pocket Books, 1957.

"Standards for Maternity Care and Employment of Mothers in Industry." Washington, D.C.: United States Department of Labor, Women's and Children's Bureau, July 1942.

"Standards of Day Care of Children of Working Mothers: Report of the Subcommittee on Standards and Services for Day Care Authorized by the Children's Bureau Conference on Day Care of Children of Working Mothers." Children in Wartime No. 3, Bureau Publication 284. Washington, D.C.: United States Government Printing Office, 1942.

Statistical Abstract of the United States, 1980–1994.

Steinmo, Sven. "American Exceptionalism Reconsidered: Culture or Institutions?" In *The Dynamics of American Politics: Approaches and Interpretations,* edited by Lawrence C. Dodd and Calvin Jillson. Boulder, Col.: Westview Press, 1994.

Stone, Deborah. "Causal Stories and the Formation of Policy Agendas." *Political Science Quarterly* 104: 281–300.

Stoneback, Sharon A. "Developing Feminist Strategies for Policy Change: The Women's Legal Defense Fund and Family and Medical Leave." Unpublished case study, Women's Studies Program, George Washington University, 1989.

Stonecash, Jeffrey. "The State Politics Literature: Moving beyond Covariation Studies and Pursuing Politics." *Polity* 28 (Summer 1994): 559–79.

Subcommittee on Labor-Management Relations and the Subcommittee on Labor Standards of the Committee on Education and Labor, United States House of Representatives, 100th Cong., 1st sess. Joint Hearings on the Family and Medical Leave Act of 1987. Washington, DC: February 25 and March 5, 1987.

Subcommittee on Children, Family, Drugs, and Alcoholism of the Committee on Labor and Human Resources, United States Senate, 101st Cong., 1st sess. Hearings on the Family and Medical Leave Act of 1989. Washington, D.C., February 1989.

Subcommittee on Labor-Management Relations of the Committee on Education and Labor, United States House of Representatives, 102nd Cong., 1st sess. Washington, D.C., February 28, 1991.

Sundquist, James. "Needed: A Political Theory for the New Era of Coalition Government in the United States." *Political Science Quarterly* 103 (1988): 613–35.

Tarrow, Sidney. *Power in Movement: Social Movements, Collective Action, and Politics*. New York: Cambridge University Press, 1994.

Tennessee State Senate. Debate on Maternity Leave in Tennessee, May 4, 1987.

Tennessee Women's Political Caucus. "WPC Legislative Highlights." Pamphlet produced in Nashville, Tenn., undated.

Thompson, Joan Hulse. "The Family and Medical Leave Act: A Policy for Families." In *Women and Politics: Have Outsiders Become Insiders?* edited by Lois Duke. New York: Prentice Hall, 1993.

Tilly, Charles. *From Mobilization to Revolution*. Reading, Mass.: Addison-Wesley, 1978.

Trzcinski, Eileen, and Matia Finn-Stevenson. "A Response to Arguments against Mandated Parental Leave: Findings from the Connecticut Survey of Parental Leave Policies." *Journal of Marriage and the Family* 53 (May 1991): 445–60.

Tsebelis, George. *Nested Games: Rational Choice in Comparative Politics*. Berkeley, Cal.: University of California Press, 1990.

United States Department of Labor. *State Maternity/Family Leave Law*. Washington, D.C.: Women's Bureau of the U.S. Department of Labor, 1993.

Van Etten, Ida M. "The Condition of Women Workers under the Present Industrial System." Speech given at the National Convention of the American Federation of Labor, Detroit, Michigan, 1890.

Verba, Sidney, Kay Lehman Schlozman, and Henry Brady. *Voice and Equality: Civic Voluntarism in American Politics*. Cambridge, Mass.: Harvard University Press, 1995.

Verespej, Michael A. "Family Leave: It's Here. While Congress Fiddles, States Step In." *Industry Week*, March 4, 1991.

Vogel, David. "The Political Power of Business in America: A Reappraisal." *British Journal of Political Science* 13 (1983): 19–43.

———. *Fluctuating Fortunes: The Political Power of Business in America*. New York: Basic Books, 1989.

Vogel, Lise. *Mothers on the Job: Maternity Policy in the U.S. Workplace*. New Brunswick, N.J.: Rutgers University Press, 1993.

Walker, Jack L., Jr. "The Diffusion of Innovations among the American States."

American Political Science Review 63 (1969): 880–99.

Weaver, R. Kent. "The Politics of Blame Avoidance." *Journal of Public Policy* 6 (1986): 371–98.

Weber, Max. "Politics as a Vocation." In *From Max Weber: Essays in Sociology,* translated and edited by H. H. Gerth and C. Wright Mills. New York: Oxford University Press, 1946.

———. *The Protestant Ethic and the Spirit of Capitalism,* translated by Talcott Parsons. New York: Charles Scribner's Sons, 1958.

Weiner, Lynn. *From Working Girl to Working Mother: The Female Labor Force in the United States, 1820–1980.* Chapel Hill, N.C.: University of North Carolina Press, 1985.

Weir, Margaret. *Politics and Jobs: The Boundaries of Employment Policy in the United States.* Princeton, N.J.: Princeton University Press, 1992.

Weir, Margaret, Ann Shola Orloff, and Theda Skocpol, eds. *The Politics of Social Policy in the United States.* Princeton, N.J., Princeton University Press, 1988.

Weisensale, Steven K. "Family Policy in the State Legislature: The Connecticut Agenda." *Policy Studies Review* 8 (Spring 1989): 622–37.

Weisensale, Steven K., and Michael D. Allison. "Family Leave Legislation: State and Federal Initiatives." *Family Relations* 38 (1989): 182–89.

Wever, Kirsten. *The Family and Medical Leave Act.* Cambridge, Mass.: Radcliffe Public Policy Institute, 1996.

"Who Stands for Children?" *New York Times,* June 1, 1996.

Williams, Wendy. "Equality's Riddle: Pregnancy and the Equal-Treatment/Special Treatment Debate." *N.Y.U. Review of Law and Social Change* 13 (1984–85), 325–80.

Wilson, James Q. *The Politics of Regulation.* New York: Basic Books, 1980.

———. *Political Organizations.* 2nd ed., rev. Princeton, N.J.: Princeton University Press, 1995.

"A Woman's Dilemma: Pregnancy vs. Financial/Job Security." Pamphlet. Winston Salem, N.C.: The North Carolina Center for Laws Affecting Women, Inc., undated.

A Workable Balance: Report to Congress on Family and Medical Leave. Washington, D.C.: U.S. Department of Labor, 1996.

"Working Families Speak: Case Studies of Americans Who Needed Family and Medical Leave." 2nd ed. Washington, D.C.: Women's Legal Defense Fund, 1991.

Ziegler, Edward F., and Meryl Frank, eds. *The Parental Leave Crisis: Toward a National Policy.* New Haven: Yale University Press, 1988.

INDEX

www.ingramcontent.com/pod-product-compliance
Lightning Source LLC
Chambersburg PA
CBHW021903020426
42334CB00013B/465